CHRISTIANITY AMIDST APARTHEID

Christianity Amidst Apartheid:

Selected Perspectives on the Church in South Africa

Edited by
Martin Prozesky

*Ad Hominem Professor and Head of Department of Religious Studies,
University of Natal, Pietermaritzburg*

Afterword by Desmond Tutu

St. Martin's Press   New York

© Martin Prozesky 1990

All rights reserved. For information, write:
Scholarly and Reference Division,
St. Martin's Press, Inc., 175 Fifth Avenue,
New York, N.Y. 10010

First published in the United States of America in 1990

Printed in Hong Kong

ISBN 0–312–03529–2

Library of Congress Cataloging-in-Publication Data
Christianity Amidst Apartheid: Selected Perspectives on the Church in
South Africa/ edited by Martin Prozesky; foreword by Desmond Tutu
p.   cm.
Includes index.
ISBN 0–312–03529–2
1. South Africa—Race relations   2. Race relations—Religious
aspects—Christianity.   3. Apartheid—South Africa.   I. Prozesky,
Martin.
DT763.C542   1990
276.8—dc20   89–34299
                                                         CIP

276.8
Chr
1990

Contents

List of Figures

Acknowledgements

As editor of the present collection of essays my appreciation to the authors who have joined me in compiling it requires special mention here in addition to the gratitude expressed towards them in my Introduction.

For details about the first known Christian contacts with Southern Africa I am indebted to Professor Eric Axelson, formerly of the University of Cape Town, through his elegantly learned publications and through personal correspondence. My own essay in this collection on the implications of apartheid for Christianity in South Africa originated as a conference paper in 1985 organised by my departmental colleague Dr Ronald Nicolson, to whom thanks are due for kindly inviting me to present a paper at that event. For valuable critical comments and other suggestions about the original paper I must also thank Dr David Chidester, Mr Patrick Maxwell, Professor Stewart Sutherland and the late Dr Alan Paton.

Next I must acknowledge with gratitude the help I received in the typing of the text of this compilation from Mrs Maureen Yardley and from my wife Elizabeth, who has been unfailingly supportive during my various literary and academic pursuits; and lastly let me thank the relevant staff members of Southern Publishers and especially The Macmillan Press for their exemplary promptness, efficiency and encouragement in bringing this book into being.

M.P.
Pietermaritzburg
October 1988

Notes on the Contributors

James Cochrane is a Lecturer in Theological Studies in the Department of Religious Studies, University of Natal, Pietermaritzburg.

Calvin Cook is Professor of Ecclesiastical History in the Faculty of Divinity, Rhodes University.

John De Gruchy is Personal Professor of Christian Studies in the Department of Religious Studies, University of Cape Town.

Denis Hurley OMI is the Roman Catholic Archbishop of Durban.

James Kiernan is Associate Professor of Social Anthropology in the Department of African Studies, University of Natal, Durban.

Johann Kinghorn is a senior lecturer in the Department of Biblical Studies, University of Stellenbosch.

Gerrie Lubbe is a lecturer in the Department of Science of Religion, University of South Africa, Pretoria.

Takatso Mofokeng is a senior lecturer in the Faculty of Theology, University of South Africa, Pretoria.

Klaus Nürnberger is Professor of Systematic Theology at the University of Natal, Pietermaritzburg.

G. C. Oosthuizen is Director of the Research Unit, New Religious Movements and Independent/Indigenous Churches (NERMIC), co-sponsored by the Human Sciences Research Council and the University of Zululand, based in Durban.

Martin Prozesky is Ad Hominem Professor and Head of the Department of Religious Studies, University of Natal, Pietermaritzburg.

Willem Saayman is a Professor of Missiology in the Faculty of Theology, University of South Africa, Pretoria.

Desmond Tutu is the Anglican Archbishop of Cape Town and Nobel Peace laureate.

Charles Villa-Vicencio is Associate Professor in the Department of Religious Studies, University of Cape Town.

Introduction
Martin Prozesky

To the best of our knowledge, the long story of Christian influence on what would later be called South Africa began with the arrival of Portuguese mariners led by Bartholomew Dias early in 1488. On 12 March, the feast day of St Gregory the Great, they erected a padrao or limestone pillar topped by a small cross on high ground at what is now called Kwaaihoek, overlooking the Indian Ocean near the mouth of the Bushman's River on the eastern Cape coast. It is possible that Mass was also said. (Brown 5: 1) In all probability the events of that day were thus the earliest distinctively Christian activities to take place in South Africa.

The first lesson from Dias's padrao-raising that day is its highly revealing blend of three interests: commercial, because the main motive behind the voyage from Portugal was to foster trade with the East; political, in so far as the padrao also carried the Portuguese coat of arms and was erected to demonstrate primacy of claim (Axelson 2: 17ff); and of course religious. As Austin recently remarked, 'the padrao was a powerful symbol of Christianity' (1: 10). Thus the arrival of the cross in South Africa simultaneously heralded the coming of a political economy that has greatly enriched many people in and from Europe but which has also involved conspicuous disadvantages for the native peoples of the land in a long process of subjugation whose climax in the present century has been the creation of the apartheid state. That too would make its advent in close association with people of undoubted Christian conviction.

It is highly likely that Muslim explorers had reached as far south down the east coast of Africa as present-day Mozambique before the arrival of the Portuguese, and trading vessels from the orient had long since made contact with those parts when Dias and his party reached the southern end of the continent from the Atlantic (Axelson 3: 2ff). Whether any of their explorers ever penetrated further southward into areas now forming part of South Africa we do not know, and certainly no monument revealing their interests has yet been discovered here. Thus it would not be the great religious systems of Islam, China or India that would become characteristic of South Africa, and we shall never know what impact their faiths might have had in the region had

1

things been different. What did happen was the arrival of people of the Christian faith, at first those fleeting Portuguese contacts, then Dutch settlers in the mid-seventeenth century with the same commercial and political motivations as their predecessors; thereafter French Huguenot refugees displaced by persecution in their homeland, and finally the British from 1795 onwards with their own characteristic blend of pulpit, rifle and empire.

What has also happened during this period is acceptance of Christianity by the black people of South Africa on a very large scale, as current statistics clearly reveal (Kritzinger 6: 22), a process involving some highly significant adaptations of that religion on their part. This forms the subject of the opening chapter in the present book by James Kiernan, while the second essay, by Willem Saayman, contains a critical review of Christian missions in South Africa. The most recent and highly important manifestation of the religious creativity of black people in this country takes the form of South African Black Theology, which is the subject of the third chapter by Takatso Mofokeng.

But to start with things were less favourable to the new religion. So far as we know, there were no witnesses to the padrao-raising from the indigenous people of the area that March day in 1488, just 500 years ago as these words are being written, nor any recorded contact between them and the Portuguese. But at other landfalls on those early voyages there were contacts, and these reveal a very mixed and often unfavourable response by the black people of South Africa to those earliest representatives of Christian Europe.

Dias first set foot on the sub-continent at present-day Mossel Bay in February 1488, and when his men attempted to draw water from a spring without prior negotiation with the local Khoikhoi people, who had originally fled, they were subjected to stone-throwing (*SA Outlook* 8: 8). To this Dias responded by firing a cross-bow, killing one of the Khoikhoi, 'the first victim of white aggression in South Africa', as Axelson remarks (3: 18). So it is scarcely surprising that the next Portuguese mariner to land there nine years later, Vasco Da Gama, had a distinctly unfriendly reception. The wooden cross his men planted was promptly pulled down by the Khoikhoi as the seafarers sailed out of the bay on their way northeastwards in a journey that would open to Europe's traders a searoute to the orient (Raven-Hart 7: 23). Later contacts included sufficiently serious fighting between Portuguese and Khoikhoi to disincline the newcomers towards any permanent base or settlement in the region, in preference for their footholds in Angola and Mozambique.

The story is not, however, one of unrelieved antagonism and conflict, and one event in particular reveals a very different kind of contact. This too befell Da Gama's party, early in 1498, when a landing on the southeast coast brought the Europeans into contact for the first time with Bantu-speaking people. The generosity of their reception led the Portuguese to name the area the *Terra da boa gente* – 'the land of the good people' (Axelson 4: 24). It is not known to what extent the visitors from Christian Europe elicited from this kindly people a similar compliment, but at least it is possible to demonstrate from near the beginnings of the history we are considering that conflict between different cultures is not inevitable.

Over the centuries since these beginnings people professing the Christian faith have become a large majority in South Africa, not just among whites but also among blacks, though parts of the country, notably Natal and the Western Cape, are also home to an exceptionally rich diversity of religions. These are the legacy of exiles, slaves, indentured labourers and settlers from the Islamic parts of the East Indies, from Jewish communities in western and eastern Europe, from the Indian sub-continent and, in very much smaller numbers, from China and elsewhere. In fact the diversity is so great that of the so-called great world religions only Buddhism has not had a numerically significant and long-standing following in South Africa. But in the main the story of religion in South Africa is the story of Christianity: brought by Europeans, thereafter interacting with the black population, embraced by them in very great numbers and permutations, and continued also by the white descendants of the first Christian migrants, with some important and in some cases disturbing adaptations of their own, the main one being the theology of apartheid, a topic reflected in most of the essays in this book but treated in detail by Johann Kinghorn in connection with the Dutch Reformed Church or NGK.

It is now half a millenium since the processes of Christian influence in South Africa and reciprocal African influencing of Christianity on these shores began, and at the time of writing the country faces unprecedented political and religious challenges at whose heart is the problem of how to achieve a harmonious and equitable co-existence. It is deeply disturbing to realise that misunderstanding and conflict manifested themselves at the very beginnings of white-black contacts despite good intentions. On the other hand it is also deeply encouraging that those early happenings included at least one luminous example of peace and well-being through humane service and hospitality.

Given the numerical preponderance of Christians in the South African population, 77 per cent of which associates itself with that religion according to the 1980 census, as well as the obviously important part these people and their fellow believers in previous generations have played in many facets of the religious and political life of the country, and given also the great challenges now facing the region, it is both timely and appropriate for Christianity in South Africa to be placed under the spotlight. The essays in this collection are a contribution to that large and urgent task. Their purpose is to provide broadly-based, critical interpretations of a selection of the most important aspects of South African life, in order to foster awareness, debate, discussion and further investigation into the subject. They summarise the basic information relating to these aspects, giving such detail as their several authors deem desirable within the limits of a critical and interpretive overview of topics which are, in every case, highly complex, and draw from that information such significant patterns, evaluations and perspectives as the authors judge will help readers to form a more informed, more balanced, more critical and more constructive awareness of the achievements, failures and prospects of Christianity in South Africa.

The essays are by leading academic and ecclesiastical writers from South Africa, two of them Archbishops, one a Nobel laureate, some of them theologians, others (including the editor) from such fields as religious studies and anthropology. In each case they have attempted to present their material in a readable manner and with the minimum of that type of scholarly apparatus which most readers find unhelpful, in the belief that a book such as this can serve a valuable purpose in a much larger community than just the academic. It is material which deeply concerns all thinking people in South Africa, whether they identify with Christianity or not, as well as the large number of those abroad for whom this country and the shape of the Christian church are matters of real interest.

The essays are grouped around five themes, starting with 'Christianity and the Black People of South Africa'. This section comprises the three chapters mentioned above, by James Kiernan, Willem Saayman and Takatso Mofokeng. The next theme is 'Christians and Apartheid', with four chapters. The one by Johann Kinghorn, giving a critical outline of the Dutch Reformed Church's position on apartheid, has already been mentioned. It is followed by James Cochrane's study of Christian resistance to racist exploitation in South Africa. Then comes a contribution treating Christianity's impact on race relations, by G. C. Oosthuizen, while the fourth essay in this group is the editor's investigation of the implications of apartheid for Christianity.

Prominent social issues provide the book with its third theme. Here the aspects covered are the impact of Christianity on the socio-economic development of South Africa, a subject discussed by Klaus Nürnberger; education, a topic handled by Calvin Cook, and a reappraisal of the meaning of evangelisation in relation to the social factor by Archbishop Denis Hurley.

Contemporary challenges to Christians in South Africa are the fourth theme, focussing on two issues of violence and its justification on one hand, and religious pluralism on the other. The authors of the chapters dealing with these two topics are Charles Villa-Vicencio and Gerrie Lubbe.

The fifth and last of the themes is Christianity and the Future in South Africa, to which the last two of the 14 chapters are devoted. John De Gruchy opens this section with an essay on the church and the struggle for a democratic South Africa, while the collection is brought to its conclusion in Archbishop Desmond Tutu's Christian vision of the future of South Africa.

Writers of such calibre require no further introduction by their editor, except to say that opinions expressed in each chapter are those of the author in question and not necessarily of them all (brief biographical notes about each contributor are provided on p. ixf). What does require explanation is the part played in the genesis of this book by the editor. This was to conceive of a collection of essays reviewing major aspects of the story of Christianity in South Africa at a significant and critical period of its history, to identify themes and topics that warranted coverage in such a book and to approach the various authors in question. The topic of Christians and violence was proposed by Charles Villa-Vicencio, and one of the contributors' names was suggested by James Cochrane, proposals which have unquestionably enriched the book and for which thanks are here recorded. Complete freedom was thereafter naturally exercised by each contributor in the writing of the various chapters, and each of them wrote independently of the others. The convergence of basic insights and emphases that is discernible in the collection is all the more remarkable for that reason. In particular, no methodological directives were proposed by the editor, though the collection as a whole contains highly significant implications for the history of religion in South Africa, through the attention which is given in various ways to the following historiographical principles: the importance of a plural-istic approach in which the history of Christianity is correlated with South Africa's other religious traditions; the equal importance, next, of an independent critical stance in relation to the subject, as free as possible from confessional and above all denominational confinements of perspective; and thirdly a no-less-vital correlating of such a history of Christianity (or any other religion) with its secular context as this changes over time, especially the political economy of the country. Issues of the greatest possible significance for believer and scholar alike come to light in no other way than through a clear appreciation of the fact that the Christian faith came to South Africa in association with – not to say dependence on – the forces of merchant capitalism. The various contributors were not asked to shape their work for this book according to those three principles, or any other, but it is a major benefit to the subject that, taken as a whole, they bring them to light with such telling effect.

Finally, as editor, let me record here my great appreciation to this group of colleagues for their interest in the project, their promptness in meeting various deadlines, for the expert knowledge and wisdom manifest in their work and for assistance in other connections. If, as a group of writers, we are able to contribute something positive to our homeland and all its people as they enter the second half-millennium of the interaction between indigenous and settler faiths and cultures, and to stimulate further study of and research into the rich and highly significant topics we investigate in this book, we shall feel amply rewarded.

REFERENCES

1.   Austin, Michael, S. J. 'History of the Dias Crosses', *The Southern Cross*, 28 February 1988.
2.   Axelson, Eric, 'Discovery of the Farthest Pillar Erected by Bartholomew Dias', *SA Journal of Science*, vol. XXXV, December 1938, pp. 417–29.
3.   Axelson, Eric, *South-East Africa 1488–1530* (London: Longmans, Green, 1940).
4.   Axelson, Eric, *Portuguese in South-East Africa 1488–1600* (Johannesburg: Struik, 1973).
5.   Brown, William Eric, *The Catholic Church in South Africa: From its Origins to the Present Day* (London: Burns & Oates, 1960).
6.   Kritzinger, J. J., *'n Statistiese Beskrywing van die Godsdienstige Verspreiding van die Bevolking van Suid-Afrika* (Pretoria: Instituut vir Sendingwetenskaplike Navorsing, 1985).
7.   Raven-Hart, R., *Before van Riebeeck: Callers at South Africa from 1488 to 1652* (Cape Town: Struik, 1967).
8.   *South African Outlook*, January 1988.

Part I
Christianity and the Black People of South Africa

1 African and Christian: From Opposition to Mutual Accommodation

James Kiernan

Christianity was for a long time the exclusive property of whites in South Africa before it purposefully reached out in the 1820s to touch the African population, the great majority of whom were settled Bantu-speaking farmers and pastoralists. How Africans perceived the approach of Christianity, responded to it and were ultimately affected by it, is the subject of this chapter. History has largely fashioned the African perception of and response to Christianity. In the earliest encounters between Africans and Christian emissaries, who were in most cases not missionaries, lasting impressions were formed by each of the other which were to have profound consequences for subsequent interaction between two very dissimilar ways of life. Each had its own closed system of ideas for interpreting the world and humanity's place in it and for organising a distinctive way of life. Each was satisfied with its own understanding of the universe and entertained no desire to change it under challenge from the other, much less to adopt an alien outlook. Yet, in conjunction with other sources of change, mainly of an economic and political kind, Christianity has been instrumental in transforming the lives of Africans in this part of the continent.

Essentially, Christianity propagates a God-centred view of the universe. Humanity, created by God, is initially at one with the rest of creation, but is wilfully estranged from the creator and is consequently at odds with its environment. God takes the initiative and provides the means of restoring the damaged relationship and the lost harmony, in the form of his who in his person unites the human and the divine. But man must constantly struggle to achieve the indwelling of the deity in his being and activities, to recreate in his own domain the fusion of god and man established by the divine-human mediator. Thus, God is the creator of all things and the focus of human striving. By contrast, an African view of the universe is basically man-centred. Man is produced by the universe: the first men emerge out of the ground, from water or through a hole in the sky. Ideally, man is in harmony

9

with his source but he can invite calamity if, by his actions, he upsets this balance. Nature is imbued with mystical force which man strives to contain. Mystical power is also generated by disharmony in human relationships which extends to include dead forebears. To be estranged from one's ancestors or to fall foul of living associates is to risk mystical retribution and the blighting of physical well-being. All lapses from a state of harmony, but health can be repaired by recourse to ritual. Man is, therefore, the product of nature and the focus of his striving is the quality of his physical and social relations in this world.

Despite the unavoidable simplification, what is clear from this presentation is the character of the opposition between these two worldviews. While the Christian's life is incorporated in divine planning and its resolution is beyond time and place, the African looks for satisfaction within his own life-span and that of his descendants, by careful observation of the rhythms of nature and the norms of society. What happens when two such fundamentally different systems of ideas come into prolonged contact with each other? The logical possibilities are limited. At the very least some mutual absorption will occur leading to a measure of synthesis in which one system may gain at the expense of the other. In fact, it was African religion which in the main gave ground to Christianity, although this process stopped well short of capitulation. Discounting an understandable tendency to invest one's own worldview with inherent superiority, it is not simply the case that a Christian set of beliefs succeeds in making better sense of the universe than does an African system of ideas. The universe is differently defined in each case and there are no grounds for supposing that African religion was especially deficient within its own context. It was when that context was transformed by innovations of a technological, political and even military nature, with which Christianity was itself associated, that Christian ideas gained the ascendancy. However, even in advance of these developments, Africans perceived that certain benefits might accrue to them from a dalliance with Christianity.

Shaka 'paid marked attention' to the account that Isaacs gave him of God as supreme being, as creator and source of life and was 'struck with profound astonishment' at his version of the origin of the world. 'We told him that we had not brought any doctors (missionaries) with us to instruct the ignorant in the ways of God: this he appeared to regret and expressed the wish for them to come and teach his people, observing "that he had discovered we were a superior race" and that he would give the missionaries abundance of cattle to teach him to read and write' (Isaacs, 7: 119–20). In more general vein, Isaacs states (301–2): 'The Zulus have no idea of a deity, no knowledge of a future state. They cannot comprehend the mystery of creation . . . and though they could not comprehend the worship of an invisible creator, they seemed to be somewhat convinced that our motives had more in them than they, poor illiterate beings, could fathom or divine'. Some extracts from the diaries of Owen, the first British missionary to arrive at Dingaan's court in 1837, are equally illuminating. In his first encounter with Africans on his way to the Zulu capital, the lines were clearly drawn between divergent preoccupations (Cory, 3: 19). He spoke to them of sin, using the imagery of strayed sheep, but they put him off by saying they would think about it. In turn, they wanted his opinion about witchcraft but he refused to be drawn on this topic. When he denied that the purpose of his journey was trading, they concluded that 'there must be something in it for the white people to take so much pains' (20). He exhorted Dingaan to 'listen to and live God's word as a guarantee of happiness'; Dingaan responded by asking 'if he should be able to learn, and whether I could teach him, to read' (39), and followed that up with a request for gunpowder (40). Dingaan subsequently applied himself seriously to reading lessons: 'He is wonderfully taken with this sure mode of communication by writing and resorts to it at every opportunity' (59). At the same time, the King pressed his interest in the acquisition of muskets, gunpowder and horses. 'Tho' he has not a horse in his dominions, he will be glad if possible to train up a body of cavalry . . . [Horse and musket combined]' (101). However, on matters of a more religious nature, Owen met with stout resistance. 'Zulus have no word in their language to express the sublime object of our worship [God]'. 'Unkulunkulu is applied by the natives to a certain ancient chief whom they suppose to have sprung from a reed' (90). When he asked some villagers nearby if they knew 'the chief above', they treated the idea with some derision. 'Is there one? Can he see us if he is in the air? He must be a good climber', 'but it appeared that they did not know I was speaking of God, they thought I was talking of King George. Of God they said they had heard from some white man, but had forgotten His name till I mentioned it' (103). This is supplemented by Dingaan's questions at their first meeting: 'Who was the first English King?' he demanded to know. 'Was God among the English Kings? Was he from the beginning' (39). On possibly the only occasion on which Owen preached to the King and his assembly, he was shouted down when he broached the subject of the resurrection. They found this so incredible that he was told not to tamper with the dead but rather attend to healing the sick, 'for this is easier than to raise the dead' (74). There was no meeting of minds on these issues; the Zulus attempted to understand the new religion by pressing the concept of God into a familiar mould, that of ancestor or first settler of a territory, while the missionary tried to usurp the term 'unkulunkulu' to convey the notion of God. Neither was successful although, in the long run, the second tendency was to prove the stronger.

There is a great deal to be learned from the record of early contact between Christianity and what was distinctively African, bearing in mind that the Zulu experience was only one of numerous similarly fascinating encounters. What seems incontestable is that, almost from the first contact, astute Africans realistically measured the material gap between the two cultures and unerringly identified the areas in which Whites were superior. They were impressed by White superiority in technology (guns and horses) and by the fact that knowledge could be stored and transmitted by means of the written word. Furthermore, they correctly divined that there was a connection between the two, the more so since the missionaries regularly emphasised the existence of 'a book', the reading of which would 'show them the way to happiness' (Cory, 3: 48), implying a better way of life. Secondly, Christian teaching was too alien to their way of thinking and to their organised existence to have any real meaning. The idea of a world above and beyond, and independent of, the human was quite incredible. It was equally incredible that strangers should travel great distances just to relate such 'fairy tales'. It followed that these visitors were impelled by other undeclared motives, a suspicion given substance by later developments. Thirdly, they readily recognised that some advantage might be gained from an alliance with the newcomers, in that it would lead to the acquisition of new knowledge, distilled from Christian teaching, which would lay bare the secret of white accomplishment and would ultimately lead to parity between the two groups. Better to acquire those skills which seemed to be the key to white superiority while turning a politely deaf ear to their ramblings about a fabulous God. In pursuit of this pragmatic objective, Africans were willing to give hostages to Christianity (mere children initially) and to make religious concessions of a superficial kind, which did not endanger the integrity of their own religious system and its adequacy to their needs. But, once set in train, the history of the exchange between Christianity and African religion and the mutual influence of the one upon the other acquired a momentum of its own and led to consequences unforeseen and unintended by either party. As Ranger has observed: 'We are beginning to realise that during the missionary period, the foundations of a vigorous African Christianity were laid. We are also beginning to realise that these foundations were laid in a concealed and mysterious manner'. 'The emergence of an African Christianity was a dialectical process, an interaction between missionary and African consciousness' (16: 182). He concludes that 'African Christianity as it evolves, corresponds neither to missionary nor indigenous hopes or expectations' (183).

While the unfulfillment, or at best partial fulfillment, of African and Christian missionary expectations was the outcome of their interaction, it cannot be stressed enough that what most profoundly influenced that outcome was the essential incongruity between the two sets of expectations, an incongruity that manifested itself in the earliest contacts and is still very much at the heart of the matter. The missionaries sought a commitment to develop an interior spiritual dimension as the wellspring of moral behaviour. Africans, however, responded to the missionary message through the filter of their own culture, not least of which was the cultural expectation that religious observance and good behaviour should bestow tangible blessings in the form of material endowment, social advancement, a better way of life in the here and now. Hence, 'the equality of all before God' had a much more mundane resonance for Africans than was contained in the more spiritual meaning conveyed by missionaries. And, as we shall see, each of the historical wrenches in the development of African Christianity, specifically the Ethiopian and Zionist departures, had its roots in the failure of Christianity to realise the promise it held out for Africans. At the same time, while the Christian message was being redirected and refined under the African lens and many Africans had become fully committed exemplars of the Christian way of life, those who stubbornly remained outside the fold did not escape its influence. 'Christianity first took root in the fissures of the local polity, initially attracting the marginal and the powerless: yet the mission by its very presence engaged all . . . in an inescapable dialogue on its own terms' (Comaroff and Comaroff, 2: 15). The spread of Christianity has meant that even those Africans who resisted its religious message internalised to some extent its categories (for example, of time and work) and values (for instance, individualism and egalitarianism). In short, there was a complex exchange of influence between the two. Christianity has modified the African worldview: on the other hand, Africans have reinterpreted the Christian message.

It would be impossible within the compass of a short essay to demonstrate this across the full spectrum of religious developments affecting Africans throughout South Africa. Since I must perforce be selective, I take my point of departure from Hastings' distinction (5: 80) between coastal and inland evangelism. For Hastings, these are the earliest of four sequential stages in the history of missions to Africa, each demanding the application of new techniques to deal with novel situations. The coastal period was characterised by the separate Christian village, a sanctuary for redeemed slaves and other social outcasts. When missionaries penetrated into the interior, they abandoned the concentrated village in favour of dispersed catechists' schools situated within African settlements. Something of the same pattern emerged in South Africa, though for different reasons. Here, coastal and inland missions were virtually contemporaneous, first appearing among Tswana and Xhosa within the same decade (Pauw, 14: 415–6), but they operated in widely differing situations of ecology, economy and habitat, to the east and west of the Drakensberg. In the relatively wetter eastern grasslands, the range and diversity of resources to be found within a very limited physical area were sufficient to support a small independent group of people, such as a kraal or a homestead, and access to such resources could be regulated locally by the headman of the group. Thus each self-sufficient homestead was set within its own pasture land and agricultural plots, which physically separated it from other homesteads. 'The Bantu East is characterised by dispersed settlement of its inhabitants whose homes dot the landscape' (Sansom, 17: 139). In the highland and arid western zones, variety of soil type and plant cover has to be sought over greater distances, water sources are widely dispersed and poorer grazing conditions must be compensated by more extensive access. To exploit this spread and separation of resources, men had to enter into co-operative arrangements wherein their investments were tightly weaved with those of others. Consequently, they lived together in concentrated settlements under centralised authority, the Tswana towns being the largest of this type, from which they journeyed to attend to fields and herds. Thus, in the west, dispersed resources went with concentrated settlement, as opposed to the eastern pattern in which concentrated resources gave rise to dispersed settlement (cf. Sansom, 17, for a more complete elaboration of this difference). The point is that missions were constrained to adapt to these environmental and social patterns. While among eastern Nguni, a mission could be set up as another small independent local unit (the village model), to the west it could only exist as part of a larger settlement or town. We can now explore the consequences of these different arrangements for the emergence of Christianity among Tswana and Zulu.

When Methodism first encountered the southern Tswana[1] in 1822, they were on the run from marauding Sotho groups, themselves displaced by the great social and political upheaval of the nineteenth century (Difikane), the shock waves of which had rolled westwards from its epicentre in Shaka's Zulu kingdom. The missionaries jumped to the conclusion that this state of instability and social dislocation was the permanent condition of the Tswana and their customary way of life, and it simply confirmed their predisposition to depict the indigenous people as benighted and backward, miserable, superstitious and inhabiting a moral wasteland. Their sense of mission was thus assured; to turn the Tswana into healthy Protestant individuals, self-determining agents of planned activity and moral accounting, and ultimately to transform them into a free and self-reliant peasantry. The Tswana themselves were trying to restore their collective independence and self-determination and the missionaries were welcomed as useful allies, both as robust riflemen and as political middlemen. Presented with the first opportunity to revert to their familiar settlement pattern, the Tswana placed the mission in the centre of a three-cornered town, an arrangement that was to pit Christianity against the indigenous political system. Methodist attempts at spiritual conversion were not notably successful; seeking a meeting ground in the identification of God with Modimo, they met with the usual incomprehension ('Where is God? How big is he? Does he have hair?'). Nevertheless, between 1822 and 1851, the missionaries drew a steady trickle of converts from among the disadvantaged and disgruntled, junior royals excluded from succession, poor men and women generally, and thus began to construct the nucleus of a state within the state. But in 1852 the Tswana again dispersed to escape the encroachment of their former allies, now the Boer Republic, upon their independence. The Christian nucleus established a new centre at Mafikeng and maintained its distinctiveness until Tswana consolidation in 1876 made Mafikeng the capital.

The confrontation between missionaries and Tswana authorities, between two ways of life, Setswana and Sekgoa, took time to develop. At first the missionaries could not function without the approval of the chiefs and hence concentrated their attacks on domestic arrangements. Under the misapprehension that the Tswana had no marriage, they made the rejection of polygyny and bridewealth a precondition of conversion. They resented the purely secular role allocated to them by the chiefs, but the Tswana understandably lumped them with other whites, motivated by material considerations. But once they attached converts in whom they sought to foster a vigorous individualism, the missionaries were committed to the elimination of public collective rites, without being fully cognisant of the extent to which these underpinned political authority. Their avowed purpose was to draw Tswana away from communistic tribal relations into healthy individualistic competition and this led them into a direct confrontation with officeholders over the control of spiritual power as a political asset. Their demonstrated capacity to draw water from the ground was seen as a usurpation of chiefly powers expressed in the rain-making ceremonies. Moreover, the rites gave collective expression to the conflation of categories which axiomatically the missionaries took to be distinct; the 'religious' with the 'political', the sacred with the profane, the symbolic with the rational, the spirit with the body. This fluid merging of what Methodism rigidly kept apart was derogatively labelled superstition. The Tswana chiefs and their subjects were in a dilemma. Christianity was undermining the political order but they had come to rely on the expertise, skills and resources which the mission commanded. Their compromises were rejected and the chiefs laboured to contain the internal threat of Christianity, putting their trust in the link with a converted royal, but without much success. For their part, the missionaries were intent on breaking out of chiefly control and, in pursuit of the formation of a stable social order within which to build a Christian peasantry, they invoked British colonial protection, thus embracing a more overt political role, which they had earlier despised.

The missionaries introduced the plough, irrigation and new crops to the converts but, of course, these were adopted more widely among the Tswana. The effects could scarcely have been envisaged by the missionaries. One was to fuse agriculture with pastoralism, the plough with draught animals, and thus to increase the economic control of men over women. Secondly, the production of grain for cash meant more extensive cultivation and land became a scarce resource, while not everyone could afford a plough. Those exercising traditional controls over land and labour had the initial advantage and, paradoxically, were able to compensate their waning political powers by extending their dominance over the sphere of production. By the 1860s two thirds of the independent townsmen had become clients of aristocratic producers. For this reason and because of other external developments, the missionary dream of an independent peasantry in biblical clothing was shattered and the disadvantaged among the Tswana were pushed into the labour market. Unwittingly, the missionaries had partly equipped them for this by transmitting to Tswana, generally, concepts of civilisation, person, property, work and time which familiarised them with categories ordering relations in industrial employment. Clearly the Methodist mission had a profound, long-term but unforeseen impact on the Tswana. The effect of the Tswana encounter on the missionaries was to make them re-evaluate the Methodist separation of religion from the political in the light of the political role they were forced to adopt in practice.

The Methodists were also present on the East Coast from 1841 onwards where they were preceded among the Nguni people[2] by American Congregationalists. They were quickly followed by Anglicans, French Catholics, German and Scandinavian Lutherans and Scottish Presbyterians. Few areas in the world had attracted such a range of missionary involvement and this made it very different to the Tswana experience of a single missionary body. Secondly, whereas the Tswana mission was directed at a single political unit, along the coast in Natal and further south the missionaries were surrounded by a multiplicity of uprooted and contentious tribal units, with the exception of the Zulu kingdom to the north. Not only did the missionaries compete at times with one another but they were the object of competition between vying African leaders. A third difference and additional complexity was the growing number of white settlers who increasingly demanded separate religious leadership from the missionaries.

It became clear that, although for Africans missionaries constituted a valued and scarce resource and were actively courted by them, it was not on account of their Christianity that they wanted them. Missionaries were coveted because they could bolster African leaders in inter-tribal disputes, act as brokers in black-white relations and render unusual services, by deploying skills in construction, agriculture, education and medicine and by facilitating the flow of material goods. They were even credited with superior magical powers. The result was the establishment of isolated mission stations on grants of a few hundred acres within which the missionary was a minor despot. All began with unrealistic expectations of success, though the envisaged manner of achieving it differed from one missionary body to another, from the mass conversion of whole tribes to the piecemeal attachment of individuals, from demanding a complete change of life from converts to tolerating a gradual adaptation and assimilation. It mattered little which approach was advocated; the result was the same, a resounding and uniform failure to win over converts in any significant numbers. One missionary lament asked 'shall we sit still and wait for better times as we have done for nearly thirty years?'

Better times had to be indefinitely postponed. The Nguni resolutely, defiantly and, at times, aggressively resisted and opposed conversion, seeing it as an act of cultural treason and of political defection. The hostility to Christian conversion was entrenched and widespread in British Natal but, in Zululand, it was extraordinarily effective because it was promoted by royalty, better organised and backed by physical retribution against the missions and their protégés. Because Christianity made an overt assault on lobola or brideprice, one of the lynchpins of customary relations, it was rightly perceived to destroy the African way of life. Conversion meant being wrenched out of the structure of customary attachments; one ceased to be a Zulu among Zulus and was accounted a loss to one's relatives. Tactics were evolved to ensure that children could have short-term exposure to education without running the long-term risk of turning into little Christians and thus into total strangers. Zulus were also concerned with Christian subversion of women, giving them expectations which ill-befitted them for a return to Zulu society, and with the individualism it fostered in converts. Nguni leaders were particularly sensitive on this latter score; to them a convert meant the loss of a follower. Christianity thus struck at the heart of political allegiance and the influence of the mission station was divisive. Unlike their Tswana counterparts, the Nguni leaders did not countenance the emergence of the mission station as a state within the state.

The general policy adopted by the Nguni was to neutralise the influence of the mission by isolation and quarantine, allowing only the secular assets of the missionary to filter through. Consequently, the physical and cultural separation of 'school' people, those residing on mission stations, from 'traditionalists' was from the beginning almost absolute. In the main, the missions attracted the misfits, the flotsam and jetsam of Nguni society, those thought not to be worth reclaiming; these first Christians were disparagingly referred to as Kaffirs, a corruption of the Zulu, iKhafulo, meaning 'those spat out' by society. Hence, the separation acquired a moral dimension. Missions were stigmatised as places of disrepute, housing renegades who flouted tribal custom and moral norms; dissolute and contaminating, they did not invite long association. The danger was accentuated by treating belief as if it were a sickness to be vomited by taking strong medicines. The policy of resistance and containment was so effective that a semblance of missionary success could be achieved only by artificial means, such as the practice of one missionary of buying children with cattle. The frustration of the missionaries eventually led them to renounce the Zulu King and actively to encourage the British invasion of Zululand in 1877.

That missions subsequently prospered throughout South Africa is due in no small measure to the steady diminution of African political and economic independence and to the gradual erosion of cultural and religious observances in black societies, under the impact of forces released by expanding white political and commercial interests. It would be facile to accuse the missionaries, imbued with humanitarian motives, of entering into a conspiracy with white expansionists, but historical circumstances did bring about an undeniable convergence of objectives and the missionaries, both to east and west, gave moral support to African subordination. They could not foresee the course of history or anticipate the extent of African repression and, faced by these historical developments, later generations of missionaries would recognise the need to reverse the tide.

Having reviewed the early stages of Christian intrusion into African society, with its attendant benefits, and the bases of African resistance to it, we can now examine the impact of African life on Christianity.

Once organised African resistance had been hobbled and a social order more benign to the missionaries had been superimposed, Christianity began to make inroads into African society. 'By 1880, although Christians still formed a distinct minority of the population, the church was well established in most tribal areas, counting many literate Bantu, including teachers, evangelists, and a number of ordained ministers among its members' (Pauw, 14: 417). One hundred years on, the official statistics of 1980 attest to the extraordinary success of a century of Christian expansion, in that no less than 75 per cent of the African population claims to be Christian (Kritzinger, 13: 253). Christian expansion went hand in hand with the steady deterioration of the power of the chiefs and the disintegration of other indigenous institutions; for instance, kinship solidarity has been undermined by migrant dispersal and self-interest, ritualised status progression has been largely replaced by the migrant experience or otherwise eliminated, and marriage and family patterns have been transformed to favour more personal contracts based on choice, in which wives are more equal and daughters more independent, while avoidance rules between in-laws have been relaxed. Africans have been inexorably drawn into a new kind of society, at once commercial, industrial and urbanised – a more overtly competitive society – in which the value placed by Christianity on individualism and self-reliance is a fillip to achievement. All of this has opened the door to Christianity and rendered it attractive. With the breakdown of the indigenous social order, the church exercises a strong organisational appeal, becoming the focus of a rich and varied pattern of associational life, to the point where it may be said to fulfil many of the functions of the ailing kinship group (Pauw, 14: 426). Furthermore, with the personnel and funds at its command, the church offers access to desirable resources, other routes being blocked; it provides amenities and services, especially in the fields of education, development and health care, which are particularly supportive in rural areas. There is evidence that Christianity attracts women to a greater degree than men (Pauw, 14: 422); they have little to lose and much to gain from embracing it. Conversion entailed a more radical dislocation for men, at least initially, and this has fostered a persisting male attitude that Christian religion is a female concern, although this is by no means an exclusively African reaction. A further outcome of missionary success, and of the ascendance of Christians in the African population, has been a softening of the cleavage between Christian and non-Christian ('school' as against 'traditional'). The original dichotomy between them has been reduced to a polarity, with a wide range of intermediate shades occupying the middle ground and a great deal of interaction and some degree of common participation in each others' rituals spanning the division between them. The mutual borrowing between these interacting poles, as well as the comparative unawareness of doctrinal distinctiveness between intermingling Christian denominations, facilitates a measure of synthesis between African and Christian religion. Those of a traditional persuasion, no less exposed to the sweeping social changes of the past hundred years, have made their compromises with Christianity. As Hexham, for instance, has shown (6: 284) the terms Unkulunkulu and Modimo have had their original meaning, that is, 'first human of our kind', superseded even for non-Christians by the sense of a creative spiritual being. Among Christians the belief in ancestors, though modified in certain ways, survives with great pertinacity and the tendency to read human malice as witchcraft or sorcery has proved to be equally durable (Pauw, 15: 109). The intermingling of these two religious streams, Christian and African, should startle nobody. It could scarcely be otherwise. And since it can be claimed that, for the believer, each operates in a different context or range of relationships (Pauw, 14: 438), in practice the choice of according one precedence over the other is rarely a cause of personal distress. Besides, the wearing of different hats for different occasions is a human rather than a specifically African trait.

But surely it is only a question of time before Christianity, with more powerful forces on its side, succeeds in completely replacing the surviving relics of an African religion which appears to be irrelevant in the evolution of modern society? Certainly those who lightly dismiss African religion as mere superstition would be inclined to think so. But it is by no means inevitable that Christianity will ever dispose of the central tenets of African religion – change them, yes, but it is doubtful if it can destroy them. Some African churchmen and other Christian leaders have become aware of this and are beginning to investigate the implications of inculturation.

Clearly, African religion is not itself resistant to change and yet there may be something within it which is. There is a distinction to be drawn between religious form, that is, the substance of belief and the pattern of observance, and the function or perceived purpose of religion, namely, to make the vicissitudes of life more meaningful, bearable and manageable. One can opt for a different form of religion while retaining the same function. Thus, while Africans have embraced Christian beliefs and practices, the expectation remains that these will yield the same kind of result as was delivered by indigenous observance. To the extent that this expectation is not realised, it makes sense to revert to more established praxis in which one has a greater degree of confidence, hence the retention of a reliance on diviners, ancestors and mystical protection from witches and sorcerers. The perduring principle is that there is a connection between religious observance and the realisation of *temporal* goals. According to this principle, formal observance of the behavioural requirements of Christianity should lead to a better way of life in the here and now, to improved conditions of health, prosperity and status, or, in a modern idiom, to jobs, income, prestige and increased well-being. It goes without saying that in South Africa the flow of these benefits to Africans has been systematically curtailed and otherwise unevenly distributed. The resultant disappointment and dissatisfaction among Christians largely explains, not only the continued appeal of revered ancestors and of mechanisms for coping with sorcery, but also the eruption of schism and the prevalence of sectarianism within Christian ranks.

These latter two phenomena account for the presence of thousands of thriving African independent or separatist churches. According to national statistics, the African independent churches presently claim 28 per cent of the African population, that is, well over a third of African Christians (cf. Kritzinger, 13: 253). The schismatics, those churches which were formed by fission from Christian denominations, have been styled 'Ethiopian' (Sundkler, 18: 53–6). The formation of these independent churches, free from white control, represents a revolt on the part of an emergent educated middle class in Christian communities and was born of the expectation that a wholehearted commitment to Christianity would lead to parity with whites. For a time, the educated Christian élite did enjoy equal opportunity for displaying leadership and initiative in the fields of capitalist agriculture, commerce and education but, when these secular opportunities were deliberately blocked by increasingly severe laws towards the end of the nineteenth century, the setback was such as to make competition for advancement in the church hierarchy especially acute (Etherington, 4: 161–2). Granted a certain reluctance to promote Africans to high ecclesiastical office and the limited number of offices to which they could aspire, the only realistic response was to create new areas of leadership by establishing independent churches under exclusively black control. Ultimately, these churches sheared off on the issue of internal church politics and the patterns of belief, worship and organisation were unaffected. Although the principle of opening up fresh leadership opportunities through schism continued to spawn new offshoots within the Ethiopian movement, it posed no challenge to Christian teachings and formally introduced no elements of African religion. It has gone into decline in the latter half of this century, possibly because the 'missionary' churches have adopted a more vigorous political stance and have elevated African churchmen to prominent positions.

If the Ethiopian churches have left the religious content of Christianity unchanged, this cannot be said of the other more powerful stream of African separatism. Here, the term 'Zionist' is employed to cover a bewildering array of independent churches which collectively have exhibited remarkable expansion and, as far as can be ascertained, continue to grow. At the core of this phenomenon are the 'true' Zionist churches stemming by descent and secession from an original foundation in the 1920s, which was inspired by a brand of American pentecostalism. But also to be accommodated within it are a multiplicity of churches based on the individual inspiration of a prophetic founder; some of these are modelled on the Zionist pattern to some extent, yet others, among them a few that are spectacularly large, have no real or pretended connection with Zionism. What they all have in common is a distinct tendency to incorporate more or less features of African religion. If Ethiopianism can be seen as a middle class protest, Zionism appears to be a reaction to, and adaptation of, Christianity on the part of the relatively uneducated working class and particularly, but by no means exclusively, of the impoverished urban proletariat. What Zionism holds out to the poor and despised is self-respect, economic and social support, a healing service and a general sense of security. While the missionary church does not actually neglect the poor, it is arguable that its ministry is not exclusively designed to cater for their needs. The church is particularly wanting in the area of health, always a major concern for the poor, in that it lacks an appreciation of the connection between religious observance and physical and social well-being, which is presupposed among Africans. Zionists not only acknowledge this connection but service it.

The belief in the mystical causation (and alleviation) of illness rests on the recognition of a number of agencies and techniques, thus, ancestors, spirits, malign humans (sorcerers), divination, sacrifice, medicines. The degree to which these features are retained, either singly or in combination, varies greatly across the wide range of Zionist churches. While the counteraction of sorcery is a concern which has scarcely abated (Kiernan, 9: 220), the influence of ancestors and the need for sacrifice have waned among some Zionists (Kiernan, 10: 311). At the same time, it is not unknown for church founders to assume the status of ancestors after death (Pauw, 15: 108) and this accords with a tendency among African Christians generally to view Christ as a kind of super-ancestor (Pauw, 15: 103). Recourse to traditional medicines is still a feature of some Zionist healing, but it is more usual to encounter a blanket prohibition on all medicines in favour of the use of water. Spirits, in combination with sorcery, remain a potent source of physical affliction. However, it is the Holy Spirit, a somewhat fallow feature of mainline Christianity, which is the supreme and distinctive source of Zionist power to do good, to overcome sorcery and to restore health, and communal prayer is the means of tapping and deploying that power. Divination is widely retained as a diagnostic technique but is commonly subsumed within prophecy, which relies on the inspiration of the Holy Spirit.

These elements of African religion are not merely tacked on to a body of essentially Christian belief. They rest not only on African precedent but simultaneously enjoy biblical legitimation. The invocation of the Holy Spirit, the causing of affliction by malicious (demonic) spirits, dependence on prophetic interpretation and speaking in tongues, the performance of sacrifice and the therapeutic use of water are all grounded in Christian scripture. Zionism thus succeeds in projecting a creative blend of African and Christian traditions. Although it applies not at all to some and unevenly to all, it can be said of Zionist churches that the bible is the well-spring of their preaching and practice. At the same time, they have given a definitively African impress to Christianity which strongly appeals to the mass of struggling workers as a means of improving their lives. Zionists have adapted Christianity to the conditions experienced by the majority of modern Africans: they are 'poor but self-disciplined people who rely on divine help and the support of fellow-members to develop themselves physically, socially, economically and spiritually and who offer the same capacity for self-improvement to others' (Kiernan, 12: 13).

It would be unrealistic to expect that African Christians would be exact replicas of the missionaries who converted them or of their European co-religionists. Their roots in a distinctive African way of life, the vibrancy and resilience of their own religious heritage together with the vigour of their initial resistance to Christian beliefs, all lead to this conclusion. Nor would it be any less naive to regard them as second class Christians on that account, for it is a fact to be regretted that many of them have grounds for believing that they are so regarded. If Africans did not yield to Christianity without a struggle, it should follow that they did not embrace it lightly and there is no reason to suspect that, collectively, their commitment to it is any weaker than that of any other population in the world. Like any other general statement which, perforce, I have had to make about African Christians in the course of this essay, this claim has to be read with some caution. No more than any other group of Christians, African Christians are not all of a kind. They differ considerably among themselves in their attachment to Christian principles and values and in the selective emphasis which is given to some elements and interpretations of Christianity at the expense of others. They are divided according to denomination and sect, divisions not all of their own choosing, although their readiness to transcend these barriers with relative ease and to join in ecumenical undertaking is perhaps more noteworthy (Pauw, 14: 426). African Christians also differ in their capacity to assimilate and express the tenets of Christianity, a product of class distinctions and of differential educational attainment. The gulf between how the Archbishop of Cape Town understands Christianity and how it is grasped by an unlettered woman in a rural reserve is as great as that between a mediterranean peasant and the Pope in Rome. Finally, Christians differ in the degree to which they accommodate features of African religion within their total belief structure, from those who consciously reject it *in toto*, to those who latently entertain some parts of it without being aware of any clash with Christian principles; from those who only in moments of great personal crisis will resort to its practice to those, like the Zionists, who overtly incorporate it into their organisation and worship.

Faced with this understandable range of variation, it is hazardous to make any generalisation about African Christians which will not run foul of the spectacular exception. Nevertheless, it seems to me that one general assertion remains which can be made without much qualification and with a greater measure of confidence. It has been noted that Africans dance their religion (Marett in Sundkler, 18: 198). The joyous celebration of the human body conveyed in African ritual dancing was condemned by the missionaries who took exception to its 'salacious' character. To the missionaries 'it proclaimed an ascendancy of the flesh that was inimical to the Puritan temperament' (Comaroff, 1: 151) in which religious observance was a means of chastening the body, subduing it and subordinating it to the ascetic spirit. African thinking uncompromisingly conflates the corporeal and the spiritual; they are mutually dependent and what affects the one affects the other. The third link in this indissoluble chain is the social. Social discord triggers spiritual mechanisms which afflict the body. Conversely, working with and upon the body in ritual releases spiritual forces which ensure natural and social harmony. Accentuating the body in worship is therefore an intrinsic feature of African piety. Nor is the corporeal dimension absent in the spirit world of the ancestors. 'Ancestors are repeatedly spoken of as being hungry and wanting attention' and were satisfied only with offerings of food and drink (Wilson, 19: 27). It is this interpenetration of body and spirit that Africans bring to Christianity and which, in a Christian idiom, constitutes a resounding affirmation of the doctrine of the incarnation. As the spirit infuses the body, the body expresses the spirit. Although this principle is most clearly stressed among Zionists, in their emphasis on bodily engagement and physical health, it remains a deeply felt concern among African worshippers of whatver persuasion and epitomises their most significant and abiding contribution to Christianity.

NOTES

1. Throughout this section on the Tswana, I draw liberally on Jean Comaroff's account of their missionary experience (Comaroff, 1: 123–56).
2. In what follows, I am indebted to Norman Etherington for his historical study of early Christian communities in Natal, Pondoland and Zululand.

BIBLIOGRAPHY

1. Comaroff, Jean, *Body of Power, Spirit of Resistance: The Culture of a South African People* (Chicago and London: University of Chicago Press, 1985).
2. Comaroff, Jean and John Comaroff, 'Christianity and Colonialism in South Africa', *American Anthropologist* 13 (1), 1986, 1–22.
3. Cory, Sir George (ed.), *Owen's Diary* (Cape Town: Van Riebeck Society, 1926).
4. Etherington, Norman, *Preachers, Peasants and Politics in Southeast Africa, 1835–1880* (London: Royal Historical Society, 1978).
5. Hastings, Adrian, *Church and Mission in Modern Africa* (London: Burns & Oates, 1967).
6. Hexham, Irving, 'Lord of the Sky, King of the Earth: Zulu traditional religion and belief in the sky god', *Sciences Religieuses/Studies in Religion* 10 (3), 1981, 273–8.
7. Isaacs, Nathaniel, *Travels and Adventures in Eastern Africa*. Vol. 1 (London: Edward Churton, 1836).
8. Kiernan, James, 'African Separatism' in A. Prior (ed.), *Catholics in Apartheid Society* (Cape Town: David Philip, 1982).
9. Kiernan, James, 'A Cesspool of Sorcery: How Zionists Visualise and Respond to the City', *Urban Anthropology* 13 (2–3), 1984, 219–36.
10. Kiernan, James, 'Dreams and Visions: Pattern and Purpose in Modes of Revelation among Zulu Zionists', *Africa* 55 (3), 1985, 304–18.
11. Kiernan, James, 'The New Zion', *Leadership: South Africa* 4 (3), 1985, 90–8.
12. Kiernan, James, 'The Management of a Complex Religious Identity: The Case of Zulu Zionism', *Religion in Southern Africa* 7 (2), 1986, 3–14.
13. Kritzinger, J. J., 'What the Statistics tell us about the African Independent Churches in South Africa' in G. C. Oosthuizen (ed.), *Religion Alive: Studies in the New Movements and Indigenous Churches in Southern Africa* (Johannesburg: Hodder & Stoughton, 1986).
14. Pauw, B. A., 'The Influence of Christianity' in W. D. Hammond-Tooke (ed.), *The Bantu-Speaking Peoples of Southern Africa* (London: Routledge & Kegan Paul, 1974).
15. Pauw, B. A., 'Ancestor Beliefs and Rituals among Urban Africans', *African Studies* 33 (2), 1974, 99–111.

16. Ranger, Terence, 'An Africanist Comment', *American Ethnologist* 14 (1), 1987, 182–5. Special Issue: Frontiers of Christian Evangelism.
17. Sansom, Basil, 'Traditional Economic Systems' in W. D. Hammond-Tooke (ed.), *The Bantu-Speaking Peoples of Southern Africa* (London: Routledge & Kegan Paul, 1974).
18. Sundkler, B. G. M., *Bantu Prophets in South Africa* (London: Oxford University Press, 1961).
19. Wilson, Monica, *Religion and the Transformation of Society* (Cambridge: Cambridge University Press, 1971).

2 Christian Missions in South Africa: Achievements, Failures and the Future

Willem Saayman

Instead of addressing the subject strictly historically, tabulating past achievements and failures, and then setting out future challenges, I would like to interpret the subject rather as an opportunity to take stock of Christian mission in South Africa at this point in time. In such a stock-taking, past achievements and failures, as well as future challenges, will obviously be addressed. Yet my approach will be rather more inclusive, without such clear divisions. I want to address the subject according to four critical issues facing the church in its African context (cf. Northcott 11: 36–40). These issues are:

(1) the fact that Christianity in Africa (also in South Africa) tends to *con*form to society, for example, in racial matters, rather than to *trans*form it;
(2) the fact of the church/mission's identity with the West and its civilisation, and the tacit assumption that Africa will do best by adopting the Western pattern;
(3) The fact of the church/mission's association with colonialism;
(4) The fact of the disunity in the church.

I

Christianity in Africa, and therefore also Christian mission in South Africa, tends to conform to societal institutions, such as racialism, rather than to transform society. Commenting on missionaries in Africa at the end of the nineteenth century, Moorhouse states, '. . . the racialism which had never been far from the surface whenever a white man contemplated a black one in Africa, was beginning to flow more freely than ever before. Missionaries had generally been no more exempt from this feeling than traders, though their professional ethic had given them a vocabulary and gestures which allowed them to camouflage their racialism with unlimited euphemism' (10: 282–3). This was unfortunately true for too long about church and mission in South Africa, and was true also of other things apart from racialism. However, because of the high visibility and pervasive influence of racialism in South African society, it is especially true with regard to racialism. From the very beginning all the churches and mission societies which became involved in mission in South Africa tended to organise such missionary efforts along racial lines. Thus George Schmidt's Moravian mission was directed only at blacks, while the Dutch Reformed Church early on in its history made provisions for separate ministries to whites and blacks. The so-called English-speaking churches have often expressed themselves very strongly against race discrimination, yet often suffer from discriminatory practices in their own life (cf. De Gruchy 2: 92–4).

It is only fair to point out that all of this ordering of their life according to societal structures was not the result of racialism only. There was also the contemporary theological understanding that mission as a separate ministry of the church could only be directed at blacks (not yet Christians), while ministry to whites (no-more Christians) was called evangelism. Yet it would be dishonest to say that racial practices in the churches were only a result of this theological misunderstanding; the racial structuring of society had a powerful influence on the practice of the church in its mission. A body preaching a message of unconditional inclusivity, therefore, very often in its own life practised overt or covert exclusivity. As McDonagh comments, 'The church did not, at least for a considerable time, see the inclusivity of faith and salvation as challenging or in conflict with political thinking about the distinction between religion and politics, the unreadiness of Africans for participation in the political process, the advantages which the introduction of European civilisation and political control offered the Africans as well as the impossibility of effectively challenging the European power structure and the church's dependence on that structure to maintain law and order and so allow the church to carry on its mission. All this was of course supported by churchmen's belief that the divine inclusivity vastly exceeded in importance and effect any human and political exclusivity and in its ultimate eternal fulfillment more than compensated for the suffering and privations of this world' (9: 106). This quotation from McDonagh points out all the various theological arguments which were often presented to rationalise racism in the church's life and mission. When all is said and done, though, the sad truth remains that instead of transforming this terrible sin in the life of South African society, the church in its mission conformed (and often still conforms) to it. 'The gospel should have the effect of judging the self-centredness of the powerful and not just of consoling the powerless. It should provide the inspiration, courage and strength to understand and finally be seen to overcome the exclusion and discrimination. Its apparent failure to do so over such a long period is partly understandable in human circumstances; it is hardly excusable to the church in the divine plan' (McDonagh 9:106–7).

And yet, despite all the gloom, this is not the full picture. Very often the Christian church in its mission was the first importer of ideas of freedom, independence and human rights. Thus no less an African nationalist than Chief Luthuli could state, 'Every part of Africa which has been subject to white conquest has, at one time or another, and in one guise or another, suffered from it, even in its virulent form of the slavery that obtained in Africa up to the nineteenth century. The mitigating feature in the gloom of those far-off days was the shaft of light sunk by Christian missions, a shaft of light to which we owe our initial enlightenment. With successive governments of the time doing little or nothing to ameliorate the harrowing suffering of the black man at the hands of slave-drivers, men like Dr David Livingstone and Dr John Philip and other illustrious men of God stood for social justice in the face of overwhelming odds' (Luthuli 7: 14). It would therefore be a simplistic judgement to state that church and mission simply conformed to society. Although very often the church which grew out of the mission looked distressingly like the society around it, Christian mission did, in its best moments, plant the seeds which would eventually grow to challenge unchristian and dehumanising forces such as racism.

II

The history of mission in South Africa gives ample evidence of the fact that church and mission were identified with the West and its civilisation, as well as of the tacit assumption that Africa would do best by adopting the Western pattern. To quote but one example of this: in his foundational work on the history of Christian mission in South Africa, Du Plessis asked the question: can the San people be

Christianised and civilised? In answer to this question he quotes Theal, 'It can now be asserted in positive language that these people were incapable of adopting European civilisation (Du Plessis 3: 269). In doing so, Du Plessis illustrates the unfortunate trend, which was rather typical of nineteenth-century missionaries, to equate Christianity with Western culture and civilisation, and therefore to equate evangelisation with acquiring the trappings of Western civilisation.

This problematical tendency in Christian mission in South Africa was very clearly embodied in the life and missionary convictions of David Livingstone. His belief that Christianity, commerce and (Western) civilisation go together, is well known and had a strong impact on generations of missionaries in South Africa. As a result of this conviction South Africa was westernised at the same time as it was Christianised; indeed, the westernisation acted really as a precondition to the Christianisation, with the result that the church came to be seen as *the* bulwark of Western civilisation in Africa. This is the context in which we should understand Majeke's serious criticism of Christian mission: 'The missionaries came from a capitalist Christian civilization that unblushingly found religious sanctions for inequality . . . and whose ministers solemnly blessed its wars of aggression. Men like Wilberforce had visions of extending this civilization to the ends of the earth' (8: 4). This is also the reason why Majeke can interpret the whole missionary effort in South Africa as the *method* by which the ultimate *aim*, namely the introduction of capitalism, was to be achieved (8:18).

Unfortunately there is much in the life of the church which confirms this negative image. What is necessary, therefore, is that, 'the Christian Church must become part of the "image" of Africa contributing its own life and vitality to the "African personality"' (Northcott 11: 38). Over the past decade a start has at least been made in this direction, largely the result of the rise of Black and African Theology. In this regard Black and African Theology have been both a continuation of as well as a contradiction to mission Christianity. They are a continuation insofar as they are Christian theology and part of the Christian tradition; but they are a contradiction insofar as they had to overcome the denial of true black Christianity in the previous identification with Western civilisation. As De Gruchy puts it, 'Black consciousness was a spiritual reawakening which drew its resources from Christianity, but also discovered new meaning in African culture, which, for many, was closer to Christianity than European culture' (2: 152). He therefore expressly links the growth of Black Theology with mission, 'It is important to realize that we are witnessing a result of the great missionary enterprise which, for all its faults, brought the gospel to South Africa in the first place. Like all theologies, it must not be allowed to turn in on itself or lose the ability of self-critique in the light of the Word of God, but it needs the freedom to express and fulfill itself for the sake of the church and society' (De Gruchy 2: 169).

Another facet of the Christian movement in South Africa in which the growth of a real African Christianity is reflected, is the development of African Independent Churches (AIC's). Originally the whole phenomenon of African Independent Christianity was interpreted as a protest against the Westernisation of the Christian mission in South Africa. More recent research has shown that the complex phenomenon of African Independent Christianity cannot be attributed simplistically to a single protest factor. Still the often latent desire for a true African Christianity did indeed play an important role in the growth of AIC's, and in this sense these churches serve today as a correction of the previous identification of Christianity with Western civilisation.

III

The historical fact of the entanglement between mission and colonialism has left the church in South Africa with a serious drawback which has to be overcome. Indeed, it is specifically in this regard, namely the entanglement of mission and colonialism, that Majeke raises her most serious charges against Christian mission in South Africa. I have already referred to the fact that she sees mission as the *method* by which the ultimate *aim*, namely the introduction of capitalism, was to be achieved (Majeke 8: 18). The liberation which early British missionaries preached was therefore according to Majeke nothing more than the liberation from feudalism to capitalism. In order to achieve this, missionaries in the classical liberal sense acted as intercessors for the blacks with the colonial government, as intercessors between the oppressors and the oppressed (Majeke 8: 26).

On the other hand one comes across commentators who regard the missionaries as everything but docile accomplices of the colonial authority. So, for example, R. Philip draws a picture of Dr John Philip, the well known missionary, as a typical pietist in his personal piety, but at the same time a fearless champion of 'native' rights (Philip 12). And Beetham states that, 'the names of Johannes Vanderkemp, Robert

Moffat, John Philip and David Livingstone recall not only preachers of the Gospel, but those who speak up for Africans' rights' (Beetham 1: 13). How is one to attempt a reconciliation of these widely divergent views?

It is undoubtedly true that the colonial government sometimes (most of the time?) used missionaries for its own purposes. On the other hand a shrewd and wise ruler like Moshweshwe made use of missionaries for *his* own purposes, using them to procure training for his people and placing them on exposed frontiers to act as agents for the expansion of his authority (Wilson and Thompson 15: 401). It is therefore only to be expected that the missionaries would sometimes be placed in an ambivalent situation. Groves recounts the case of J. Williams of the London Missionary Society (LMS): 'Colonel Cuyler, the landdrost of Uitenhage, desired regular interchange of information about Xhosa thefts and complaints against colonists, but Williams resisted this attempt to treat him as a disguised Government agent with secular authority . . . Williams pointed out that if he were to attempt to exercise a secular authority in the way suggested "the natives would say that I was come to entrap them, instead of instructing them in the truths of Christianity"' (4: 242). Groves therefore goes on to say that 'it is impossible to pursue this story of missionary beginnings at the Cape without realizing that a major factor in the situation was colonial policy towards the African peoples and the resultant attitude of the Government to the Missions. This was indeed a sinister background to all their endeavour, even threatening their continued existence if they were not conformable to official desire' (4: 250).

It is against this background that the role of the missionaries *vis-à-vis* the colonial authority has to be judged. Seen in this context, the missionaries did indeed from time to time act as sincere advocates of black rights. So, for example, the directors of the LMS 'emphatically condemning the acts of cruelty and rapine perpetrated against the colonists, . . . were courageously outspoken: "The Kaffirs are charged with robbery and encroachment; but whose lands have they sought but the lands of their fathers? What soil have they claimed but the soil that gave them birth? Why should the love of home and the love of country be eulogised as the virtues of patriotism in the civilized, and be branded as crimes and rebellion in the savage?" ' (Groves 5: 133). And it is for this reason that Sithole can come to such a positive evaluation of the role of the missionaries: 'If the Bible teaches that the individual is unique, of infinite worth before God, colonialism in many respects said just the opposite, so that biblical teachings were at variance with colonialism, and it became only a matter of time before one ousted the other. The Bible-liberated African reasserted himself not only over tribal but also over colonial authority' (Sithole 14: 86).

On the other hand the missionaries were as much children of their time as any Westerner who lived during the era of colonialism. They therefore paternalistically saw many benefits in the whole process of colonialism and the acquiring of Western civilisation, and therefore often, consciously or unconsciously, acted as agents of the colonial authority. Simply writing them off as stooges of the colonial authority will therefore be as mistaken as simply eulogising them as fearless fighters for the rights of oppressed colonialised peoples. Their relationships with the colonial government and its subjects were characterised as much by moral ambivalence as is the whole of our human predicament.

IV

The disunity of the church in South Africa is a serious obstacle to effective mission. South Africa has been described as the most over-denominationalised mission field in the world – undoubtedly an apt description. Not only were all the confessional and theological divisions of the world church transplanted in South Africa by the missionaries, but the situation is further complicated by the racial divisions in the church, as well as the fissiparous tendency in the African Independent Churches. The church in South Africa, being born mainly out of the missionary wing of Western Protestantism, is by and large evangelical in character. Evangelical ecclesiology is charac-terised by a strong tendency to view church unity mainly in spiritual and invisible terms. Especially in the specifically South African situation of racial divisions, however, the visible, organic unity of the church is of the utmost importance. In the words of De Gruchy, there is a 'direct connection between the unity of the church and the social situation in South Africa . . . To regard the unity of the church largely in spiritual and "invisible" terms is to misunderstand the teaching of the New Testament, and in the end, to compromise the witness of the church as it struggles against racism and other forces that divide and separate people on the grounds of culture and ethnicity' (2: 101).

In defence of the tendency to view the unity of the church mainly in invisible terms, it is often argued that visibly expressing the unity of the church in acts of joint worship, for example, is nothing more than a mistaken 'demonstration' of a unity which is basically spiritual in nature and therefore not in need of 'demonstrations'. 'This serves to underline the validity of De Gruchy's statement quoted above. The struggle for the visible unity of the Church in South Africa should therefore receive the highest priority. In the specific South African situation, churches whose witness is compromised to such an extent by racial divisions cannot expect to fulfill the mission of Christ – not because "demonstrations" of unity are required, but because the Church *is* and *must be seen to be* one' (Saayman 13: 126). The reason why the church must be *seen* to be one is closely allied to the mission of the church. According to John 17: 20–23 the acknowledgement by the world of Jesus as Messiah and Lord is directly linked to the unity of the church. And as the world does not possess an organ to perceive spiritual unity, it has to be visible, organic unity. Therefore 'if racial (and other) divisions are allowed to destroy this unity to the extent that the Church has to evade the demand for unity by taking refuge in a platonic, invisible unity, the Church in South Africa cannot expect to enjoy credibility in its mission' (Saayman 13: 126).

Unity in the church is therefore of the utmost importance for the sake of the mission of the church. This search for the unity of the church 'can only be credible if it is *in itself* a witness to Christ. In the same way, the fullness of the mission of the Church demands *in itself* the search for unity . . . It is impossible (therefore) to choose in favour of *either* unity *or* mission. The only possible choice for the Church, or any part of the Church is *for or against both*' (Saayman 13: 127).

V

A stocktaking of the past history and achievements of the Christian mission in South Africa leaves us therefore with a chequered picture. No single simplistic judgement of either good or bad can do justice to this history. Many things happened which the church today has to confess in a spirit of repentance – and it is not always clear whether the church already acknowledges this. It is especially the consequences of the entanglement between mission and colonialism, resulting in a mistaken relationship between church/mission and state, which urgently needs to be corrected. In order to achieve this, many methods of executing the mission of the church have to be radically altered. If the church is willing and able to acknowledge and face honestly its past mistakes in mission, it may find in its mission history the makings of a firm foundation on which the challenges of the future can be faced.

BIBLIOGRAPHY

1. Beetham, T. A., *Christianity and the new Africa* (London: Pall Mall Press, 1967).
2. De Gruchy, J. W., *The church struggle in South Africa*, 2nd edn (Cape Town: David Philip, 1986).
3. Du Plessis, J. *A History of Christian missions in South Africa* (London: Longmans, Green, 1911).
4. Groves, C. P., *The planting of Christianity in Africa* Vol. 1 (London: Lutterworth Press, 1948).
5. Groves, C. P., *The planting of Christianity in Africa* Vol. 2 (London: Lutterworth Press, 1954).
6. Hastings, A., *A history of African Christianity 1950–1975* (Cambridge: Cambridge University Press, 1979).
7. Luthuli, A. 'Africa and freedom' in *Africa's Freedom* (London: Unwin Books, 1964).
8. Majeke, N., *The role of the missionaries in conquest* (1952).
9. McDonagh, E., *Church and politics. From theology to a case history of Zimbabwe* (Indiana: University of Notre Dame Press, 1980).
10. Moorhouse, G., *The Missionaries* (London: Eyre Methuen, 1973).
11. Northcott, C., *Christianity in Africa* (London: SCM Press, 1963).
12. Philip, R., *The Elijah of South Africa* (London: John Snow, 1852).
13. Saayman, W. A., *Unity and mission. A study of the concept of unity in ecumenical discussions since 1961 and its influence on the world mission of the Church* (Pretoria: Unisa, 1984).
14. Sithole, N., *African Nationalism*, 2nd edn (London: Oxford University Press, 1968).
15. Wilson M. and L. Thompson (eds) *A history of South Africa to 1870* (Cape Town: D. Philip, 1982).

3 Black Theology in South Africa: Achievements, Problems and Prospects*
Takatso Mofokeng

INTRODUCTION

In any review of the impact of Christianity in South Africa the emergence of black theology must surely qualify as a development of very great significance indeed, and such a review must begin with a realistic sense of contemporary realities in this country. The people of South Africa live during difficult times when crucial decisions have to be made. With the state of emergency widened to embrace the entire black South Africa (there are no signs of it in white towns) there is no doubt any more that there is a great measure of intransigence and desperation on the part of the white state. Large-scale indiscriminate detentions of black leaders and activists of all ages; the tear-gassing of people in churches and at funeral services and the brutal shootings of unarmed school children provide irrefutable concrete evidence of this desperation and intransigence. The entire black South Africa has been forced to retreat to a low level of resistance because of increasing and deepening repression and harassment. This situation of crisis has brought black politicians, economists, social scientists, religious leaders and theologians who are in prison as well as those who are still outside, to a tactical stop. They have had to stop and review the situation of stalemate and search for new and more meaningful answers to pertinent questions which are posed by it and devise new strategies of advancing the cause of liberation.

The present setback which we are experiencing in our exodus is also an opportunity that cannot be missed. It is a setback in what appeared till recently as an unstoppable thrust to bring about the emergence of a new future, and the birth of a new nation has been abruptly and ruthlessly intercepted. While it is a lamentable setback, it is one that can and has to be converted into an opportunity which if properly and carefully utilised can benefit the struggle for liberation. The state of emergency is for black people an epistemological moment to which all

37

thought and language have come. It is not certain anymore that old theological language and communal activity will continue to be the best way of expressing the presence of God among the oppressed in the most effective manner in and beyond the present state of emergency. It is not certain any more that this language, which used to kindle the light of hope and the fire of active faith in the oppressed, will continue to be the most effective witness to God as He continues to bring down opposition to his sovereignty and to the liberation of His oppressed creation. It is also not certain any more that this theological language which we now use will continue through the entire state of emergency to give appropriate expression to and inspire new 'emergency' responses of black people to God's command to engage in a radical discipleship in pursuance of justice and liberation.

It is therefore imperative that in our attempt to be theologically vigilant and our continuing obligation to test and reconcile black concrete discipleship with verbal articulation of that discipleship we should grab the epistemological moment which has been forced upon the black theological community and struggle. While standing firmly in the present, we have to re-examine the past in order to fashion a better and more crisp and sharp theological language that can cut open the door to a future of liberation for black people of South Africa.

LIGHT ON METHODOLOGY IN BLACK THEOLOGY

From 1978 when, according to S. Biko, 'essentially the black community is a very religious community, which often reflects on being, in other words, what is my purpose in life, why am I here, who am I?,'[1] going through 1980 when Bonganjalo Goba stated that '. . . black theological reflection as a communal praxis cannot be separated from the ongoing commitment to political change in South Africa'[2] to 1986 when Itumeleng Mosala asserts that Black Theology has to be a theoretical weapon of struggle in the hands of the exploited black masses,[3] this theology has always been one of praxis which emerged in the heat of the historical struggles of black Christian workers and peasants and has always retained that base. Initially, however, the link with this praxis was not pronounced and vivid because black praxis had not yet evolved into a deliberately organised historic project. But as soon as the South African Student Organisation (SASO) and the Black People's Convention (BPC) launched the earliest concrete social projects for purposes of economic improvement and psychological liberation under the banner of Black Consciousness, this important methodological link became explicit and visible. It immediately had a direct and forceful impact on the determination and arrangement of theological themes in order of priority. In fact Black Theology, as a theological articulation of black consciousness in the religious realm became one of the many projects of increasing awareness. It continues to play an important role in the ideological formation of black political agents. This is evinced by the successful leadership of Archbishop Desmond Tutu, Dr Alan Boesak and other black pastors.

This complex relationship was misunderstood by white theologians, who wrongly attempted to link Black Theology with some European theologies in order to acquire the right of placing it on their agenda in the arena of their struggle for orthodoxy.[4]

As a matter of fact the blame can not be put entirely on the acquisitive instinct of European and other Western theologians. Black theologians in South Africa are also to blame. They did not make the distinction between their theology and others sufficiently clear. They also continued to use dominant theological categories which are household categories in European theology without even explaining the difference that emerges when the same categories are used in their theology. Neither did they make a total break epistemologically with European theology. They continued to be dependent on it for a long time and thereby opened their theology for European theological meddling, long before they were ready to deal with critique from outside.

James Cone, a black American theologian, was very clear from the very beginning that he was not satisfied with Euro-American theology and that he was attempting to leave it behind him. His book, *A Black Theology of Liberation*, is evidence of this noble effort. Other black theologians, who shared the same concern, became involved in assessing whether he had succeeded in his goal or not. This is how G. Wilmore and C. Cone came into this debate and assisted J. Cone through their critique to go further and complete the epistemological break which he had initiated, making a real new beginning for Black Theology.[5]

On the issue of the identity of Black Theology, Wilmore asked what factors made black theology black, and thus distinguished it from white theology. He pushed Cone to get to the basic issue of the sources and the norm, which is what determines the identity, content and methodology of a theology.

In the above mentioned book J. Cone can be seen vigorously

grappling with the theological constructions of K. Barth, P. Tillich and to a lesser extent that of R. Niebuhr. He criticises some parts of their theology in the light of the social challenges and theological needs of the black community and appropriates some of its useful methodological elements. In that way Cone released himself from the grip of Euro-American theology and went further in his development of Black Theology, as is evident in his book, *God of the Oppressed,* especially.

South African black theologians were not so fortunate in that regard. They did not have a Wilmore at the very early and crucial stage of the development of their Black Theology. Consequently their theology suffered from a lack of self-critique which did not last very long, as we can see from the present debates among black theologians in South Africa.

When, as a matter of priority, most black theologians focussed their entire attention on the black community and its praxis as sources of material for reflection, and neglected public methodological debates, B. Goba plunged into these debates in which he was later joined by I. Mosala and B. Tlhagale who lifted the debate to a higher level. At a time when the acting subject in the struggle for liberation was not yet clearly identifiable in group or class terms, B. Goba, M. Buthelezi, D. Tutu and others, consistently identified the entire black community as the acting subject of its liberation.[6] It was only later when black trade unions for both men and women made a forceful appearance on the labour scene and took their rightful place at the forefront of the fierce battle for a society of unshackled people that Mosala and B. Tlhagale identified our interlocutor as the black workers.[7] It is necessary to say that this change of the identity of the acting subject did not imply disillusionment with or a rejection of the black community. It was a necessary deepening of the concept 'black community' whereby this community is named in relation to the primary activity – economic activity – that determines its oppression and also serves as a trustworthy criterion of national liberation. Black people have been dispossessed of their land, which is the basic means of all production and subsistence as well as a source of power. They have been turned into dispossessed workers whose only possession is their labour power. By identifying black people as workers these theologians have lifted our struggle beyond civil rights to human rights from an exclusive struggle against racism to a social and national revolution.

This deepening in the identifying of the black interlocutor is very important for Black Theology. It introduces into the area of theology its material basis, which has been rather largely neglected by Euro-

American theologians in favour of spiritualisation. This is to my mind, an important theological deepening and corrective.

Recent publications by our American brothers and sisters also show evidence of a further development in this area.[8] In the earlier stages of the development of their version of Black Theology the interlocutor was the black community as an undelineated whole. The acute and urgent problem was racism as it affected the entire black community and as it permeates the entire fabric of American society. This viewpoint was carried forward into international theological dialogues, especially into the dialogue with Latin American theologians, where it was presented forcefully by Cone and Wilmore among others. Latin Americans for their part approached theology from the class paradigm and also forcefully presented class as the determinant in society.[9]

In the ensuing difficult debate that took a long time before positions softened, each side acceded to the point made by the other. Black theologians recognised that racism is not the sole problem facing blacks and that capitalism posed a serious problem and that it has to be addressed theologically, combated socially as well as politically and eradicated simultaneously with racism. What is important for us at this stage of our discussion is that in addition to convincingly presenting the painful, concrete issue of racism and acknowledging that the Latin Americans had a point about capitalism, black Americans also addressed the issues of religion of the oppressed as well as the culture of the oppressed within the framework of marxism. They pointed out that these two areas are the achilles' heel of marxism.[10] In fact as far as religion is concerned, marxism generally regards it a negative factor in the life of oppressed peoples, that is, as an ideological instrument that is used by the dominant classes against the dominated. And as we all can attest from our own experience as well as that of many people in our black communities, this is not completely true. Oppressed black people continuously remould religious ideas which are imposed upon them and produce a religion that is capable of functioning as a defensive as well as combative ideological weapon.[11]

This position is based, as we know, on the marxist principle that the dominant ideas in every society are the ideas of the dominant class. This leads to ignoring the ideas of the oppressed or relegating them to a position of insignificance, thus clearing the field for dominant ideas to continue to dominate unchallenged. The experience of the oppressed is that their ideas, in the present case their dominated religion, continue to survive and play a sustaining role as well as that of contesting the hegemony of the religion of the dominant classes. (So far the Italian communist party is the only marxist party that has acknowledged the positive role of religion, especially the religion of the oppressed.)

The implication of the above for black social analysts is that black theologians and other social analysts should not rely exclusively on marxism in their attempt to understand their predicament in a capitalist and racist world. They have to find within their own cultural heritage other tools which will be used complementarily with marxism.

This is a lesson which is very important for South African black theologians because there is a significant section of the oppressed in South Africa today that insists on the validity of the orthodox marxist assertion that race is not a co-determinant of oppression of black people. Those who hold that view are bound to ignore the culture and religion of black people in their search for weapons of struggle.

The redefinition of the identity of the black community also coincided with a new issue of the agenda – women's oppression and their struggle against it. Black Theology had up to that point not addressed this issue and for this gross neglect black theologians should hang their heads in shame and ask for God's forgiveness and that of our mothers and sisters.

All attention had up to that point focussed entirely on national issues in which black people as a group stand over and against white people, the white economy and the white state. Many black women, especially at a time when they too were in the forefront of the battle facing the wrath of the army and the police and suffering equally if not more, demanded the issue of their subservient position during times of relative peace to be addressed. The entire black community, especially men, was challenged to widen and deepen sanctificatory processes within itself and practise internal justice and distribute power to effect equality in order to enhance the external thrust of communal praxis and theology in combat against oppressive forms of white theology. Black women who have tasted equality in battle, in suffering and in victory are not prepared to return to their former status in the community and at home after combat or when the struggle is over. They call for internal dialogue to redress this situation so that the gains of their struggle will not be lost.[12]

The church and theology have not escaped from this justifiable critique. It is indeed true that black women constitute the largest group in the church and also that they provide the material means for its survival. But paradoxically, they are the objects of a male-created, -

monitored and -imposed power structure and theology. Women are in most cases not allowed to exercise power in the church wherein they are almost the sole audience and activists, be it political, religious, financial or theological power.

They are allocated some space, yes, but it is space at some remote corner and not at the centre stage of the church. That remote corner is the only space they are allowed to use for articulation of their own theology, a theology which they create in response to the challenges which face them specifically, as well as those which face their families and community.

Black women in South African churches are starting to stand up against this exclusion in church and theology. They have started to articulate their theological thoughts and demand an audience and dialogue.

As we are all aware and have come to accept, pursuing a relevant theology demands a rigorous analysis of society. This is the area in which the overwhelming majority of black women in South African churches are in my opinion not yet well grounded. And this is the area in which .black American women are well developed. They can therefore be of great assistance to black South African women, church women and theologians.

As we have stated above, the advance to which we are referring is in the area of the analysis of society and that determines the questions and priorities for the theological agenda. We have noticed that black female theologians in the US distinguish their predicament from that of white women. This is because of the peculiar way in which racism operates in a capitalist society. It leads to more suffering for black women in society. On the other side, capitalism in a racist society favours white women and exploits black women together with black men as well as the entire black community.

This understanding of their society has led to a development of black theology from a feminist perspective which is different and separate from white feminist theology.[13] Its agenda is also different from that of white feminist theology because black women stand in the black community and the black church. They are not undistinguishable members of American society and church. This is what most black South African women of the church still have to learn, accept and defend. Since feminist theology came to South Africa wearing a white garb and was introduced by white feminist theologians at a time when the black consciousness perspective had lost ground to the so-called progressive democractic perspective, women's theological reflection has also been dominated by the dominant perspective and the questions and priorities of white society and the white church. Black questions take a back seat as a result.

Social developments in South Africa have inevitably led to a greater appreciation of the value of the social sciences and their analytical usefulness in bringing clarity to an often muddy and confusing situation. Calls in this regard were repeatedly made by Goba in the past and are presently renewed by Tlhagale and Mosala. They loudly call for a search for an appropriate biblical hermeneutic which would deal with these new issues satisfactorily. It is especially Mosala's timely critique of Black Theology for its failure to become the property of the masses that really hurt. Black Theology, he said fairly recently quoting Karl Marx '. . . has not yet become a material force because it has not gripped the masses'.[14] He called for a new way of going about with the biblical text, a way that will enable the hidden and silenced but struggling, oppressed people in biblical communities to become visible, and to break their silence and speak up clearly and loudly enough to be heard by the equally silenced black people today as they stand up to demand God's justice and liberation. As history shows, radical calls of this nature are not readily heard or speedily responded to black theologians in South Africa are, however, slowly responding and in their struggle to read Scripture in the light of the perspective of the black working people as their loyal 'organic intellectuals' they are amazed at the dynamite that lies hidden deep in the bowels of the scriptural text. It will, however, take some time before the results of this new effort reach the international theological market in large consignments.

Inevitably, the above hermeneutical question raises again a related issue which, we thought, had been adequately dealt with and closed in the 1970s by A. Boesak, T. Mofokeng and others, namely the relationship between scripture and a social praxis which is informed by the social sciences, especially by dialectical sociology of marxist derivation.[15] While Boesak in his argument with Cone in the 1970s insisted that 'the light of the Word of God' is the only final judgement of all action and reflection, other black theologians disagreed and contended that light shines both ways because of the unifying and enlightening presence of Jesus the Messiah in the struggles of faith of both the communities in the biblical text as well as that of the suffering black people in South Africa whose text is being written with their blood.

It is interesting to see that black theologians in the US have also had a similar debate. I'm thinking here of J. Cone and Deotis Roberts.[16] In this debate Cone took the position that God is not absent from the life of the oppressed as they struggle in life and as they read the scriptures in the light of their actual concrete actions. And consequently, that practice is of revelational importance. In other words the light of that practice shines on the scriptural text making certain things in the text perceptible as it does on the practice, improving it qualitatively and driving it forward. Roberts, I think, takes the traditional reformed view that light can only shine from the bible, which is the view propounded by Boesak in his first book *Farewell to Innocence*.

I'm of the opinion that, when discussing this matter, we should bring the Spirit of God into the picture and ask what the role of the spirit is in the communal practice as the spirit that dwells among those who are occupied with being obedient to Jesus' command of loving their neighbour. If this spirit is God and if this God is, as the bible teaches, involved in that practice in both its concrete and theoretical forms, is it too far-fetched to conclude that spirit brings the two practices together? To put it differently, I don't see how and why the spirit of God can be involved in the life and practice of the biblical community of faith as well as in contemporary community of faith and not be involved in bringing the two communities together when the contemporary community desires to dialogue with and learn from its predecessors. I think that the God who has promised us His presence continues to use our own practice to enlighten our reading of the scriptural text. I would therefore agree with Cone on this matter.

For those who would fear contemporary textual domination of the biblical text and would want to protect it, I would say that we should emphasise the dynamic character and nature of the spirit of God in the community of faith. God's spirit cannot be held hostage or prisoner in the practice or life of the contemporary community just as this spirit could not be imprisoned in the biblical communities. The bible witnesses to many occasions and situations where people or communities were abandoned by God and whom the spirit of God deserted. The spirit of God is free and frees.

Coupled with the above issue is the closely related one of the 'authority' of scripture as a whole, which especially Mosala addresses very provocatively, posing very pertinent questions. According to him, too many black theologians still approach the text with awe as the 'Word of God' and consequently use uncritically texts which can have no other impact than that of frustrating the total liberation of black people.[17] This mystification of the text still stands in the way of a rational and liberating reading and appropriation of it. It hides the class struggles which were going on in biblical communities of which the biblical text reports. It also hides the fact that the text itself is a product of such struggles, one that has to be approached with great analytical care lest black theologians make wrong textual connections. Unfortunately we can only report that not many of our theologians, especially biblical scholars, have entered this discussion. It is therefore not evident whether this proposed approach will make Black Theology grip the black Christian masses and enhance their faith as well as stimulate and radicalise their struggle for justice and liberation.

Black American theologians approach the scriptural text from within the black church and read it using all the available tools from within this church. This is important because it is this church or Christians within it who read that text and have to be helped to understand it better or go further with it. So far evidence has shown that this community has always read this text in such a way that it contributed to their struggle to survive in a society which militated against the life of black people and denied their humanity. Their reading has even encouraged them to engage, as Wilmore has shown so clearly in his *Black Religion and Black Radicalism*, in acts of rebellion, in the past and present. There was therefore no general opiating influence of the bible evident.[18]

But since many black people who belong to the working class and are aware of their class position and class interests have to be reached with the biblical text, it remains a question whether they can be reached and impressed with the traditional reading of this text. I have my doubts. I suspect that they would prefer to read it in such a way that they would hear it addressing their working class problems, which are not absolutely identical with those of the black community *per se*. If that be the case, then black American theologians will benefit from engaging in the dialogue which Mosala is calling for.

DEEPENING THE SOURCES

Right from the inception of contemporary Black Theology the definition of the concept 'black' has been problematic. While there was unanimity at the beginning that all the oppressed people of South Africa, that is, Africans, Coloureds and Indians, are black people, the same cannot be said regarding inclusion of black culture, black history and African traditional religion as formative factors in Black

Theology. M. Buthelezi explicitly and emphatically talked about the culture of blacks having been totally destroyed – and was followed by A. Boesak in that he excluded it in his first book while including black history. S. Biko, on the other hand, firmly held that black culture had only been severely damaged but not totally erased from the memory of the oppressed as well as removed from their daily lives.[19] Many theologians, including those who contributed towards the publication *A relevant Theology for Africa*, concurred with him on this.[20] At the end one was confronted by two parallel streams in our black theological thinking which still persist, despite slight narrowing lately. Many black theologians of the former persuasion have come to acknowledge the pervasiveness of black culture and recognise the importance of black history for Black Theology. Those who were first in regarding black culture as important were already sifting through it to distinguish useful elements from those which, if displayed to whites, wrongly give an impression of our readiness to submit to white oppression. Others were searching for cultural parallels with the culture of the Hebrew people of the Old as well as the New Testament and identifying concepts like 'corporate personality' and 'solidarity' which are central to African and Hebrew perceptions of being human. S. Maimela even explored the contribution which an African concept of salvation can make towards Christianity in general and to theology in particular.[21]

The case of African traditional religions was more difficult, especially as found in the African Independent Churches – the principal religious custodians of African culture and traditional religion. Some students in SASO during the early days of the black consciousness movement were rightly very critical of the African Independent Churches for their apolitical stance, which significantly reduced the numbers of black Christians in the forefront of the struggle. They subsequently advocated the total eradication of these churches, a task which would have been impossible given their closeness to the black working class and to working class conditions that still exist. The situation has fortunately changed, though not significantly. Notwithstanding persistent criticism of these churches' intolerable neutrality, which is seen as tantamount to support of the racist state, there is an increasing understanding among a significant number of black theologians of these churches and appreciation of their positive role in enabling the lowest in the black community to at least absorb the sting of oppression and survive.[22] We therefore anticipate an increase in research interest in this area of church activity as well as dialogue with theologians and religious leaders of these churches on the part of black theologians. One can only caution that this new appreciation should not lead to idealisation of these churches. They still have great problems like all the historic churches.

As we all know, the areas of African culture, history and traditional religions have been both areas of unhappy separation as well as possible bases of Pan African dialogue, co-operation and unification of black people in the world. In the 1970s there was unfortunately less success in the dialogue between Afro-Americans and many Africans who took part in it. While G. Wilmore and J. Cone tried hard to bridge the differences by pointing at areas of possible common interest and cross-fertilisation, J. Mbiti on the African side seemed irrevocably bent on widening the gap by stressing the differences between these theologies at the expense of commonalities.[23] It was not until Desmond Tutu entered this discussion as an African and a black person, that is as one who combines in his life and thought African culture and politico-economic commitment on the African continent, that prospects for Pan-Africanism in theology improved. Since that intervention by a black South African, many of his countrymen have joined the discussion and more African theologians in free Africa accept the validity of the critique made by J. Cone that African theology is impoverished by neglect of socio-political issues. We are thinking here of people like J. Chipenda, Kwesi Dickson and Jean Marc Ela. This shows the key strategic position in which our situation of oppression and our struggle have put South African black theologians in regard to this Pan-African theological dialogue. It remains to be seen whether we will live up to the challenges that face us and use the opportunities which are open to us.

In their own appropriation of African culture, history and traditional religion as formative factors, some black theologians in South Africa are going further and consistently apply class analysis to them in order to eliminate their negative elements and discover positive ones. This they do notwithstanding their recognition of weaknesses in marxism on issues of culture and religion. Mosala asserts, for instance, regarding culture and black theology, that 'for this reason the task of a black theology of liberation is, amongst other things, to identify the distinctive forms of working class culture and use them as a basis for developing theological strategies of liberation'. When doing that we should search in the past struggles of our working people how this culture informed and transformed their struggles so that we can deal critically with their contemporary culture. It is necessary to do that because, as Marx says, 'the history of all hitherto existing society is the history of class struggles'. We should therefore investigate the cultural history of the struggling classes and learn from it. This is how Cornel West and J. Cone deal with black culture in the US.[24]

As far as African history is concerned, I am of the opinion that while we accept the symbolic importance of certain African personalities of the past as bearers of the traditions of struggle against oppression in its many different manifestations, we should dig deeper and unearth the real bearers of those struggles, the lowest men, women and children in our African societies of the past and be informed by them in our reading of scripture and our subsequent formulation of black theology. We should not get stuck in valorisation of African feudal kings, especially in present day South Africa where most of their descendents are being co-opted into the apartheid system and are consequently a serious distortion of the history of their forbears.

As far as African traditional religion is concerned, as it is practised inside as well as outside of the African Independent Churches, we should be very careful, especially now. Too many missionaries and former missionaries who were denying the validity of these religions and actively campaigned against them are now glorifying them. In the past they tried hard to elicit black support in their campaign to eradicate these religions; now they are asking for black support in their rehabilitation. This we should not give. Instead we should follow our own path and critically appropriate only those elements which appeal to and sustain the black poor and most powerless in their struggle for survival. These we should consider incorporating into Black Theology.

DOMINANT THEMES OF THE PAST AND PRESENT

Racist oppression and capitalist dispossession of blacks in South Africa have undergone a historical development and manifested themselves differently during different historical periods. This happened, of course, in such a way that the suffering of our people broadened and worsened progressively. Not only men and women became the victims but old people and babies as well. The different official names which were used to refer to the indigenous people reflect this. They were initially kaffirs, then natives, later bantu and now blacks (with a truncated connotation). Black theologians worked hard to create an appropriate psychological resistance among blacks and also made necessary adjustments to means of resistance, continually evolved new strategies in order to be more effective in such worsening conditions. Since the assault on blacks was not limited to the economic, social and physical areas but extended to include ideological manipulation, which took – among many others – a theological form, black Christians, pastors and theologians were called upon to respond theologically to counteract and restrict the mental damage to black Christians. They had to join hands with black sociologists, economists, psychologists and other scientists.

In the field of Black Theology it is evident that the selection of themes and determination of priorities was related to the historical development of objective conditions as well as the subjective state of the Christian faith of the oppressed. At no point in time did Black Theology follow the European and white American agenda, because it was part of the problem. That would not have helped to build theological resistance against further corrosion of the mind of the oppressed. And as S. Biko aptly put it 'the mind of the oppressed is the most potent weapon in the hands of the oppressor'. To deprive the oppressor of this precious mind Black Theology had to determine its independent agenda which, more often than not, contradicts that of most white theologians.

In the actual systematic development of Black Theology two poles of reference stand out: the Exodus and the praxis of Jesus, the Messiah (Christology). Much of the earlier Black Theology revolves around these events that provide a powerful paradigm of liberation. In both cases the notion of history, which is generally insufficiently dealt with, if not totally neglected by traditional white theology, is regarded as very important. A historical approach to those events brings out their dynamic theological character. All the different theological concepts which are dealt with – creation, liberation, justice, reconciliation – are injected with a dose of historicity by a people for whom history and time had stood still until they decided to move them. Black people have been awakened to regard 'the world as history in the making' and themselves as active participants in its making and moulding. To them history is not simply harmonious but conflictual as well because of inherent contradictions and antagonism amongst blacks and whites. It is dialectical and stumbles through moments of harmony and conflict in its forward movement. In opposition to a notion of history which moves independently of the human agency, with God alone in action, a notion that creates passivity among the oppressed who cannot wait an extra day longer for change, black theologians emphasise black people's agency as co-workers with God. They work with God in the historical destruction of structures, institutions and attitudes that make acquisitions of life and dignity by black people impossible. Black Christians – men and women, young and old – are shown biblically that they should be on the cutting edge of the struggle to create new structures and institutions which they can use to gain their economic justice, social equality and political empowerment as a people and as individuals. It is their Christian vocation to do this in anticipation of the coming of the Kingdom of God. To stimulate this active discipleship, Black Theology emphasises people's God-given potency for revolutionary action and encourages black people to believe in themselves as well as in their abilities to define, shape and reshape their world and social relationships. It is in connection with these emphases that A. Boesak discussed the biblical basis of black power in the middle 1970s and S. Maimela does today at the end of the 1980s. (As things are today in South Africa this notion of black power in various forms – its channelling, direction and utilisation – will continue to be emphasised by Black Theology.) An understanding of the central position and role of the modern racist state in organising and utilising power to foster injustice and violently resist all efforts towards peace makes these emphases imperative.

In this area Cone and Albert Cleage have remained loyal to the earliest positions of black consciousness and black power. When Cone enters dialogue with black marxists he does so without abandoning that position which deals so aptly with racism. He complements it with a paradigm that is capable of dealing better with capitalism. In that way he is strengthened instead of weakened. C. West is open to critique in this area.[25] For him racism is only responsible for the extra suffering of black people and not for their basic suffering. The tragedy with many black South African theologians and activists is that in a situation in which racism is still rampant and promises to be more so as the struggle hots up they have dumped black consciousness in favour of the more attractive and fashionable orthodox marxist paradigm. They believe that it is more adequate in dealing with both racism and capitalism in spite of the absence of evidence supporting that claim. These groups can learn from the American experience that these two paradigms complement each other and be more open in their dialogue with fellow theologians of the former persuasion.

Black Theology also deals at length, as is evident in the writings of the period around the 1976 Soweto uprisings, with the experience of suffering and death both within the Exodus journey as well as in Christology as the major fountainhead of the Christian faith. Since

1976 the cross continues to hang heavily over black South Africa. Institutional resistance (sin) which violently confronts all followers of the radical prophets and Jesus the black Messiah in the Exodus of black people, results in inconceivable suffering and genocidal killing of our people all over our country. Their suffering through heinous forms of torture, shootings and callous rape of our school children is related to the suffering of Jesus and his death at the hands of the state that acted in the name of the economically, politically and religiously powerful. As early as 1974 the endless killing of so many young people before their time, let alone the invisible internal bleeding of millions of our people as a result of economic and psychological torture, already constituted a crucial theological problem for M. Buthelezi. Dying in the path of a radical discipleship was made even more of a problem because there was then no visible convincing sign that the wall of apartheid was cracking. Instead it was toughening and thickening day by day, making it imperative for theology to descend deeper and deeper into the dark mysteries of the suffering and death of Jesus in search of the presence of God and his promises for our people. Black theology cannot but continue to search for the christological meaning of their suffering and death because their innocent blood continues to scream to God for justice like the blood of Abel. Within the South African valley of the death of innocent black children who try to do God's will by following in the footsteps of Jesus the Messiah, Black Theology is bound to stand on both feet. It will have seriously to explore in this overshadowing atmosphere of death and despair a new and meaningful way of understanding and articulating the faith of a resurrection that denies death a word of finality in the world. Black Theology owes this to the black departed, the living and the unborn whose history is characterised by death and the absence of God. The power of resurrection which is produced from the tomb of Jesus is desperately needed to break the bonds of racist oppression that tie black people to the South African inferno.

NOTES

*This essay, except for minor changes, first appeared in the *Journal of Black Theology in South Africa*, November 1987, and is used here with the permission of the author and editor.

1. Biko, S., 'Statement made in court during the SASO-BPC trial' as quoted by A. Millard. See his *Testimony of Steve Biko*' (New York: Panther Books, Granada, 1979) p. 94.
2. Goba, B., 'Doing Theology in South Africa: A Black Christian Perspective' in *Journal of Theology for Southern Africa*, June 1980, p. 25ff.
3. Mosala, I. J., 'The use of the Bible in Black Theology' in J. Mosala and B. Tlhagale (eds), *The Unquestionable Right to be Free* (Skotaville, Johannesburg, 1986) p. 175ff.
4. See Bosch D., 'Currents and crosscurrents in South African Black Theology' in G.S. Gilmore and J. H. Cone (eds), *Black Theology, a Documentary History 1966–1979* (New York: Orbis, 1979) p. 233ff.
5. See G. S. Wilmore's *Black Religion and Black Radicalism* (New York: Anchor, 1973) p. 295f. Also see Cone's *God of the Oppressed* (New York: Seabury Press, 1975) p. 252f: also see Cone's *My Soul Looks Back* (Nashville: Abingdon, 1982) p. 82.
6. See Mokgethi Mothabi (ed.), *Essays on Black Theology* (Johannesburg: UCM, 1972).
7. See B. Tlhagale's 'Towards a Black Theology of Labour' in C. Villa-Vicencio and J. W. De Gruchy (eds.), *Resistance and Hope* (Cape Town: Dave Philip, 1985) p. 126ff.
8. See C. West, *Prophecy Deliverance* (Philadelphia: Westminster Press, 1982), Cone's *My Soul Looks Back*; see also Frances Beale's 'Double Jeopardy: To be Black and Female' in *Black Theology: A Documentary History*.
9. Sergio Torres and John Eagleson (eds), *The Challenge of Basic Christian Communities* (New York: Maryknoll, Orbis, 1981).
10. See especially Cornel West's paper in *The Challenge of Basic Christian Communities*. Also see Cone's *My Soul Looks Back* as well as in *For my People*.
11. See I. J. Mosala's 'African Independent Churches: a study in socio-theological protest' in *Resistance and Hope*.
12. Bernadette Mosala's 'Black Theology and the Struggle of the Black Women in South Africa' in *The Unquestionable Right to be Free* is along these lines.
13. See the articles by Frances Beale, Jacqueline Grant, Theressa Hoover, Pauli Murray and Alice Walker in *Black Theology: A Documentary History*.
14. Mosala's article, entitled 'The use of the Bible in Black Theology' in *The Unquestionable Right to be Free*, addresses this issue.
15. See Mofokeng, T. A., *The Crucified Among the Crossbearers: Towards a Black Christology* (Kampen: J. H. Kok, 1983) and Boesak, A., *Farewell to Innocence* (Kampen: J. H. Kok, 1976).
16. See J. Deotis Roberts, *Liberation and Reconciliation* (Philadelphia: Westminster Press) and Cone in his *A Black Theology of Liberation* (New York: J. B. Lippincott, 1970).
17. See *The Use of the Bible in Black Theology*. See Cone's *God of the Oppressed*, and also J. Deotis Roberts' *Roots of a Black Future: Family and Church* (Philadelphia: Westminster Press, 1980).

18. See G. S. Wilmore's *Black Religion and Black Radicalism*.
19. See *Farewell to Innocence* for Boesak's position and *Essays on Black Theology* for that of M. Buthelezi. S. Biko's position on this issue comes out clearly in his 'Black Consciousness and the quest for true humanity' in *Essays on Black Theology*.
20. See Hans. Jurgen Becken (ed.), *Relevant Theology for Africa* (Durban: Lutheran Publishing House, 1973).
21. S. Maimela, 'Salvation in African Traditional Religions' in *Missionalia*, Vol. 13., August 1985, No. 2.
22. See I. J. Mosala, 'The Relevance of African Traditional Religions and their relevance to Black Theology' in *The Unquestionable Right to be Free*.
23. See Sergio Torres and Kofi Appiah-Kubi (eds), *African Theology en Route*, (New York: Orbis, 1978). Also see Cone's *A Black Theology of Liberation* and Cornel West's *Prophesy Deliverance*.
24. See C. West's *Prophesy Deliverance*.
25. Ibid.

Part II
Christians and Apartheid

4 The Theology of Separate Equality: A Critical Outline of the DRC's Position on Apartheid

Johann Kinghorn

In assessing the role of Christianity in Southern Africa, the DRC (as I shall call the Nederduitse Gereformeerde Kerk), undoubtedly merits special attention for its part in the religious expression of the apartheid world-view. Being by far the most popular church among Afrikaners (and in fact among all whites), it was inevitable that attempts to give religious expression to the apartheid world-view would manifest themself primarily within the DRC. Enough has already been written on the popular religious expression of apartheid. In this chapter we shall therefore concentrate on the *theology* of apartheid according to the *official* self-understanding of the church. We shall start with an interpretative historical outline of the growth of the theology of apartheid, followed by a description of the anatomy of this theology and conclude with some evaluative remarks.

THE GROWTH OF THE THEOLOGY OF APARTHEID

The era of non-doctrinal segregation (1652–1927)

The DRC became involved with the history of Africa when the Dutch established a small colony at the Cape of Good Hope in 1652. However, it was only in 1824 that the church in the Cape formed its own synod and became institutionally independent of the mother church in Holland.

After 1836, when the trek of a number of boers into the interior began, the church naturally accompanied them. Eventually indepen-

dent synods were established in those regions which in 1910 became
the northern provinces of the then Union of South Africa – the
Transvaal, the Orange Free State and Natal. These synods were,
however, relatively unimportant until the 1930s. The main body of the
DRC remained in the Cape Province and for all practical purposes the
Cape synod was the DRC until the 1930s. Although a co-ordinating
Federal Council had existed since 1905, the DRC was united under the
umbrella of a general synod only in 1962.

When the ideologues of apartheid describe the history of South
Africa, they invariably state that apartheid started in 1652. That,
however is an ideologically inspired misrepresentation. No doubt a
class consciousness existed. What else might be expected of the
seventeenth to the nineteenth centuries? But it operated on a personal
level and was not institutionalised. Moreover, the class consciousness
prevalent in the Cape never fully coincided with colour. The division
ran along the lines of civilisation and education as it did in almost all
colonial territories. There was what one might call a 'natural'
segregation which is not to be confused with apartheid.

It is also fairly common to ascribe the so-called apartheid of the
previous centuries to the influence of the DRC and particularly to the
'Calvinist' theology promoted. The fact is, however, that until 1857 the
DRC officially tended the opposite way. Decisions taken between
1824 and 1852 at the Cape synods all clearly indicate that the church
officially ignored racial differences. There could be one church only,
for whites as well as blacks (Borchardt 1: 75).

Yet, unofficially, during the middle of the nineteenth century a
growing lobby in favour of separation *within* the church did occur. It
arose from the practical situation in various congregations. Blacks
were all first generation converts and very often totally ignorant of the
church's traditions. Differences in language, culture and hygiene also
created friction. Gradually, some whites began to promote the idea of
one church, but separate services, and perhaps even separate congregations for the 'members from the heathen'. At the synod of 1857
things at last came to a head and it was decided that '. . . although it
was desirable that our members from the heathen be assimilated into
existing congregations . . .' some who are 'weak' [read: whites] had
opposed this and, therefore, '. . . impeded the propagation of
Christianity among the heathen'. Thus, for the sake of reclaiming
white support for mission work, synod decided that those Christians
from the heathendom would henceforth '. . . enjoy their Christian
privileges in a separate building . . .' (Handelingen 6: 60).

Evidently, a separate church was not foreseen, either in theory or in practice. Yet in 1881 the Dutch Reformed Mission Church (DRMC) was formed in order to provide some cohesion to the appendages to the white congregations which had sprung up since 1857. However, some blacks still remained members of the DRC and two black congregations chose to retain affiliation with the 'mother church', one of which to this day is a member of the Cape DRC synod. Even the separation of the DRMC was not total, as it still depended on the DRC for financial support, drew its clergy from the DRC, and until the 1960s decisions taken by the DRMC were subject to ratification by the DRC.

The history of the origin of the DRMC illustrates the ambivalence that prevailed from the nineteenth century to the 1930s. In principle, the DRC accepted the factual unity of the church – and therefore implicitly, the equality of humanity. In view of the practical situation, however, it was prepared to make exceptions for tactical reasons.

There are some who take the view that the formation of the DRMC in 1881 was the historical beginning of apartheid and that political developments later on had merely followed the lead of the church. Convincing as this may seem, it nevertheless does not hold true. As was pointed out, neither in 1857 nor in 1881 was the separation interpreted as permanent or correct in principle. It was explicitly recognised as a concession to 'weakness' and regarded as a deviation from the church's tradition. Moreover, the separation of the DRMC happened in an era when all the so-called civilised world believed in natural segregation.

On the other hand, it cannot be denied that the separation of the two churches did play a significant role in later developments. In the 1930s prominent DRC theologians started to justify the events of 1857 and 1881 theoretically. Although it was never officially argued that the separation presented a *model* for the social policies of SA, the event was interpreted as the first step in a process which was coming to fruition in the policy of apartheid. Identifying providence with their reading of *the* tradition of the DRC (as one of separation along racial lines as experienced since 1857), they propounded the idea that the 1857 decision was correct, despite the fact that synod had, at the time, advanced the wrong reason for it. Synod, so to speak, anticipated (by God's grace) the tradition of separation and thus proleptically enacted God's will for the church.

It was, of course, an interpretation of the events contrary to the intentions of those who were involved at the time. But after 70 years the intentions were drowned in the effective tradition of separation. In a climate where an ideological approach had become dominant, the events of the previous century could be construed as historical legitimisation for apartheid.

And so, what was originally considered to be no more than a matter of strategy and functionality, became a matter of *tradition and therefore of doctrine*. Henceforth anybody who advocated the structural unification of the various DR Churches, would have to face the question whether the tradition of separation since 1857 had been a *sin*.

Meanwhile the ambivalence of the nineteenth century continued into the 1920s when there were even signs that the DRC would make the quantum leap of a radical shift in anthropology away from a feudal class consciousness to a modern concept of equal democracy. In the 1920s the rudimentary elements on which to build this anthropology were present in the DRC. This is evident in the following extract from the minutes of an important ecumenical conference organised by the general mission committee of the DRC held in Bloemfontein in 1926:

> It is the opinion of this conference that the general principle applicable to all Christians concerning the relationship between Whites and Blacks today, is one of *co-operation* between them for the good of *the fatherland*. From this follows: 1) that it goes against Christian principles to put general constraints on the progress of natives; 2) that it does not necessarily conflict with such principles to attempt to uplift Blacks apart from Whites; 3) but it nevertheless remains the responsibility of Christians to scrupulously monitor such divisions in order to ascertain that all sections of the population be treated fairly.
>
> This conference, in obedience to the teachings and Spirit of Christ, emphatically emphasizes the *divine dignity* of natives as men and women created in the image of God. Thus they shall never be used as instruments to be exploited in order to enrich others. (Handelinge 7: 50) [My italics and translation.]

The conception of an ideological theology (1927–48)

However, during the next eight years, drastic changes took place. New, younger members of the DRC were appointed to the mission committee. After some wheeling and dealing, they produced a newly formulated mission policy for the DRC which was adopted by the Federal Council in 1935. The essence of the guiding philosophy is clearly articulated in the following paragraph:

The *traditional fear* among the Afrikaner of 'equalisation' of black and white stems from his abhorrence of the idea of racial admixture and anything that may lead to it. On the other hand, the Church does not deny the native and the coloured a social status as honourable as they may be able to achieve. Each nation has the right to be itself and to attempt to develop and uplift itself. Thus, while the Church rejects social equality in the sense that the differences between races are negated in the normal run of things, the Church would like to promote social differentiation and spiritual or cultural segregation (Handelinge 8: 99). [My Italics and translation]

The contrast between this and the previous statement, is profound. Clearly, the era of apartheid had dawned. The word apartheid was only used three years later by one of the main personalities behind the new mission policy. However, the idea was very clear and in the final sentence the will to institute a massive social revolution – which is what apartheid eventually turned out to be – to engineer reality in accordance with the idea, is explicit.

Of all the many factors and their intricate interplay which created the climate and dynamics conducive to the growth of the apartheid ideology, only the two most important, namely, the economic and the ideological factors, are briefly mentioned here.

Since the Anglo-Boer War (1899–1902) Afrikaners, living mainly on the farms in the interior, were caught up in a slow but relentless process of impoverishment. There were many contributing factors, among others the international economic crisis, local droughts and over-population of rural areas. This resulted in massive urbanisation over a relatively short period. And, as the poor whites moved to the cities, the slums, unemployment figures and the psychological feeling of inferiority grew (Van Jaarsveld 13: 312–17).

By 1929 the problem began to assume the proportions of a national disaster. The American-financed Carnegie Research Project on the so-called 'poor white' problem showed that one third of all Afrikaners were living below subsistence level. The majority of Afrikaners could be classified as poor, and it was debatable whether they could be integrated into an industrial culture, since they lacked the necessary skills and perhaps even adaptability, it was stated.

The poor whites were not the only poor. Many poor blacks also migrated to the cities and ended up in the same slums as the whites, which, in the 1930s in South Africa, were racially mixed.

It was in this context that the factor of ideology entered. A racially defined ideology of nationalism imported from Germany, Spain,

Portugal and Italy penetrated Afrikanerdom like a veld fire. It found a situation well prepared by the British colonial legacy: the belief in the superiority of the Western European (for which in South Africa, read: white), which was given some institutional legitimacy by the British by excluding blacks from the voters' roll when the constitution of the Union of South Africa was drawn up in 1909. Now, however, it became possible to legitimise separation of black and white on ostensibly scientific grounds. After all, racially defined nationalism teaches that humanity is *genetically* divided into inferior and superior groups. White superiority could be considered a fact of nature.

The new philosophy of Afrikaner nationalism which quickly developed in sympathy with these ideas meant that, for the first time in South Africa, a racist world view was introduced (Kinghorn 11: 54). This provided the basis for a relentless campaign by all and sundry, including the churches, to separate black and white permanently, comprehensively, and by means of force if need be. According to this ideology, such a separation was the absolute prerequisite for maintaining the natural world order and consequently for saving the Afrikaner from the depths of the slums, as well as from a total loss of self-respect. The suffering of the Afrikaner, accordingly, was the result of the sin of admixture, of a higher culture stooping down to a lower culture – thus defiling both. In this respect the Rev. P.J.S. de Klerk wrote in 1939:

> Equalisation leads to the humiliation of both races. Mixed marriages between higher civilized Christianized nations and lower nations militate against the Word of God . . . This is nothing less than a crime, particularly when we take note of the very clear lines of division between the races in our country. The Voortrekkers constantly guarded against such admixture and because of their deed of faith the [Afrikaner] nation was conserved as a pure Christian race up to this day (De Klerk 3: 61). [My translation.]

Undoubtedly, this kind of language is crude, but for some Afrikaners it did then what Black Theology has done for some blacks since the 1970s: it affirmed the humanity of the outcasts and served to spark some measure of self-respect. But, *unlike* Black Theology, and typical of all racism, it accomplished this by denigrating others and legitimising their subjugation. The racially defined ideology of nationalism is after all inherently incapable of affirming an equal and inclusive humanity. It can only affirm one's humanity by stressing other people's inferiority.

Thus, the idea of apartheid was born in the 1930s. It was enthusiastically supported by the church right from the start, as we shall see. But, it must be added that the church's conscience very soon became uneasy about the elements of denigration and subjugation inherent in racism. And, in 1950, that led to a reinterpretation of apartheid to which we shall soon refer.

Apartheid as a racially defined doctrine of nationalism eventually legitimised a policy that resulted in possibly the most comprehensive programme of social engineering the world has seen this century. Within less than three decades a total reconstruction of South African society, politics and the economy enabled the poverty of the poor whites to be converted into great affluence.

This process only began in 1948 when the National Party came into power and started to implement measures to consolidate whites geographically, economically and politically. As early as 1942, however, delegations of the DRC visited the then Prime Minister, General Smuts, pressing for legislation to effect this consolidation. On several occasions government was approached on the issues of racially mixed marriages, separate suburbs, separate education and separate industries. Contrary to popular belief, Smuts did not respond negatively to these submissions, but he could not agree to legislation as the proper means of achieving the desired separation. (*Sy ontstaan* 12: 73–4).

The period of rationalisation and doctrinalisation (1948–82)

When the NP came to power in 1948, it speedily implemented the first three of the four measures mentioned above. Clearly, socio-political lobbying by the church became unnecessary. This meant that the church could now apply more time and energy to the theoretical and theological expression of its point of view. Because the church's support for apartheid was initially based almost exclusively on the concept of tradition – as was made clear in its mission policy – for some time the nagging need had been felt to explain that this tradition was, at least, not in conflict with God's revelation in Scripture. Now the church could attend to this need at leisure.

Moreover, for some time critical voices had been objecting to the church supporting the political programme of apartheid on *theological* grounds. For example, Ben Marais argued that practical considerations might perhaps necessitate apartheid, but the policy could not be presented as a Biblical obligation. Thus a debate on the theological grounds for apartheid was sparked off which continued for more than a decade after 1948. The debate centred mainly on the most satisfying exposition of the theological grounds for apartheid. As a result, influential conferences on the 'native question' (as it was called in the 1950s and 1960s) were held, numerous study commissions were appointed and a succession of reports and documents written.

It is, of course, impossible to review this documentation here. In any case, despite countless variations as to details, they all operate within the same paradigm. For our purpose we only need to refer to two documents.

In 1948 the Transvaal Synod after a stormy debate accepted a report entitled *Racial and national apartheid in the Bible* (Handelinge 9: 279–84). This was the first exegetical attempt made by the DRC to point out that the tradition of separation, as practised since 1857, was indeed in accordance with the Scriptures. Written by a prominent New Testament scholar, the report bore the stamp of authority. It was soon rewritten and finally replaced by much more sophisticated and doctrinal documents. Yet there was no deviation in them from the fundamental propositions set out in the 1948 report. It was after all the original formulation of the theology of apartheid thereby defining the paradigm and informing the scope of successive documents.

The 1948 document stated that Scripture posed the 'unity of humanity'. Yet Scripture also 'recorded and presupposed the division of humanity in races and nations as a deed of God'. This division comprised the totality of life: constitutional, social and religious. God therefore 'graced those who obeyed this apartheid'. Regarding the church, the document affirms the 'unity in Christ' but sees this unity as a spiritual communion with Christ and not as a physical communication of believers beyond the boundaries of one's own nation.

Finally, the document affirmed the 'principle' of 'trusteeship'. It admitted that 'direct' Scriptural proof was not in evidence, but maintained that it could be inferred from the historical role of Israel that 'one nation should take responsibility for another' – that is, the stronger should see to the needs of the weaker, materially as well as politically. We shall come back to the 1948 document. But at this point it is appropriate to turn our attention to the second document, as it represents a significant reinterpretation of the 1948 document as regards the issue of trusteeship.

The second document was drawn up in 1950 at a 'People's Conference' in Bloemfontein. The significance of this conference, once again initiated by the mission committee of the DRC, cannot be overestimated. It was a mammoth gathering from all over South Africa and from abroad – although, of course, no black delegates were invited. Even the WCC was represented. Many papers were read and discussed. A great number of resolutions were adopted and eventually submitted to parliament. These resolutions were all-embracing – dealing with religion, economics, education, social welfare, politics and many other aspects affecting blacks in South Africa.

The formula developed in Bloemfontein was later adopted by Dr H. F. Verwoerd when he became prime minister in 1958 and was introduced to the world as *separate development*. The formulation of the policy of separate development in 1950 was the one and only occasion in the history of apartheid when the DRC was demonstrably the first to initiate and propagate a certain concept. In all other cases the Church merely reflected broad opinion, or even trailed the political process. But, for once, in 1950 it was at the forefront. And although it remained within the parameters of apartheid, it did effect an important reinterpretation of apartheid, which has had more than merely theoretical significance. To understand this, we need to interrupt our historical outline briefly.

Since 1799 mission work had been very high on the agenda of the DRC. This emphasis on mission work has played a far-reaching and as yet underestimated role, not only within the DRC, but also in the development of a social theory in Afrikaner circles. When all is said and done, the essence of mission theology during the nineteenth and twentieth centuries lies in the implicit recognition of the dignity of every human being. After all, Christ had died for all. From that point of view every human being shared a basic dignity before God. On this basis fully fledged racism is untenable. Add to this another aspect derived from Calvinist theology. Despite the impression created by certain wayward schools of Calvinist theology, Calvinism stresses the equality of all people before God. Combined, these two concepts make it impossible to entertain the notion of racial inequality – and thus the factual inequality and inferiority – of some. In fact, it makes the logic of racism fundamentally suspect.

These theological perspectives, absent in the 1948 document, came to the fore at the conference in 1950. As the ideology of apartheid was already entrenched, it was, however, impossible to break the paradigm as such. But they did provide a stimulus strong enough to change the character of the DRC's concept of apartheid. In the end, what amounts to a compromise between a racially defined concept of apartheid on the one hand and a recognition of the equal human dignity of every human being on the other, was reached at the 1950 conference, thus bringing about a correction of the statements about trusteeship in the 1948 report.

The compromise was articulated by the 1950 conference in terms of a detailed system of social ethics. The underlying formula was: all people were equal, not as individuals, but within the confines of their particular nationhood. All nations were also equal – at least in principle, if not at the level of their cultural development. Exactly for this reason a God-given responsibility rested on the more developed to ensure the development of the less developed – without violating their individuality and dignity.

Thus Christian trusteeship was redefined. It was no longer a matter of merely seeing to the needs of the inferior. Removing the status of inferiority altogether was the aim. The less advanced had to be supported in order to develop to levels of advancement equal to those of the more advanced. This approach seemingly eradicated the negative connotation of apartheid. Henceforth, no one who cared for the good of humanity could dispute the Christian character of apartheid or the obligation to practice apartheid any longer. In fact apartheid could even be considered a way of liberating the subjugated.

But it was a compromise. The recognition of the fundamental equality and human dignity of all human beings was integrated into the notion that humanity is divided into a number of nations. That the division of humanity into different nations was a providential deed of God and that the separate existence of nations was therefore the intended order for humanity, was taken as an immutable truth. It was not separation that was wrong. Inequality had to be combated.

Thus, the DRC's mature concept of the meaning and purpose of apartheid was born. Convinced that apartheid was based on sound principles once the notion of inherent and permanent (that is, racial) inequality was discarded, the DRC began to develop an intricate theological edifice in support of their perception of apartheid. What emerged was: *the theology of humanity as equal because of separation.*

In an information brochure reflecting these perspectives drawn up by the Cape synod just before 1950, this reinterpretation of apartheid is aptly proclaimed.

The Church accepts the existence on earth, of nations and races as separate entities through God's providence. This is therefore not the work of human beings. . . . Although God created all nations on earth from the same blood, He gave each one *its own national intuition and soul* which must be honoured by all and which may not be destroyed by the superior in the inferior (Kinghorn 11: 92). [My italics and translation.]

In this spirit the Bloemfontein congress (1950) could, for example, declare:

> The policy of autogenous development which we advocate . . . is no static condition but dynamic in its *separate development*. It proposes a process of development which seeks to lead each population group to its purest and speediest autonomous destination under the hand of God's gracious providence. The policy is the means to an end, namely an independent status. It envisages the elimination of conflict and friction, of the *unhealthy and unequal competition between the more and the less developed* (Naturellevraagstuk 5: 20). [My italics and translation.]

Note that the concept of race was substituted by 'group' or 'volk'. Very soon after this congress the word race disappeared almost entirely also from other church documents – only to make way for the concepts 'nation' and the 'diversity of nations'. Note also that here, probably for the first time, the idea of independent black nation status surfaces. Henceforth separation would no longer be effected along horizontal lines, leaving some (whites) at the top and others (blacks) at the bottom, but vertically, leaving people next to each other. According to the 1950 vision humanity did not consist of permanently inferior or superior people but of more or less developed nations.

The 'problem' of South Africa was thus in theory redefined from a racial to a nations problem. In particular, the question which was afterwards most hotly debated was the nature of the *relationship* between different nations. For the next 30 years this question was to be the shorthand indication of the paradigm within which all social analyses, ethics and theology took place.

In theory race, as the principle of division, was hereby discarded. In actual fact, however – in church as well as state – this was not the case. And when one closely analyses the theory itself, it turns out that even in theory it was not true. The notion of race had merely been absorbed into the notion of nation. But viewed superficially, and most definitely from the viewpoint of the mature apartheid theologians, the concept of race was eradicated and with it the elements of denigration and subjugation inherent in racism. This is the reason why, during the past three decades, the DRC has never felt guilty in the face of all the complaints about racism. And, in the mid 1970s, when politicians admitted to some institutionalised forms of racism in society, the DRC promptly responded by outrightly condemning racism. In 1986 it even managed to call racism a 'grievous' sin (Church and Society 2: 20). But, all the while, racism and apartheid were never equated.

In passing, it is opportune (although I would suspect, in some quarters not popular) to note that the combination of mission theology and the Reformed emphasis on equality, leading to the shift from 'race' to 'nation' effected by the 1950 congress, contributed largely to saving South Africa from total submission to racism. The restraining influence of this theological input has not, as yet, been adequately understood. The reason, I submit, is that popular writers on the Afrikaans Churches' involvement with apartheid tend to interpret the church's viewpoint in the light of popular religious pronouncements on social issues. It is only recently that serious analyses of the official documents of the DRC have been made.

Looking back on the 1950 congress, one has to come to a strange conclusion. *If* apartheid is defined as a system of social separation based on *race*, intending to entrench the superiority of some and resulting in· oppression and inequality, then it had already been rejected by the DRC in 1950. But the 1950 congress did not define apartheid in these terms. Instead a dream was constructed. Theirs was an apartheid called separate development. It was the dream of 'separate freedoms', equal development for all nations and affirming human dignity.

By redefining the present in terms of an ideal end, the reality of apartheid was substituted with a fantasy that over the years had very little in common with the real policy of apartheid. And through the years, in ever growing theoretical abstraction, the dream persisted. However, in the actual experience of day-to-day life for a black person this dream turned into a nightmare. This is the tragedy of the South African saga. While blacks were treated as inferiors and lived in a culture of marginalisation and insecurity, whites believed that they had established a peaceful and just society by the establishment of homogenous black nations and states.

Having provided the platform for this illusion, the DRC participated in its perpetuation by pronouncements of synods, policy declarations, and even ordinary sermons. As recently even as 1987 an editorial in the official church organ *Die Kerkbode* (4: 6) hailed the establishment of independent black states (such as Transkei, Venda, and such like) as milestones on the road of justice in South Africa, disregarding the multitude of sociological and economical evidence to the contrary. Not that it was intentional though. It was just one more example of the discrepancy between dream and reality in the DRC.

A final, but very important comment still has to be made in connection with the 1950 congress, without which the events of 1986 become incomprehensible. As pointed out above, the 1950 congress formulated its theology of apartheid in terms of a detailed (although illusionary) social ethics. This was to be the last time for more than 30 years that an ethical approach to the situation was adopted. After 1950 the mode of reflection was to be highly philosophical and doctrinal.

Even the 1974 document *Human Relations in the Light of Scripture*, which was an attempt to formulate the church's position in a way comprehensible to its members, was too theoretical ever to be popularly understood. Significantly, the 1974 document contains no references to the contemporary situation. It comes across as an attempt to express eternal truths.

It certainly was not as if the church was trying to avoid the issues in South Africa. On the contrary, all the theorising and doctrinalising was done to aid the search for a solution to the country's problems. But, drawing on the (utopian) social analysis of 1950, a rigid system of social ethics was developed, eliminating the need to engage in further analysis of the situation. Over the years the social ethical framework devised in 1950 was simply assumed all along. Although a few synods since 1950 have adopted some *ad hoc* resolutions of a social ethical nature, it is safe to say that the ethical *mode* of reflection and an ethical *approach* to apartheid were lost after 1950. Supporting apartheid was no longer a matter of volition. It had become a creed.

The time for revision (1982 onwards)

Dreams or fantasy cannot be maintained forever. Sharpeville in 1960 could still be attributed to ungodly instigation but by Soweto (1976) even government was prepared to accept the findings of a board of enquiry into the causes, stating that the real reasons for the upheaval were material and political. After tremendous wheeling and dealing behind the scenes, the era of reform was ushered in.

More than just party politics was, and still is, at stake. The fundamental question underlying all the rumpus of the past six years is whether the failure of apartheid was a result of the application of the policy or of the policy itself. Apartheid had clearly failed. But in order to rectify the situation, was an adaptation or a transformation of the South African social order called for?

Until now it seems that whatever reforms the government has instituted, they were motivated by considerations of expediency. Most definitely the government is opposed to a transformation of society. Many reforms have taken place, more or less nullifying statutory petty apartheid – namely, keeping individuals apart (prohibition of mixed marriages, separate amenities, and so on). At the same time the idea of humanity being inherently divided into separate groups was constitutionalised in the 1983 constitution. Thus, whereas apartheid on the micro level is almost extinct, it has been strengthened on the macro level, resulting in the ironical situation that all efforts at present are directed at maintaining apartheid *without* racism.

What was the DRC's response to these developments? In 1982 the Church appointed a commission to revise its previous policy document published in 1974. The revised edition was discussed and accepted at the General Synod of 1986 and published under the title of *Church and Society* (CS) promptly generating a tremendous rejection from the ultra-right. Eventually a very small group, but including more pastors than expected, broke away to establish the Afrikaans Protestant Church (APK). Other objectors, presumably a much larger group, remained in the DRC but openly formed the Dutch Reformed Association to campaign actively against the 1986 document in order to have it declared null and void in 1990. The Association's chances of success, however, are slim. During 1987 only one of the 11 regional synods of the DRC rejected the 1986 document. Eight synods accepted it forthwith and two pressed for even more reforms.

Does all this indicate a fundamental swing in the DRC? Does it represent a paradigm switch or is it just another example of reforming and reformulating the apartheid idea?

Sadly, the answer to the first question remains firmly in the negative. The hot air aside, the old paradigm is still intact and is as decisive as ever. Even so, within this paradigm, two shifts with the potential to eventually erupt and to tear the apartheid paradigm apart have taken place. Sensing this, and in anticipation of this eruption, those who oppose it took action – and in good time too, from their point of view. What are these two shifts?

The first has already been pointed out. Under international pressure, but primarily because of local conflict, recognition that at least some elements of the policy of the separate development of nations were indeed nothing but discrimination on the basis of race, slowly dawned on some leading supporters of apartheid. Since 1980, therefore, in public rhetoric one hears that discrimination (which is deemed negative) should be distinguished from differentiation (which is considered to be natural). Following this distinction, a speedy end was brought to so-called discriminatory measures, the best known example being the abolition of the prohibition of mixed marriages act (1985).

In 1986 the DRC followed suit by not only endorsing (however reluctantly) the abolition of this law, but it also rid itself of the only purely racially motivated church law in its own corpus. Since 1986 membership of the DRC has been open to anybody regardless of race, or any such criteria. The only prerequisites concern confessional matters, which is fair enough.

But note that the DRC did not decide in favour of uniting with its own so-called 'daughter churches', that is, the DRMC (the 'coloured' church) and the DRC in Africa (to which blacks belong). Structurally, the 'DRC family' of churches, divided along racial lines, remains intact. The decision to open up membership of the (white) DRC equals the political scrapping of racism on the micro level in South African society. Maintaining separate 'national' churches on the other hand, runs parallel to the trend to intensify the 'group character' of South African society. Thus, at the Western Cape synod held in Cape Town in October 1987, it was decided that synod, while rejecting apartheid out of hand, could find no objection to the differentiation of society, provided this was agreed to mutually.

So the paradigm is still intact on the macro-level. But on the other hand the 'whiteness' of the DRC has, at least in theory, come to an end. Will this lead to better communication with black Christians and in time to a willingness to let the structural barricades down? This remains to be seen.

The second shift is much more subtle, but also potentially much more explosive. It concerns the resurgence of a social ethical approach.

In *Church and Society* under the heading 'The Practical Implications' one finds a subparagraph entitled, 'The DRC and political models'. Here one reads the following (which is held by its critics to be the main evidence of a total abandoning of apartheid by the DRC): the church '. . . is convinced that the application of apartheid as a political and social system which does injustice to people and which leads to one group being unjustifiably privileged above another, cannot be accepted on Christian ethical grounds. . . .' (*Church and Society* 2: 47). [My translation.]

One should not go overboard with this quotation – presuming that one is in favour of the DRC rejecting the present social system in South Africa. The real significance of this passage does *not* lie in what it says but in what it signals.

Starting with what it says, it does *not* say that the socio-political system of South Africa is fundamentally wrong. Only apartheid, moreover only the application of apartheid, is condemned. The fact is, as is evident also from the above reflections, that the concept of apartheid in the quoted passage does not refer to the all encompassing life experience of the oppressed in South Africa. Given the whole of CS, it is fair to say that apartheid is taken only to refer to discrimination on the individual level on the grounds of race. But the idea of an inherent differentiation of humanity into separate nations is not questioned. Even a superficial reading of this passage makes it clear that the fundamental group approach is assumed throughout. For this reason CS nowhere even remotely attempts to apply this statement to the *structures* of South African society. The concept of apartheid employed here and the concept of apartheid in the Belhar confession or in the Kairos document are still miles apart.

Yet this paragraph does signal a fresh approach. The universal theological concepts of equality, dignity and justice, which we already noted in connection with the 1950 congress, are evident in this quotation too. Now the difference is that here, at last, these concepts are used to *evaluate* apartheid, not to *define* it as was the case in 1950. While it is true that only the *application* of apartheid came under scrutiny, even that had not been done for three decades.

The original Afrikaans version (*Kerk en Samelewing* 10: 52) is not as clear as the English translation above. It can, in fact, be read in two ways, either as the above, or as a statement condemning apartheid as such. The ambiguity is intentional. It was an (unsuccessful) attempt to keep the different factions in the DRC together. Predictably, considerable confusion followed and eventually an exposition of the meaning of the Afrikaans version was given which favoured the interpretation reflected in the above English translation. Be that as it may, the very fact that the original was intended to be ambiguous, signals an oncoming debate on the question stated above: is the failure of apartheid due to its application or to the nature of the system?

What does this signify? At the very least it signifies that the slow but irresistible movement among a growing number of Afrikaners away from doctrinal ideology to pragmatic ideology, and perhaps even away from ideology itself, has also penetrated the DRC significantly. At long last the DRC is willing (if somewhat reluctantly) to evaluate apartheid. And that means that, after many years, the DRC is opening up to an ethical, as opposed to a doctrinal, approach to the problems of South Africa. If this tendency persists, it must inevitably lead to a reassessment of the concept of apartheid itself and eventually also of the social analysis implied.

Yet in the mean time the ideological framework is still intact. We shall now turn to an outline of the anatomy of the theological expression of this ideology.

THE ANATOMY OF THE THEOLOGY OF APARTHEID

The appeal to scripture

Since 1947 many attempts have been made to prove theological support for apartheid. Initially, these attempts were in the form of exegetical treatises. The best known, and certainly the most influential, attempt was the 1948 report referred to above. Linguistically, as well as logically, it was not very sophisticated. But soon the various reports and documents became highly sophisticated as apartheid theology took the shape of a doctrinal theology.

Although the doctrinal element was there from the beginning, its upsurge can be attributed to the influence of theologians such as B. B. Keet (Stellenbosch) and B. J. Marais (Pretoria) in the early 1950s, and Beyers Naudé in the late 1950s. They tried to halt the development of a theology of apartheid by pointing out the invalidity of the use of Scripture to support the apartheid concept. All of this had the sole effect on the exponents of apartheid theology of treating the Bible with much more circumspection, or of applying it less directly. Scaling down the number of direct applications of Biblical quotations was not very difficult and did not pose a serious threat to apartheid theology – provided a minimum of quotations could be maintained.

And so, over the years, the direct *textual* basis of apartheid theology diminished until the critical minimum was reached. To understand the essence of apartheid theology, one has to take one's point of departure in this critical minimum and the arguments built thereupon.

To isolate this critical minimum, it is instructive to compare the 1948 document with *Church and Society* in 1986. The question then is, what of 1948 is still maintained in 1986? This is not difficult to ascertain. In all CS's 64 pages *direct* references to Scripture are made in only two paragraphs. In both cases the issue dealt with concerns the theo-cosmological paradigm on which the document, as a whole, depends. When analysed, the same use of Scripture and the same conclusions are drawn in CS as in 1948, the difference being that whereas the document of 1948 had yet to state a new case, CS merely takes things for granted. In 1948 it was argued thus:

1. *Scripture poses the unity of humanity.* All of humanity is from Adam, from one blood. Gen 1: 26; 6: 3; 7: 21; 10: 32; Mt 19: 4; Rev 17: 26; Rom 5: 12; 1 Cor 15: 21; 45.

2. *Scripture records and presupposes the division of humanity in races and nations as a deed of God.*

The diversity of races and nations is grounded in the predestination of God and serves the glory of His name. The attempt to maintain humanity as a homogeneous entity, results in God's intervention leading to the confusion of languages and the establishment of diversity. Gen 11. Furthermore, God apportioned to Abraham's posterity, Gen 15: 19, and other nations, Amos 9: 7, their territories, as He did for all other nations by decreeing their times and territories, Acts 17: 26 . . . (Handelinge 9: 279–80).

In 1986 *Church and Society* asserted that:

When the origin and Biblical evaluation of ethnic diversity is discussed, Genesis 10 and 11: 1–9 as well as Deuteronomy 32: 8 and Acts 17: 26 are often referred to. Without entering into detailed analyses in this regard, the following findings must be stated.

* In Gen 11 the confusion of languages is described as a judgement act of God on the sinful hubris of humanity. However, this judgement also contains grace and blessing in as much as the existence of humanity is thereby safeguarded and God's purpose with the creation of humanity is reached.

* Sin and the spiritual bankruptcy of the nations is the background against which the calling of Abraham as patriarch of the people of God and the man in whom all nations will be blessed, is the better illuminated.

* In Deuteronomy 32: 8 and Acts 17: 26 it is emphasized that God is the One who apportions the nations their territories. The former is

part of a psalm on the glory of God's graceful dealings with Israel. The latter is part of a mission sermon stressing God's omnipotence and His proprietary right to the nations and rejecting any concept of fate or chance.

* This means that issues such as the policy concerning nations or the conservation or annulment of the identity of a nation are not points of discussion in the Bible. Whether the autogenous identity of a nation is maintained or not, depends on that nation's zeal to conserve its own cultural values. The *way* in which this is done must, however, be in accordance with the requirements of the Word of God (*Church and Society* 2: 19–20). [My translation.]

Thus, exegetically, apartheid theology revolves around Genesis 1–2, 10–11, Deuteronomy 32: 8 and Acts 17: 26. Quantitatively, as well as qualitatively, this is a very thin base indeed. Especially noticeable is the absence of a *constitutive* Christological component – without which no theology can rightly be called Christian theology.

Systematic comprehensiveness

From this, however, it must not be inferred that apartheid theology is simple in terms of its inherent logic and its underlying assumptions. On the contrary: it is the expression of a comprehensive concept of reality and life – the constituent elements of which are rigidly integrated. Attempts to overcome apartheid theology (or ideology) by criticising one element at a time (for instance, pointing out the untenable textual base) will, therefore, prove to be fruitless.

An analysis of the comprehensive thought system involved shows that apartheid theology is the conceptual integration, within the parameters of the protestant faith, of three sets of ideas dealing with cosmology and anthropology derived from the European tradition. Its uniqueness does not lie in its conceptual ingredients but in the way in which they were integrated and contextualised. For our present purposes, these three sets of ideas can be called evolutionary idealism, harmonious balance and intrinsic collectivism.

Evolutionary idealism
In the theology of apartheid the 'unity' of humanity is always stated as a point of departure. Without doubt, this is interpreted in a Platonic way as an ideal unity. This is probably best illustrated in the way the

unity of the church is treated. The unity of the church is said to be found in 'the trinitarian God' to which is usually immediately added that this unity does not negate the diversity in God's creation. Rather, it 'supersedes' it, as CS puts the matter. Thus, the unity of the church is '. . . something different from an artificial and forced unity which is pursued merely for the sake of a visible unity' (*Church and Society* 2: 16). (For 'an artificial and forced unity' read *institutional* unity.)

When apartheid theology deals with human history, an idealistic anthropology is likewise employed. From Genesis 1 and 2 it is inferred that 'mankind' is an 'essential unity'. However, this does not mean that all individuals are 'one'. On the contrary: when humanity is viewed synchronically, a multitude of 'forms' (that is, nations) becomes visible. Ideally people are 'one', but in reality they are diverse.

The reason for the diversity of human forms is explained in terms of a concept of history according to which, in the course of time, different human families emerged from the original one pair of ancestors. These families developed differently, each according to their own intrinsic qualities and, thus today, they all stand at different levels of cultural achievement.

According to apartheid theology, this view of history is supported by the story of Babel told in Genesis 11. The story of Babel is interpreted as the first historical attempt to thwart God's creational will by uniting, instead of dividing, the different nations. This had forced God to intervene to ensure that the course of human history complies with the intended order of creation. The story of Babel therefore serves to confirm the belief that human pluriformity (of language as an audible sign of inherent factors of division) is, in fact, the aim of God's creation. The legacy of German romanticism is very clear in this point of view.

Harmonious balance – the cosmological paradigm for social analysis
Following the thought pattern described above, it is only logical to ask what the purpose is of the evolving diversification of the original unity of humanity. Why could the original unity not simply be perpetuated?

To explain the answer given by apartheid theology, another quotation from CS is appropriate. 'Within the framework of God's acts of mercy the diversity of peoples is . . . applied to highlight the magnificence and the glory of God's all-embracing salvation' (CS 2: 19). In this ostensibly innocent remark a profound theological cosmology is deeply embedded. Here, in theological garb, we have an expression of a very specific view of reality which can be termed the idea of the primal balance. For example, at its simplest it can be found in the statement that day cannot exist without night, or that summer is inconceivable without winter, or in the well-known statement by Aquinas that the glory of Christ's redemption could not be revealed, had it not been for the reality of sin.

In apartheid theology this concept of the primal balance is applied to social groups. The result: humanity is conceived of as a constellation of different entities delicately counterbalancing one another, which, if successful, produces harmony. Consequently, in dealing with human life, conduct and ethics, apartheid theology pays prime attention to (correct) *relationships*. The delicate network of counterbalances should not be disturbed.

The concept of the horizontal balance of groups is integrated with that of vertical balance. God and creation are also in balance. On the implicit premise of the medieval dictum – *finitum non capax infiniti* (meaning that the finite cannot encompass the infinite), it follows logically that no single entity of creation (in our case a nation) could share or reflect the totality of God's glory. God needs total reality. In other words, God needs the entire diversity of reality to reflect all His glory. God being Spirit, what is one in God must therefore of necessity be many and diverse in the realms of space and time.

It follows that all types of integration, which would result in diminishing the existing diversity, must be combated vehemently. From the above it is clear that such an integration must be viewed by apartheid theologians not only as an infringement on the order of the cosmos, but ultimately as a malicious act of man to deny God his legitimate glory. Therefore, integration could only be the devil's work and thus be propagated only by the devil's own liberals and communists. From which the conclusion can easily be drawn that those against the diversity of nations (or apartheid) must necessarily be against God!

Intrinsic collectivism – a naturalist anthropology
One question has yet been left unanswered. Why is the concept of nation taken to be the entity fundamental to all human life?

The concept of nation employed in apartheid theology is derived from the nationalist philosophy of nineteenth-century romanticism, according to which a nation is an extended family integrated historically, as well as genetically, by a particular and unique identity. Nationalist philosophies always have difficulty in describing the nature of this identity. Generally mutual language (disregarding dialects or related languages) is the only outward sign which indicates such an identity. Apart from language the concept of identity becomes very vague and mystical.

Nevertheless, according to this type of anthropology and sociology, every individual is subordinate to a specific identity of which the individual is merely a particular expression. By means of this identity, the individual is bound to others who share the common identity. The group is thus much more than merely the sum total of individuals belonging to it. The group is the individual's primal ground of being.

With the introduction of biological naturalism into anthropological reflection during the nineteenth century, it became ostensibly easier to define the identity of nations. Whatever their shortcomings, racial theories seem to be scientific, pretending to deal only with *natural* phenomena in a neutral way.

The marriage of racism and nationalism has reinforced the group concept considerably. It has created an unchallenged presupposition in the ranks of nationalist ideologues and theologians that the nation's identity, even though conceptually vague, is nevertheless a *natural* phenomenon. The *immutability* of a world order based on nationhood is thereby established. If there is to be any form of freedom of association (and speech, and mobility, and so on) this can only be within the confines of one's 'own' group. And so, accordingly, every individual human being, directed by an inherent, natural force, gravitates toward one group identity or another and in this way the diversity of nations takes on form.

CONCLUDING EVALUATION

This is not the place to evaluate the impact of the DRC on South African history at length. Only a few very general remarks can be made here.

Contrary to popular opinion, the direct influence of the DRC was never as significant as it is purported to be. Not being a state church and structured in a non-hierarchical way, it is extremely difficult for the DRC to act as a single-minded pressure group in society. That was the function (and in some cases still is) of cultural and political organisations such as the Afrikaner Broederbond, National Party, Helpmekaarvereniging, and so forth.

The real contribution of the DRC as an institution was not at the level of activism. The real contribution lies in the fact that the DRC had allowed the apartheid world-view to be expressed in theological language, thereby legitimising it and eventually, through the process of doctrinalisation since 1950, canonising it in terms of the all-embracing conceptual framework of the diversity of nations.

How much influence did the theology of apartheid have on social issues in South Africa? Here again it must be stated that the *direct* influence was small. The reason for this is that the DRC by and large followed an *escapist* course in dealing with explosive social issues. This is not readily recognised, however, because outwardly it appears as if the church has been and remains deeply involved in serious reflection and lobbying on social matters. But at closer quarters we see that this reflection was mainly doctrinal and very seldom ethical in nature. One should not scorn doctrinal matters. But when people are deprived of their humanity, the issue will not be solved by doctrinal reflections. Then it is time for action and for ethical reflection on the prevailing social realities. A doctrinal approach under these circumstances amounts to escapism.

The congress of 1950 could perhaps be cited as an exception. Here at least specific social issues were discussed openly. Even so, in connection with this congress, we noted the chasm between the reality of SA and the dream of the DRC's ideal of separate development. The ideal definition given to apartheid in 1950 was in effect just another way of escaping from facing the issues squarely.

But what about the mission policy of 1935 and the submissions made to government before 1948? No doubt these are examples of active participation in political matters. However, one should bear the contents of this participation in mind. The main thrust all along was to disentangle the Afrikaner from the social dynamic of South Africa. A trend that had started in 1857 was perpetuated in 1935 and afterwards: to avoid conflict, isolate.

On the whole then the main point of criticism is not that the DRC has been too much involved, but rather that it has not been consciously involved enough. And this is probably the strongest accusation that one can level at the DRC in this respect. For, in the absence of a serious attempt to come to terms with the real social dynamic of South Africa, the church was nevertheless forthcoming with 'general principles'. These 'principles' gave legitimacy to political activities, some of which history will sentence harshly. But the church did not monitor the political use that was made of its 'principles'. Had it done so, the DRC would have found that its version of apartheid was nothing more than a flight of fantasy. However, in the absence of this recognition, the DRC kept on promoting apartheid as a means of fulfilling the Christian norms of respect for human dignity, equality and freedom – thereby legitimising in reality more or less the opposite of what it had meant to promote.

Finally, the escapist approach is evident also in the separation of church structures since 1881. This also has had an indirect effect on the broader South African situation. In the long term the separation of black and white in the DRC has had the effect that long before 1948, *spontaneous* and *sustained* contact on an *equal* footing between Afrikaners and blacks was severely curtailed. Because of separate church structures, the intimate knowledge and intuitive loyalty resulting from close interaction characteristic of church life never materialised between Afrikaners and blacks. Of course, there was and still is contact at work and in the streets. But interaction as one human being with another was effectively terminated. What remained was suspicion, if not outright fear.

Fear and escapism can be redressed in only one way: through opening up to others. Perhaps the decision of 1986 to open up membership and the slowly growing greater ethical awareness signal the dawn of a new era for the DRC.

BIBLIOGRAPHY

1. Borchardt, C. F. A., Die 'swakheid van sommige' en die sending, in Kinghorn, J (ed.), *Die NG Kerk en Apartheid* (1986).
2. *Church and Society* (Bloemfontein: 1986).
3. De Klerk, P. J. S., (*et al.*) *Rassebakens* (1939).
4. *Die Kerkbode*, 139/6 (Cape Town: 18 February 1987).
5. *Die Naturellevraagstuk* (Bloemfontein: 1950).
6. Handelingen van de Synode (Cape Town: 1857).
7. Handelinge van die Federale Raad (1927).
8. Handelinge van die Federale Raad (1935).
9. Handelinge van die Nederduits Hervormde of Gereformeerde Kerk van Suide-Afrika (1948).
10. *Kerk en Samelewing* (Bloemfontein: 1986).
11. Kinghorn, J. (ed.), *Die NG Kerk en Apartheid* (Johannesburg: Macmillan, 1986).
12. *Sy ontstaan, doel en strewe die sendingraad van die NG Kerke in Suid-Afrika* (1944).
13. Van Jaarsveld, F. A., *Van Van Riebeeck tot Verwoerd 1652–1966* (Johannesburg: 1971).

5 Christian Resistance to Apartheid: Periodisation, Prognosis

James Cochrane

INTRODUCTION

'It is our belief that civil authority is instituted of God to do good, and that under the biblical imperative all people are obliged to do justice and show special care for the oppressed and the poor. *It is this understanding that leaves us with no alternative but to conclude that the South African regime and its colonial domination of Namibia is illegitimate*' [my emphasis]. These two sentences from the Lusaka Statement, issued in May 1987 by a wide spectrum of participants meeting in Zambia at the invitation of the WCC's Programme to Combat Racism, deny the right of the South African government to consent from its citizens in carrying out its public policies.

Towards the end of that year at a workshop in Cape Town on 'Theology and Violence', Frank Chikane, General Secretary of the SACC, addressed the same issue. His keynote speech drew from the book launched at this workshop, indeed from his own contribution to the book entitled *Where the Debate Ends* (F. Chikane, in Villa-Vicencio 15: 301ff).

Chikane made three central claims. First, that the matter of violence must be discussed in relation to the problem of legitimate authority: thus he questioned the use of authority to legitimise force and spoke of the need for the transfer of authority away from the present government. Second, Chikane demanded, if the churches genuinely believe in non-violence, then they must announce and follow through a non-violent programme to end apartheid. Third, he argued that the question of violence cannot be separated from the problem of the 'space' available for the exercise of effective non-violent action. Some have this space, others not. Thus the two options of violence and non-violence should not be discussed as if they were strict alternatives. As Chikane puts it in his essay,

81

What concerned the Kairos theologians about the stance of the official church was that church theologians were talking about the morality of the use of violence in the war instead of doing something to stop the war by tackling its causes. (Villa-Vicencio 15: 305)

Standing back from the immediate issues, there are certain general observations to be made. Christian resistance to apartheid expresses itself here in ways beyond anything issuing previously from official quarters of the South African Church. Yet a long tradition of protest and challenge to the state stands behind the judgement that the ruling authority is illegitimate.

At the same time we find here key aspects of the recent development of that tradition as a result of massive repression, strengthened armed struggle against the ruling power on the part of liberation movements, and two states of emergency (one still continuing at the time of writing).

The Lusaka Statement builds upon the Harare Declaration of 1985, itself influenced by the process that led to the now historic *Kairos Document*. The *Call to Prayer for an End to Unjust Rule* stirred up controversy and reaction at about the same time; it helped set a new agenda, and it created an awareness of the difficult new territory the churches needed to map out.

If the government of the day is no longer to be regarded as legitimate, then Christian ethics must include processes that delegitimise long-standing and deep-seated patterns of obedience and authority – a heavy burden indeed. In turn, the focus of political morality has to shift to the question of an alternative authority capable of legitimate rule over the nation. Judgements here will of necessity carry with them risks and uncertainties, and they will place hard choices before the Church as it battles to relate the demands of practical reality with its hopes for a kingdom of God not realisable by any human institution or order.

Before this point had been reached, however, Christian reflection upon apartheid generally still moved in the realms of dogmatic theology. This is best seen in the declaration of apartheid as a heresy by the World Alliance of Reformed Churches meeting in Ottawa in 1982, and the Confession of the black-based Dutch Reformed Mission Church formulated at Belhar, a suburb of greater Cape Town. In both cases, the issue was the legitimacy of any theological defence or support for apartheid. It could only be a matter of time before this spilled over into ethical considerations of the legitimacy of the state itself.

These 'turning points' in recent Christian resistance to apartheid lead to a second observation. The development of strategies and theological formulations in the struggle of the churches against racism is not uniform, and this development is also connected to what is actually going on in the society. Thus any one formulation of the meaning of Christian resistance cannot be understood without grasping the particular historical dynamics which make certain things possible and others not.

We should therefore assess the past failures of the churches sympathetically. However, resistance and struggle *outside* the churches reached a point some 25 years ago of including armed struggle; only now is this acknowledged in official theological thinking. One's sympathies for the churches lessen again, and the long delay in accepting the choices made by liberation movements only emphasises the problematic nature of the churches, considering that almost all of them have no pacifist tradition.

Perhaps sympathy is not what is needed. Perhaps a proper understanding of the limitations of the churches as social institutions within the total society will help locate the nature of their failings, identify the ongoing aspects that will continue to bedevil any attempts of the churches to carry into action the implications of the most recent and far-reaching statements, and assist analysis of the possibilities that nevertheless exist within the churches for making those statements the basis of practical activity.

What then counts as Christian resistance to apartheid in South Africa? A speech? A delegation to the State President? Lying in front of a bulldozer to stop it smashing down a squatter shack? A synodical or assembly resolution? Support for an illegal strike? A call for the unbanning of liberation movements such as the ANC? A march to parliament to protest an action? Holding a prayer-vigil? Financing community organisations or development projects? Civil disobedience and a willingness to stand trial for one's convictions? Actively supporting those who engage in a guerrilla struggle? Taking up arms?

All of these actions and many others have been adopted by one or another Christian or church body over the decades. An assumption is often made that to be part of any denomination or Christian group which has denounced apartheid (as have the member and observer churches of the South African Council of Churches, for example) is to partake in resistance to apartheid.

But the meaning of resistance will depend upon what one means by apartheid. Thus, those who regard apartheid primarily as a special form of capitalist exploitation will speak of resistance as a struggle against a ruling white minority and an exploitative political economic system. Perhaps others will define resistance to include actions aimed at promoting the mixing of ethnic groups in an unchanged political economy; the former group is likely to describe this as mere reformism.

I will argue that neither the notion of resistance, nor the slogan of apartheid, have in general been adequately analysed by those who make or break policy in the churches. There is a need to identify more effective strategic interventions to give weight to the declared aim of many mainline denominations to rid South Africa of the apartheid disease before it destroys more than can be borne.

The method of my argument is to present a set of hypotheses (which others may wish to test) aimed at periodising the development of 'resistance' to apartheid. I will attempt to differentiate historic forms of resistance and their possibilities, and thus allow some conclusions to be drawn about the nature of Christian resistance as we currently experience it. This, in turn, will open up some crucial ecclesiological and missiological issues for discussion.

A PERIODISATION OF CHRISTIAN RESISTANCE TO APARTHEID

Initially I use the term 'resistance' very loosely to express attempts by Christians and churches to oppose, however mildly, the development of apartheid policies. By apartheid I mean a set of political economic realities characterised by the exercise of power on behalf of privileged groups, using ethnic categories to legitimise policies and actions.[1] This is not equivalent to official apartheid policy since 1948 (though it includes it); rather, I refer to a pattern of developing policies and socio-economic programmes whose origins are prior to Afrikaner accession to formal political power in 1948, and for which all white South Africans bear direct responsibility, as does the British colonial power of earlier times.

As long ago as the second decade of this century, prominent black nationalist leaders confronted white South Africa and the colonial churches with their demands, in clearly articulated form. Many of these blacks were leading members of churches, many of them took part in the formation in 1912 of what became the African National Congress (ANC). They had their sympathisers among white Christians. But though their demands by all standards were moderate (a qualified franchise, which would have excluded most blacks from participation in deciding their future, was, for example, quite acceptable to many of them), white sympathy was strictly limited. It certainly did not extend to black workers. Moreover, churches frequently demanded that actions and statements be kept within the bounds set by colonial priorities and interests – prior to the union of the four provinces of South Africa – and by the needs of unification between Afrikaner and English-speaking whites thereafter (for detail, cf. Cochrane 4: 55ff).

Above all, the first two decades of the century were marked by an ideology of separation or segregation, finding a legal climax in the Land Act of 1913 and its partition of the country into 'Native Reserves' (Bantustans) and 'white South Africa'. With this act and its ruinous effects, the English-speaking churches became increasingly uneasy about formal policies of separation (they often backed informal practices as the best method of achieving the desired end).

In the meantime, many black Christians took things into their own hands, forming their own, separatist churches in protest against conquest and colonial domination. One may distinguish here between the 'Ethiopian Movement' (whose leadership came largely from the African élite and wealthy peasant farmers; on this movement, cf. Kamphausen 9) and the 'Zionist movement' (strongest among peasants who resisted proletarianisation, these churches must be distinguished from the 'churches of the Spirit' of the Zionist-Apostolic framework; cf. Villa-Vicencio 16: 78–9). These 'African independent' churches (usually known in the vernacular as 'churches of the people') are evidence of the first major form of Christian resistance – *separation* from the institutions of the ruling élite to construct an alternative institution under independent control – to the policies that laid the foundations of apartheid.[2]

Some years later, black aspirations were again high on the agenda of churches as the Herzog Bills bit into the meagre rights blacks then had in the Union of South Africa. In addition, the first major effort at the unionisation of black workers, in the Industrial and Commercial Workers Union, had challenged the society at a vulnerable point. But once again, the churches could not escape their overriding interest in a stable white-governed South Africa, now under the banner of *'Christian Trusteeship'* over blacks. Such trusteeship implied a role in *supportively pleading* the case of blacks in public, particularly by way of appeals to the government and to the assumed humanitarian or liberal conscience of the English-speaking white electorate.

As time went on it became clear that the churches could not function without particular structures to carry out daily tasks of communication and investigation in respect of racial and political issues. *Specialised institutions* began to emerge, the most prominent being the Christian Council of South Africa (established in 1936 out of the General Missionary Council), an ecumenical co-operative endeavour of the main English-speaking churches and the Afrikaner Dutch Reformed churches originally set up to handle new demands of mission.

Changed times soon led the CCSA to address the central political issues of the time, in particular the problems of racism. 1936 was indeed the year in which Africans were legislatively removed from the voters' rolls of the Cape Province, a privilege enjoyed by those few who met the qualifications of the franchise since 1853 (Regehr 13: 154ff). Similarly, the Anglican church (CPSA) set up a commission with the 'task of defining what it believes to be the mind of Christ for this land' which issued in a major report on the church and the nation (Regehr 13: 156). In these and other cases, an emphasis on *formal representations* to government and requests to discuss contentious legislation is evident.

Many more years passed before the churches were again fundamentally challenged by a black nationalist movement grown impatient with decades of talk and representations. The catalyst came with the election of the first wholly Afrikaner-dominated government in 1948, and the formal institution of the apartheid policy. This policy set out to make systematic that which had been built largely upon more flexible British political practices and mechanisms of separation and control.

Resistance from the English-speaking churches to such developments increased. With the loss of any intimate contact to the reigning government, the churches turned more and more now to *formal protest* as a stream of new legislation that began to extend government control over the lives of the indigenous people, via both intensified racist regulations and stepped-up security measures. It was not long before events pushed formal protest into channels of *passive resistance.*

Spurred on by its Youth League (among whose numbers were Mandela, Mbeki, Sisulu and Sobukwe), the ANC shifted their concern primarily from talking to the authorities about their grievances and aspirations to a programme of public persuasion and activity. The 'winds of change' were blowing. A few leading clerics felt these winds early and – building on a time-honoured tradition of individual prophetic courage – began to move into new forms of resistance. Perhaps the most prominent of these was Trevor Huddleston, then priest in the black township of Sophiatown in Johannesburg.

In the late 1940s black mineworkers launched the biggest strike yet seen in South Africa. In the early 1950s, the ANC launched a Defiance Campaign, a non-violent resistance programme aimed at forcing some recognition of their demands upon white South Africans and the international community. The South African Council of Trade Unions (SACTU) also grew in political significance after its formation in 1955, adding an organised political challenge of workers to the ruling powers. In the same year a large gathering of the Congress Alliance met to draft the Freedom Charter at Kliptown, today an important plank of the ANC and its claim to a legitimate struggle. A new stage had been reached in the modern resistance struggle of blacks, and it galvanised many churches into action.

Suddenly, issues that had long been the subject of debate, public representation and formal resolutions became urgent enough to demand a more substantial engagement of the churches on the side of the oppressed. What precise form this engagement should take was not obvious, and many meetings and conferences were held to clarify matters. Indeed, the Afrikaner Dutch Reformed churches even took the initiative in 1953 to organise a major ecumenical conference on the 'racial problem' (De Gruchy 5: 56ff.). However, like so many meetings of the time, it was inconclusive, largely because the desire of the English-speaking churches to keep up dialogue with the Afrikaner churches continued to play an inordinately strong role in ecumenical relations, especially when compared with the almost complete lack of contact with the African independent churches, some of whom had a strong tradition of protest.

The judgement of Trevor Huddleston, some 30 years ago, is interesting for its indictment of the resistance of the English-speaking churches to apartheid, and its evidence of a new sense of urgency among some Christians who were willing to align themselves with acts of non-violent resistance of the ANC and its various allies. He wrote of these churches that

> There should be no question of the power of their witness on the racial issues. Why, in fact, is it so ineffective? . . . All I can say is that, over the years, I took my share in framing and speaking to resolutions of Synod which condemned apartheid or which urged advance in opening up opportunity for Africans or which called upon the Government to redress obvious injustices. . . . It was only as the years slipped by, that I began to wonder whether in fact it meant [that this would prevail to break down the hideous barriers]. (Huddleston 7: 54–5)

Passive resistance to the unfolding policies of apartheid took form most frequently in resolutions from the high courts of the churches. The tone of these resolutions varied, but they built upon a long tradition of confidence in the establishment churches that they could thereby influence policy and public opinion sufficiently to see right done. However, while this may have worked to some extent while church leaders of English-speaking denominations still had good connections to government, the weakness of the method soon became apparent to many, at least outside of the churches. One author of the 1950s quoting the well-known Christian ethicist J. H. Oldham, noted that

> The practice of passing resolutions and making pronouncements is beset with dangers and may often be a sheer waste of time. . . . Reliance on mistaken or futile methods of procedure cannot but weaken the influence of the Church for good. Pronouncements which do not have behind them a solid body of considered and convinced opinion can have little effect on public action. . . . Secondly the habit of passing resolutions, carried to excess, defeats its own·purpose. . . . Christian assemblies must not allow themselves to become involved in futilities of this kind if the influence of the Church is to count in a world in which there are movements which are in deadly earnest. (Taylor 14: 63)

By the end of the decade, when the horror of the Sharpeville massacre had burst upon the world, the last fully ecumenical conference was to take place at Cottesloe near Johannesburg (1960). There Afrikaner and English-speaking churches in effect parted company, the former to back the apartheid regime, the latter to wend their way fitfully from one challenge to another as they sought to give some kind of expression to their pleas for justice and reconciliation.

That the old questions and problems had not yet been solved in the churches is clear from assessments made in a study of methods of mission in southern Africa published in a book requested by the Anglican Provincial Board of Missions and blessed by Archbishop Joost de Blank. The author, John Carter, notes that 'we must declare that South Africa's racial structure of society is incompatible with Christian values. But pronouncements are not enough; the social order must be changed' (Carter 2: 22). Further along Carter uses characteristic verbs of public pronouncements and resolutions: 'we criticize . . . we deplore . . . we find it tragic . . . we regret . . . we declare . . . we are concerned . . . ' (24–5). But, noting the failure of the churches to move beyond the point of statements to doing something independently about the conditions they criticise, he also stakes out a position that has been the mark of the churches until the publication of the Kairos Document:

> We may find ourselves under fire from both sides, attacked by the rival nationalisms, white and black. We cannot identify ourselves with either side, for the false premise of racial domination is accepted by the extremists of both. In such a situation we are called to be a Confessing Church. . . . (Carter 2: 28)

In the meantime, the major black organisations had been banned, an armed struggle for liberation had been launched, and most black leaders found themselves either in prison or in exile. Tension subsided during the 1960s under the twin impact of successful repression and a booming economy, while the churches continued on the way already mapped out.

The twin themes of '*identification*' and '*reconciliation*' emerged as the dominant concepts guiding Christian ethics for this period. Many concerned Christians began to call for 'costly reconciliation' and an 'identification with the suffering of the poor and oppressed'. Identification meant much the same as that which Trevor Huddleston had called for in the mid 1950s. As he put it then:

> Apart from the need to arouse the Christian conscience in the world, there was in my heart . . . the desire to identify myself with the African people in their struggle for human rights and personal freedom. . . . But identification means more than word, more than speeches. For the Christian, so it seems to me, it is part of the life of faith itself. . . . Surely, if the Incarnation means anything at all, it must mean the breaking down of barriers not by words but by deed, by act, by *identification*. (Huddleston 7: 57–58)

Reconciliation as a concept guided many experiments in 'crossing the colour line', a line which had by now become a rather rigid wall and a mark of the granite-like policies of premiers Verwoerd and Vorster. It seemed that everyone jumped on the bandwagon of reconciliation without thinking through very carefully the naive, even cheap, way in which this concept might be invested with flesh and blood. Thus the recent critique of the Kairos Document that reconciliation has too often meant an 'easy peace' between parties whose fundamental conflict is not properly addressed and whose vastly unequal position is not redressed (Kairos 8: 9ff.).

Finally, the time of the debate on building a confessing church had also come, with the experiences of the Church in Germany an important and constant theme. By and large, however, the churches left to the Christian Institute (formed out of the Cottesloe Consultation by Beyers Naude and those around him) the struggle for a confessing community, the role of developing the prophetic mission of the church, while keeping their distance from the Institute's more threatening programmes and projects. Later the South African Council of Churches (SACC, formed on the foundation of the CCSA) took up the challenges of operating on the frontlines as well, though necessarily always with a wary eye on its more conservative constituent churches.

The Christian Institute has proven to be a powerful catalyst in the development of the concept of Christian resistance in South Africa, with an impact way beyond what might be expected from a rather small group of people (cf. Walshe 17; De Gruchy 5: 103ff.). Initially concerned to woo disaffected elements in the Dutch Reformed churches, and with communication towards the African independent churches, the Christian Institute later found itself closely connected to the young generation of blacks who launched the *black consciousness* movement upon an unsuspecting white population. Now the old challenges broke into the open again, with young blacks determined to rid their people of the subservient attitude that years of conditioning and moderate politics had thrust upon them.

Black theology emerged as part of this dynamic new phenomenon, and in doing so it threw the theological hegemony of the white churches into confusion. Influences now also began to come from Latin America and elsewhere, captured best in programmes of 'consientisation' outlined by Paulo Freire and other radical educational theorists. Conscientisation thus became a hallmark of the period for Christians attempting to contribute to the new political ethos. SPRO–CAS,[3] for example, in its second phase of activity, structured itself around Black Community Programmes and a White Conscientisation Programme.

Workers began to find new muscle as well, and the early 1970s witnessed the beginnings of what is now a powerful independent, non-racial trade union movement led by blacks. Taken together, these new forces challenged the dominance of old stereotypes and paradigms. In effect, they represented a determined programme of action and public persuasion certain in the longer run to threaten the legitimacy of much of apartheid policy and practice. Questions about the claim of the governing authority to obedience began to arise, spreading into the white community as well in respect of the conscription of males into the South African Defence Force (cf. CIIR 3).

In the churches, too, these questions took on an urgency not seen before. Given a massive boost by the launching of the WCC's Programme to Combat Racism (PCR), the debate about the role and limits of the churches was enveloped in a heightening emotional climate of charge and counter-charge. In an article of the time reflecting on the grants of the PCR to liberation movements in southern Africa, Moltmann noted that 'responsible political action in love is selfless to the point of sacrifice of personal innocence, to the point of incurring guilt. . . . The engagement to resist,' he pointed out, 'remains a "bitter engagement"' (Moltmann 10: 143).

Throughout this time, however, the churches were at pains to stress their acceptance of the legitimacy of the governing authority, and their willingness, albeit under protest, to keep within the limits of debate and action set by the regime. Only fringe groups such as the Christian Institute began to act as if there were a case for the legitimacy of the liberation struggle of the oppressed, rather than merely verbally to address that case. Challenges to the legality of government policy (under the rubric of the rule of law), and a change in the concept of resistance from identification with suffering to solidarity with the struggle marked this time.

The story from there on is well-known. Bannings and restrictions upon the key movements and people of the black consciousness era (including the Christian Institute and its leaders) followed upon the uprisings in Soweto and elsewhere during 1976 and 1977. A climate for revolution arose that has yet to reach its climax. Student rebellion, increasingly militant workers, a growing capacity of the liberation movement to mount a guerrilla war, and a dawning horror among the international community of what is going on in South Africa have brought the pot to boil. The lid has been screwed down as tightly as possible; the pot itself is being hammered by repression; yet the fat is in the fire and the flames are now unquenchable.

Once again the churches have had to face a resurgent black nationalism, only now the stakes are very high indeed, the moral complexities of the situation are immense, and the costs (especially in black lives and social infrastructure) already frightening, to say little of what lies ahead. The challenges facing the churches are not new. My numerous references to material from the 1950s and early 1960s in part is intended to indicate just how much time has passed without any substantial resolution to problems for long recognised by the churches in their attempts to resist apartheid. Indeed, when one recounts the past as I have here, the question must be raised whether all moral right to address those challenges on the part of the churches has already been forfeited.

This the future will tell. As many have pointed out, there is a dual history to the churches in South Africa – one characterised by a conservation of the status quo and one characterised by bold and courageous protest and action against it (cf. for example, Cochrane 4: 223ff.; Villa-Vicencio 16: 81ff.). I wish to suggest that this duality is best understood not as two contradictory threads of church history, but as a reflection of the human character of church institutions and their location in a development of thought and practice influenced diversely by struggles for influence and claims for legitimation by a variety of social actors in the wider society. Thus, what was understood as 'resistance' once may no longer appear as anything other than anachronistic activity now, or at the least, as something far less than is demanded by new circumstances.

Given this approach, I hypothesise a periodised typology of Christian resistance to apartheid. Space precludes me from testing the model in detail, but much of the discussion above serves to indicate the developmental phases I regard as characteristic of Christian resistance in South Africa. Perhaps aspiring church historians and ethicists may find some grist for their mills here. If one relates these phases to major periodic changes in the political economy of South Africa, then the following picture appears:

Boxed events in Figure 5.1 represent what I judge to be particularly critical points for my purposes, while the two columns labelled 'YRS' indicate approximate durations of particular phases. It is worth noting the rapid contraction of time-intervals as one moves into the present. This one would expect as the crisis in South Africa has deepened and resistance has grown (despite increased repression). Of course, the interesting question is whether this hints at an approaching climax to South Africa's trauma – but this is not a necessary conclusion. All one can say is that the time scales do show the growing intensity of the crisis.

The elements of 'resistance' outlined here are not wholly discrete, but there is reason to believe that they do identify particular phases in the understanding and practice of those churches traditionally understood as anti-apartheid. These phases in turn indicate that the understanding of the meaning of 'Christian resistance to apartheid'

Phase	Yrs	Periodisation	Dates	Yrs	Characteristic form of 'Resistance'
1		Post-Anglo-Boer War → Union	1903–12	9	*SEPARATION* 'Ethiopian Movement'. later 'Zionist Movement'
2		LAND ACT → Hertzog Bills	1913–26	13	*SUPPORTIVE PLEADING* 'Christian Trusteeship'
3	35	Pact Government → National Party Victory	1926–48	22	*SPECIALISED INSTITUTIONS/ FORMAL REPRESENTATIONS* Christian Council of SA
4		NAT GOVT → Sharpeville	1948–60	12	*FORMAL PROTEST/ PASSIVE RESISTANCE*
5	28	Cottesloe → 'Message'	1960–68	8	*'IDENTIFICATION'/ RECONCILIATION* 'Multi-racialism'/ 'Crossing the colour line' Confessing Church
6		SPRO-CAS → CI Banning	1968–77	9	*BLACK CONSCIOUSNESS/ CONSCIENTISATION* 'Black Theology'. Human rights issues
7		'SOWETO '76' → Tricameral Parliament	1977–83	6	*CHALLENGE TO LEGALITY* 'Solidarity with the struggle'. Apartheid as heresy
8	10	UDF/NF etc → Emergency	1983–86	3	
9	?	KAIROS DOC → ?	1986–?		*DELEGITIMISATION/ CIVIL DISOBEDIENCE* 'Church as a site of struggle' ?

FIGURE 1 *Periodic typology of resistance*

changes developmentally over time in direct proportion to developments in the society of which the Church is part.

Moreover, most of these elements of resistance, once having acquired legitimacy, do not disappear, but become alternative strategies in the present. Thus, we should expect to find groups and individuals representing all of the phases outlined in the present; perhaps a developmental view of Christian resistance to apartheid may help each rethink their position, and investigate its antecedent history, thus allowing for a sharpened critical assessment of their role.

The model I suggest implies that any particular historical phase carries with it a fresh perspective on the strategies needed to deal with apartheid, alongside existing strategies. New perspectives, in turn, are shaped by ideological constraints and a changing constellation of forces, among them the counteracting forces of the state and its supporters on the one hand, and the oppressed majority membership of these churches on the other. The churches are in this sense a site of struggle between the forces which contend for the future of South Africa, as much as any other institution.

Recognition of this reality is clearly the reason for the rapid acknowledgement of the liberation struggle by many churches in recent times, though in fact it is essentially the same struggle as it was a quarter of a century ago. Indeed, the division in the churches existed latently a long time ago, experienced by many individuals but not the subject of any public acknowledgement of confession. Crisis has heightened latent polarities, forcing Christians into harder choices and more demanding ethical reflection.

One might expect, therefore, that a further intensification of the crisis in South Africa will be accompanied, firstly, by a growing tendency in the churches to legitimise the liberation movements, and secondly, by feverish work on the part of those who represent the forces of the old order to prevent this happening at all costs. Attempts to strengthen and extend the influence of conservative or reactionary forces in the churches, with a consequent sharpening of internal polarities, will equally strain the resources and challenge the credibility of Christianity.

RESISTANCE AND THE CHURCH

In a recent essay, Villa-Vicencio asks if the Church in South Africa is 'a protagonist for change or a reluctant ally? (Villa-Vicencio 16: 71ff.).

He reviews a range of Christian churches in South Africa, from the white Dutch Reformed group to the variety of African independent churches. In each case he attempts to show that a single dynamic is present in all – the dominant tradition of the churches *vis-à-vis* political life tends to maintaining the status quo, while a contradictory tradition of 'restless subversion which disturbs complacency in every social order' (83) is also present.

It is this latter tradition which falls under my categorisation of resistance to apartheid, and it is this tradition that Villa-Vicencio believes 'keeps alive the possibility of the churches being activated, under certain circumstances, to support social change' (72). While not disagreeing with him, I have tried to argue that there is a systematic link between what the churches may countenance and the state of resistance in the wider society. Moreover, I have indicated that this link must be understood via two equally pertinent corollaries of the historical analysis, namely, that the churches as human institutions tend to reflect rather than challenge their social milieu, and, that they do so in accordance with the prevailing symbols of social and political legitimacy.

In addition, I have suggested that the state of resistance to apartheid in the churches has a developmental character in its history, directly related to the variety of pressures placed upon these churches. Thus, the churches can only be expected to lag after popular resistance, and the role of those who keep up with such resistance or even enter into the *avant-garde* will likely never be anything but peripheral to the institutional churches – the activity of a relatively small group.

Idealism and naivete

The extent to which such people can influence the churches and utilise their resources prophetically or radically will be directly related to the extent to which the secular resistance movements gain credibility within the churches. In short, the two traditions Villa-Vicencio has designated as 'status quo' and 'radical' represent also two sets of ecclesial power. Up to now, the question of the use of power remains a problematic one for many Christians who are used to seeing in the exemplary model of Jesus of Nazareth the one who forsakes power, or at least turns the normal conception of power upside down.

But the situation is not simple. Power is wielded all the time in the churches: whether funds are being allocated, withheld, or given in particular ways; whether some make decisions and policies and not others; whether the managers of the synods and assemblies of the churches allow some to speak but not others; whether syllabi or curricula for theological education and training are being constructed or altered, and so on.

It is the naive and idealistic (removed from practical experience) Christian who is shattered by the filibustering, lobbying, infighting, graft and manipulation which appear to mark the internal politics of the church as much as any other social institution. Perhaps the veneer of brotherly (seldom sisterly) language which surfaces so frequently at these levels makes the discovery of the hard realities even more difficult to bear.

But it is important to recognise its existence, and in doing so to keep one's theological perspective on the Church: the Church is not the kingdom of God and Christians would be mistaken to aspire to such a vision of the Church (this the history of Christendom has surely taught us). In recognising the ambiguous, contradictory, wholly worldly character of the churches, we are in a better position to recognise that the gospel is not defined by, even necessarily within the ambit of, the churches. We are therefore also in a position to see that the churches, insofar as they exist to testify to and maintain the tradition of the gospel, are a legitimate battleground for the truths proclaimed in the gospel.

If we then further grant that there are strong theological grounds to support at least the general aims and intentions of the historic secular movements of resistance and liberation in South Africa, we must see that these general aims and intentions have implications for the church as another of the human institutions representing and reflecting the social order. The primary implication is that the churches themselves are sites of struggle (cf. J. M. Bonino 1: 159). In this case, the struggle in the churches – parallel to that in society as a whole – is for its own soul, and there are theological reasons to undertake it (there may also be political reasons, of course).

To avoid this implication is to hide in false ecclesiologies or to dismiss the human character of the Church and the realities of ecclesial power. Perhaps an argument exists for an ecclesial model that escapes both problems in parts of the anabaptist tradition, but this possibility does not undermine the observations made in respect of the great bulk of Christian tradition and organisation.

With this implication accepted, the meaning of Christian resistance must also change, for it has usually been understood as that which the churches exhibit towards a particular, apartheid state. Now it is seen also to have the character of a theoretical and practical challenge to the ecclesial institutions themselves. They are not equipped to deal very well with something like this, except by way of discrediting the use of power in the Church (while utilising power to counteract the efforts and claims of those who may threaten).

Many outside the churches have long ago analysed the nature of the churches in much the terms I have used, but largely, they have also seen no point in working at an institution felt to be incapable of substantial transformation. The development of base communities in Brazil and elsewhere, as well as a strong Christian presence in various forms in several liberation struggles around the world, challenges this wholly negative judgement of the Church. But at the same time, it is clear that this alternative tradition, where it succeeds on any scale, is accompanied by much hard, political work in the churches.

A differentiated analysis

If, then, the churches are a site of struggle, they must be understood strategically and tactically. This the Kairos Document begins to do in its provocative critique of 'church theology'. How far this will go is not yet clear. But it is true to say that a growing number of Christians are beginning to realise that naming the churches as part of the problem is not yet to define how they are so, and what might be done about it. A significantly more differentiated analysis of the churches in South Africa than we currently have available is thus an urgent task for such Christians.

Elsewhere, François Houtart asks in similar vein 'why is it that Christianity, a proclamation of humankind's total liberation, historically finds itself in opposition to the movements which attempt to give concrete expression to this liberation and almost always identifies itself with the forces of oppression?' (Houtart 6: ix). His own analysis of the role of churches in various historic revolutions begins with the French Revolution and ends with the events of May 1968, in France; included is a chapter on revolutionary movements in southern Africa (317ff.).

Relating his key questions to a sociology of revolution, he suggests that the habitual opposition between revolutions and the ecclesiastical institutions evince not just a conflict about the choice of means, but more fundamentally about social values (Houtart 6: 318). Understood sociologically, religions have normally tended to refer to the divine as 'the decisive element in the system of legitimation of both natural and social mechanisms'; this Houtart calls 'sacral totalitarianism'.

Revolutionary movements, struggling against all that upholds the social system, therefore also struggle against one of its central institutions of legitimation – religion (320–3).

The Church fits this analysis, by and large, tending always to revert to that which it knows and feels able to exist with rather than risk its own interests in the hands of an unknown quantity such as a revolutionary movement already suspicious of the Church's motives and history. In Houtart's eyes, this has to do with

the way [the Church] envisages the pursuit of its particular objectives. When it defends a given society, it is very rare that it is simply defending a system as such. More often than not, it does so because it sees that system as one which provides it with the possibility of communicating the message it believes to be essential to human beings. The Church, then, will resist change all the more strongly if it has reason to fear being deprived of its means of action (326).

This lesson has been learned the hard way in post-revolutionary Nicaragua, and needs to be learned in South Africa as well. Without pursuing Houtart's analysis further, it is sufficient to note the relevance of the insights he offers, but more importantly, to take cognisance of the way in which he goes about developing these insights. They are essentially the result of a sufficiently differentiated social analysis, indicating the kind of work required to understand the nature of Christian resistance (or lack of it) and its possibilities and constraints in the search to overcome apartheid and the system it reflects.

Ecclesiology and mission again

This essay, like many others in this volume, seeks to assess the contribution of Christianity to South African history since the landing of Dias on our shores 500 years ago. I have tried to unravel the nature and extent of Christian resistance to apartheid as one strand of this history, and in the process I have ended up directing the question of resistance to apartheid into the theme of the churches as a site of struggle.

My reason for doing so is not simply governed by personal convictions about the current situation of the churches in South Africa, but also by a desire to suggest that the resolution of the contradictions in the churches themselves will directly affect their future in this

country. Put another way, the extent to which the churches integrate
the contribution of their 'prophetic', or 'radical', or 'revolutionary'
elements will govern the extent to which they will continue to hold any
relevance for the future of the region, and equally, the extent to which
they will end up playing a reactionary role against any reconstruction
of the society. At the same time, those who carry the heaviest burden
of Christian resistance against apartheid will determine the outcome
just as much insofar as they are able to sustain their specific
contribution as Christians, while persuasively penetrating the ecclesiastical institutions of which they are part by virtue of their integrity,
theological substance and intelligent assessment of the nature of these
institutions.

That this is not a matter of rhetoric or linguistic niceties may be seen
in the well-organised, deliberate campaign of the current regime and
its fellow-travellers to utilise a wide variety of church resources and
people to further legitimate their policies and practices. National
security ideology and its mechanisms are both a practical and a
theoretical challenge to the meaning of the gospel. The 'Church as a
site of struggle' is not an empty phrase nor, in practice, a mere
addendum to the liberation struggle as a whole, but quite literally
another field within which that struggle takes place.

The churches are still a powerful force for legitimisation, and this
force should not be allowed to be the prerogative of those who have
not seen in the gospel a tradition of hope and empowerment for the
poor and the oppressed. If anything, this issue alone indicates as
clearly as anything might, the point to which Christian resistance to
apartheid has come in the South Africa of the 1980s.

NOTES

1.   Some now refer to apartheid by the phrase 'racial capitalism', while
        others – usually representing the liberal tradition in South Africa – are
        chary of the idea that capitalism itself is a key factor in reproducing the
        history of apartheid. The latter prefer to argue that free enterprise (if the
        market really was allowed to be 'free') counteracts apartheid. The
        debate still rages in South Africa between these positions; ironically, a
        recent book from a gathering of liberal academics sees those to 'the left'
        as a greater threat to liberal ideas than the present regime. I accept the
        arguments for a rational connection between the strength of apartheid
        over many decades and the development of a capitalist political
        economy in South Africa.

2. It should be kept in mind that another element of resistance in these churches concerned the attempt to overcome the suppression of African culture by colonisation, and to restore it in different forms – thus the great difficulty of European-origin churches to understand or accept much in the independent church tradition that has been of great importance to it (cf. Mosala 11: 98ff).
3. Special Programme for Christian Action in Society; the first phase was called the Study Project of Christianity in Apartheid Society (Randall 12). Both names use the acronym SPRO–CAS.

BIBLIOGRAPHY

1. Bonino, J. M., *Revolutionary Theology Comes of Age* (London: SPCK, 1975).
2. Carter, J., *Methods of Mission in Southern Africa* (London: SPCK, 1963).
3. CIIR (Catholic Institute for International Relations), *War and Conscience in South Africa: the Churches and Conscientious Objection* (London: 1982).
4. Cochrane, J. R., *Servants of Power* (Johannesburg: Ravan, 1987).
5. De Gruchy, J. W., *The Church Struggle in South Africa* (Grand Rapids: Eerdmans, 1979).
6. Houtart, F., *The Church and Revolution* (Maryknoll, New York: Orbis, 1971).
7. Huddleston, T., *Naught for Your Comfort* (London: Fontana, 1956).
8. Kairos Theologians, *The Kairos Document: Challenge to the Church* (Johannesburg: Skotaville, 1986).
9. Kamphausen, E., *Anfaenge der kirchlichen Unabhaengig-keitsbewegung in Suedafrika: Geschichte und Theologie der Aethiopischen Bewegung, 1872–1912.* (Frankfurt: Peter Lang, 1976).
10. Moltmann, J., 'Racism and the Right to Resist,' in *The Experiment Hope* (Philadelphia: Fortress, 1975).
11. Mosala, I. J., 'The Relevance of African Traditional Religions and their Challenge to Black Theology', *The Unquestionable Right to be Free* edited by Mosala and B. Tlhagale. (Johannesburg: Skotaville, 1986).
12. Randall, P., *A Taste of Power* (Johannesburg: Ravan Press, 1973).
13. Regehr, E., *Perceptions of Apartheid* (Kitchener, Ontario: Between the Lines Press, 1979).
14. Taylor, J. V., *Christianity and Politics in Africa* (London: Penguin, 1957).
15. Villa-Vicencio, C. (ed.), *Theology and Violence: the South African Debate* (Johannesburg: Skotaville, 1987).
16. Villa-Vicencio, C., 'The Church in South Africa: a Protagonist for Change or a Reluctant Ally?', *A Question of Survival* (Johannesburg: Jonathan Ball, 1987).
17. Walshe, P., *Church Versus State in South Africa: the Case of the Christian Institute* (Maryknoll, New York: Orbis, 1983).

6 Christianity's Impact on Race Relations in South Africa

G.C. Oosthuizen

Theological and church discussions of the vital questions of race relations in South Africa have often been far removed from the actual situation in which people experience the consequences of state and church decisions, many of which deeply affect their lives. By contrast, a scientific approach to religions should study people's actual situations, ideals, visions about the future, longings, cultures and world views, for without reliable information very little advance will be made in the field of human relationships, especially race relations because these are so often disturbed by stereotyped myths far removed from actual events.

Christianity professes to give meaning to life and to assist people to understand their existence. Like any other religion, it is ultimately measured by the quality of the direction it gives people on the vital issues they encounter, including their relationships with others. It is mostly this that qualifies a religion as a constructive or destructive force. In some respects its destructive potential could be worse than that of anything else.

The religious elements in society used to be accepted as the light of the world and the salt of the earth. So often, however, religion has covered itself under the blanket of existing social circumstances, thereby becoming part of the problem instead of retaining its prophetic stance and through this giving direction to people. The result so often is that secular and new religious movements fill the vacuum, as has actually happened in the South African situation. Marxism itself came into existence because of the neglect of the common person by the Christian churches in Europe at that time. When churches or religions forsake their task or water it down, when they are not related to the issues which affect the lives of those they should serve, then they have failed. The churches in South Africa have a sad history in the context of race relations – some more than others.

A BRIEF HISTORICAL BACKGROUND

In order to assess Christianity's influence on race relations in South Africa, a brief reference to its historical role is necessary, especially during specific, crucial stages. Five such stages will be discussed.

Early polarisation

The Dutch Reformed Church (NGK) never initially highlighted the race issue or played a divisive role in this connection. In 1857, however, it decided, because of the weakness of some, to have separate places of worship for non-whites. It was never the intention, however, 'to exclude non-white members from white congregations and vice versa' (20: 16). This was symptomatic of what would follow in the NG Church's subsequent mission history, in spite of autochthonous development given as the reason for its separate churches.

The first secession from a missionary-dominated church in South Africa itself, (a small group seceded in Basutoland in 1872), is ascribed to Nehemiah Tile who in the 1870s worked as a Wesleyan evangelist in the Transkei. The first conference of the Wesleyan Methodist Church in South Africa failed to admit Tile into full connection in spite of a lengthy probation period and in spite of the fact that he was a man of considerable charismatic gifts, a conscientious and efficient worker. His greatest disqualification was that he was not a 'yes man'. Tile founded the Thembu Church in 1884, the first African to lead an independently established church of consequence in this part of Africa, and thus the father of the independent church movement in South Africa. He was accused by the Methodist missionaries of indulging in politics but had merely protested against the white domination of the Thembu Chiefdom in political and religious terms. The Methodist Church was associated with the imposition of white rule over the Thembu Chiefdom in 1875 through magistrates, and the Chiefdom was annexed to the Cape Colony in 1885. Tile expressed the deepest grievances of the Thembu people. The missionaries were co-responsible for his imprisonment, but the Attorney-General ruled that his arrest was illegal. Missionaries were thus implicated in the arrest of a brilliant man in their church, who became the father of a church movement today numbering nearly eight million members and adherents. Here, too, then Christianity showed weakness in the context of relationships with the indigenous people of the country. Tile's movement was a liberation movement 'to free the Native from

European control'. To this end he emphasised 'a conception of common blackness' (Saunders 17: 569, 570), that is, black consciousness, held that the Gospel message should be interpreted in the African context, and pioneered in his thinking something which would receive close attention in the contemporary church situation a full century later, namely Black Theology. He was a black theologian a century before the contemporary black theologians of this country. His secession led to further secessions, which led to the influential independent Ethiopian Church movement, especially after Moses Mokone left the Methodist Church in November 1892 and founded the Ethiopian Church in 1893. Only in the early 1960s did John Xaba's Anglican Church, with its so-called liberal stance, induct the first African Bishop, the Venerable Alpheus Zulu. The reluctance to accept African leadership at the highest level in this church was due to racial prejudice.

Tile set in motion a movement which would react strongly against white control working at the expense of African potentialities, initiative, self-determination and understanding of their own situation and their people. It helped to prepare the soil for the formation of the South African Native National congress in 1912 (renamed the African National Congress in 1925) to work for African unity, extension of political rights and socio-economic advancement (Oosthuizen 13: 81). One of the main reasons for its formation was the fact that blacks were completely ignored with regard to the discussions that led to the formation of the Union of South Africa in 1910.

The African Independent Church (AIC) movement, which Tile started, has proliferated among blacks, and with its 'Ethiopian' section – Ethiopia being a symbol of liberation as the only age-old independent black state at that time – its 'Zionist' section (started in 1897) and its 'Apostolic' section (started in 1908), it has grown into a massive independent or indigenous church movement with a membership of about eight million (35 per cent of the black population) and about four thousand denominations. It has established its own leadership, its own organisations supported by its own funds, and has become a mighty ecclesiastical force in South Africa – to such an extent that some of the mainline churches look like dwarfs against this movement, to which they have lost a considerable number of their members. Many of these have received positions of leadership in the independent church movement.

The general contention is that the AIC movement if not apolitical, is definitely 'anti-revolutionary'. There is a dialectic between the belief system of any people and the socio-political conditions in which they find themselves. Religious expression is also people's attempt to explain events especially where they find themselves powerless in dealing with temporal forces. The Ethiopian church movement drew inspiration from the unfavourable situation in which blacks found themselves in the last century. The main objective was to redress inequities. The emergence of the AIC movement was not merely religiously inspired but also socio-politically inspired: an attempt to delegitimise the existing socio-political order. Thus the alleged socio-political apathy within the AIC movement contradicts its social origins (Zulu and Oosthuizen 21: 3). Reaction against racial discrimination in the mission context has started a movement in which Africans rely completely on themselves, bypassing the mainline African and interracial churches.

The churches face the development from segregation to apartheid

The apartheid phenomenon is obviously another phase in the history of the church in South Africa which needs attention. Segregation, an earlier, milder, non-legalised form of South African society before apartheid, was a generally accepted but also harmful *modus vivendi* with regard to group relations. Apartheid, however, changed it into a rigid ideology with demonic tendencies concerning the destruction of intergroup relationships. Apartheid was virtually an unknown word when Dr D. F. Malan used it for the first time in parliament on 25 January 1944. A certain Ds S. J. du Plessis claimed that he used it in 1929 in a speech during the Dutch Reformed Church (NGK) Synod that year as the guiding principle of separation of the racial groups for the church's missionary work. Whatever the history of this negative word in the context of human relations, the harm it has engendered and the image it has created abroad will never be fully comprehended.

The whole emphasis was on forcing separation at all cost. Blacks (and other so-called non-white groups) had to develop on their own lines, and education should teach the blacks that they could never be whites, as Dr H. F. Verwoerd repeatedly emphasised. Dr W. W. M. Eiselen, Secretary of 'Native Affairs' at the time, emphasised the technical development of blacks (Eiselen 5: 3). Unfortunately hardly any technical development of black pupils has in fact taken place, as these subjects were practically eliminated from their curricula.

Most of the churches reacted against the introduction of legislation based on race or colour. Such legislation was motivated by a distorted concept called 'Western Christian civilisation'. One also heard at this time opposition from the NG Sending Kerk (DR Mission Church), the separate DR Church among coloureds, the fruit of the above-mentioned 1857 development. Their Wynberg Circuit stated there is no scriptural basis for colour apartheid. And yet, there were those in the Afrikaans-speaking white churches who emphasised that apartheid finds support in the Bible. In 1949 Professor Ben Marais had stood alone in the Northern Transvaal Synod emphasising that nowhere does Scripture subscribe to the separation of people on the basis of race. At its October 1949 Synod the DRC (NGK) expressed deepfelt appreciation for the government's attitude towards mixed marriages and suggested that these should be forbidden by legislation.

The rapid deterioration of race relations in South Africa

With the rapid deterioration of race relations in South Africa after 1949, some churches started to realise that they themselves had to put their houses in order and eliminate all forms of racialism if they wanted to oppose the evil inherent in the apartheid ideology. Racial reconciliation now gained a new emphasis. When the Mixed Marriages Bill was under discussion it was not condemned by the political party to which most of the English-speaking white church members belonged. Africans, coloureds and Indians felt more and more that they were thrown upon themselves to struggle for a just and civilised place under the South African sun. This led to even more intense polarisation. When riots between Africans and Indians broke out in 1949, leaders of the African and Indian Congress movements came together, resulting in a joint council of the African National Congress and the South African Indian Congress (13/02/1949). The Indian presence in the ANC is still relatively strong.

Polarisation of blacks against the Afrikaner was usually ascribed to the 'poisonous' English-language press. The Prohibition of Mixed Marriages Act was promulgated in spite of warnings from respected leaders in all sections of the community and from recognised church leaders, except the Afrikaans churches. Dr D. F. Malan associated miscegenation with mission work, holding that the loss of racial identity would disable whites from bringing Christianity to the 'heathen' (15: 1 April 1954). With this level of thinking concerning interrelationships, not much headway would be made with core issues in the area of race relations. The same applies to the doubtful means and methods used to get the Population Registration Act of 1950 through parliament whereby each person had to register under his or her ethnic group. *Die Kerkbode's* editorial of 12 October 1949 accuses the reaction of the Christian Council of South Africa of 'humanistic Christianity' and of course associated it with 'communism'. The tragedy is that it is precisely these laws and the attitudes behind them that have prepared the ground for communism. The call for racial equality was always associated in these circles with communism, which of course contributed to making it attractive to blacks. The unfortunate fact is that *Die Kerkbode* had at the time an editor whose prophetic insights did not go further than the archives of his church.

In an editorial in *Die Kerkbode* of 11 January 1950 he, however, rightly castigated the 'English brethren' for passing judgement in theory on matters which they themselves practised. There was a certain amount of double talk in those circles but this was detected, highlighted and criticised by both white and black colleagues – not defended or left unchallenged. The Episcopal Synod of the Anglican church in October 1949 expressed the conviction that 'persons of all races, who have an adequate education' should have 'some effective voice in the government of their country' and the bishops specially admonished 'all church people to recognise the truth that all men and women of whatever race are made brethren in Christ by baptism, and to face fearlessly the implications of this truth in the life of parish and Diocese' (1: 1949).

Are words enough to counteract an inhuman policy?

P. W. Botha and his assistants struggled in the 1980s to dismantle the apartheid ideology in the minds of those who had supported it. But more than three valuable decades of tragically missed opportunities for establishing an economically, socially and politically healthier South Africa have gone by. This ideology was often ruthlessly applied and the prophetic voices of the time were bulldozed by what became for many a system of oppression. It is no wonder that the Defiance of Unjust Laws Campaign started in 1952. Any generation which accepts laws which dehumanise it and its future progeny will be termed totally gutless by future generations. How many millions have suffered unjustly – thousands upon thousands were thrown into jail because of unjust apartheid laws which some churches insensitively endorsed.

All kinds of dubious methods were used to enhance apartheid, such as with the introduction of the Separate Representation of Voters Bill 1951 concerning the disenfranchisement of coloureds. When it was declared null and void by the Appellate Division of the Supreme Court, the government slapped its own highly respected legal system in the face and introduced a so-called High Court of Parliament, a strange twist, in order to promulgate this Bill. The Afrikaans Churches were again non-committal. Only a small group in the Dutch Reformed Church (NGK) felt that the church should not yield unconditionally to the state but that the pronouncements of Scripture should be adhered to.

The so-called non-whites boycotted the Jan van Riebeeck Tercentary Festival in 1952 commemorating his arrival 300 years before in order to establish a half-way station between Holland and the Far East. They organised instead a Defiance Campaign holding mass meetings on 6 April 1952, the main day of the festival. Not having the slightest insight into what blacks felt as atrocities against their future, *Die Kerkbode* of 19 March 1952 vilified them. A dangerous situation had been created.

The promulgation of apartheid laws continued, of which the Bantu Education Act, No. 47 of 1953 evoked the greatest reaction from blacks. This Act transferred the control of black education from the four Provincial Administrations to the Union Government Department of Native Affairs. The blacks wanted a single department under the central government like the white schools in order to ensure the same educational opportunities for their children. In retrospect Bantu Education has left the black child practically totally unprepared to meet a modern technical society. Up to 1985 only 1 per cent of the pupils in black high schools had any technical subjects in their curricula. If the Afrikaans churches and the English-language churches had launched a united front with regard to the education of black children, if the missions could have retained some say in this education, the black community would have been more prepared to help themselves and improve their living standards. There would have been many other professions open to blacks than practically only teaching as at present. Blacks would have been able to compete at the market place had they not been debarred from white areas and so-called white jobs. This is what the preservation of 'Western Christian civilisation' implies in the apartheid ideology. R. H. Tawney's thesis with regard to *Religion and the rise of Capitalism* applies to the Afrikaner in this country but a more appropriate title with regard to the blacks would be *Capitalism and the rise of Marxism in South Africa*. Religion can either retard or enhance development. Calvinism in South Africa has contributed to the retardation of black development in South Africa – as would be evident in an objective, analytic study of the processes that contributed to the situation in which the black community finds itself today.

The entire existence of black human beings in South Africa has thus been governed by a comprehensive, selfish and demonic ideology. Apart from what is euphemistically called petty apartheid – segregated buses, trains, post offices, restaurants, platforms, hotels, escalators and so forth – there was *demographic* apartheid involving the Prohibition of Mixed Marriages Act (1949), the Immorality Amendment Act (1950) and the Population Registration Act (1950); *political* apartheid, involving the abolition of the Natives' Representative Council and the Asiatic Representation Act (1946 – under United Party rule), the Bantu Authorities Act and the Separate Representation of Voters Act (1956); *residential* apartheid involving the Group Areas Act (1950) and the Natives' Resettlement Act (1954), and *educational* apartheid, involving the Bantu Education Act of 1953 (cf. Clarke 2: 840). J. G. Strydom as prime minister unashamedly emphasised 'baasskap' (masterhood), meaning that the white man remains the 'boss'.

What better means could be applied to make South Africa a hotbed of marxist communism? Certainly not those missionaries and others who tried to assist the blacks in this situation, nor those in the NGK, such as B. B. Keet, B. J. Marais, P. V. Pistorius and others who warned about what was happening (Marais *et al.*: 10). To act presently as if 'only a small mistake' was made during those horrible years – the 'Stalin era' of South Africa – is to evade the issue. Millions were jailed because of the pass laws and other issues, so that the jails of South Africa were bursting at their seams; the family life of many was destroyed, hatred developed especially for the Afrikaner, whites disappeared from black townships, even white missionaries, as it became too dangerous for them to venture there.

If there is an objective assessment of the harm done through these insensitive acts, then it will be agreed that a period of repentance in South Africa would not be out of place. How any church could acquiesce in a situation of injustices committed for the sake of self-preservation, is beyond comprehension. Romans 13: 1–3 could easily serve to rationalise either cowardice, complacency or involvement. The church can never wash its hands in innocence when principles affecting the lives of millions are trampled upon as if they can be manipulated at will and are expendable. There were attitudes in the English-language mainline churches which also cast their shadow on race relations but consistent warnings in these churches did take place, such as a South African Catholic Bishop's Conference statement in 1957 which *inter alia* reads: 'we are hypocrites if we condemn apartheid in South Africa society and condone it in our own institutions' (16: 16). This spirit of self-searching was the only hope in the situation.

The DRC (NGK) takes a stand

The churches made an impact for the first time with their resistance to The Native Laws Amendment Bill Clause 29 (c), the famous 'Church Clause'. This entirely new section, Clause 29 (c), proposed to prohibit '. . . any meeting, assembly or gathering to which a native [sic] is admitted or which is attended by a native . . . without the approval of the Minister given with the concurrence of the urban local authority concerned, which approval may be given subject to such conditions as the Minister may deem fit . . .' (19: 1133, Col 1).

Now, what does a church say about this? No wonder that the cabinet minister in question, Dr H. F. Verwoerd, when prime minister removed all hope from those who longed for improvement in race relations. Fortunately, the 'Church Clause' brought the mainline churches into remarkable unanimity in their resistance to it. For the first time the DRC also took a definite stand. The non-implementation of the Act, which ruthlessly affected the principle of religious liberty and the church's sovereignty, was due to the threat of a unanimous disregard of it by the churches. One of the respected African ministers of the black wing of the Dutch Reformed Church, Rev S. S. Tema, stated already in 1954; 'Because of our disunity, we have opened the door to the enemies of Christian unity to find new means to strengthen the sin of racialism' (Clarke 2: 1017).

This also indicated that the only answer to apartheid is resistance. Through all the trauma that the apartheid laws developed, the Nationalist Party felt secure because it received support from the three Afrikaans churches, especially the DRC (NGK). From 1956 the idea developed among a section of the leaders and theologians of the DRC that apartheid cannot be proved from the Bible but could only be presented as a practical arrangement. It was, however, only in 1986 that this church took a definite stand against apartheid as an attitude to life and declared it a 'sin'. Ironically, it was not the DRC leadership who blazed the trail for a more critical stance on the apartheid ideology but some of the nationalist politicians themselves. They realised better than the church how near to destruction this ideology has brought the

South African situation. The rationalisation of apartheid was often supported with the idea of churches developing on ethnic lines because of cultural differences, but the deepfelt motive of many was to keep the DRC white church white. Equality between the races was seen by many as a dangerous principle.

After 1956 some changes in approaches to apartheid were to be discerned among DRC leaders and theologians. They questioned some of the motives behind the DRC's emphasis on separate churches for the racial groups as unscriptural. Interest in ecumenical deliberations on the basis of the unity of believers in Christ was evident. In 1960 at Cottesloe in Johannesburg mainline churches gathered, concentrating on the race issue. The Cape Dutch Reformed Synod which followed this conference took a stand against its decisions on interracial contact in spite of the recommendations of the committee of this church, which represented it at the Cottesloe Conference (Lückhoff 8: 32). In order to accomplish this negative decision, Dr H. F. Verwoerd prepared the way in his New Year's message and then Dr Koot Vorster, arch-conservative who was detained during World War II, influenced the Synod to decide against the recommendations of Cottesloe. While many well-meaning and thinking South Africans condemned the inherent polarisation of black and white because of the apartheid ideology, forces within Afrikanerdom emphasised *kragdadigheid* (overruling power) as the only basis for the administration of the country.

The United Party, whose members were mainly English-speaking, unfortunately compromised on the apartheid issue in a number of respects. Many in this party then sought advice rather from church leaders than politicians. This also strengthened extra-parliamentary organisations which at the same time reflected on the weaknesses in the church's lack of a united witness against apartheid. The reluctance of many white congregations to accept black ministers in their pulpits, the third-grade stipends and conditions of service black ministers often had to contend with – all this reflects on the racialism which the leaders in these churches had to counteract in sections of their churches and in the context of the socio-economic and political world. Most white church members know nothing about the realities with which black fellow Christians are challenged daily. In spite of the activities of institutions like the Christian Institute to effect dialogue between the groups, very little real contact has been achieved through the years. Living and being kept apart do not enhance such important contacts. Eventually everything worked up to the revolutionary stage, and now that this stage could come to fruition, deeds and not merely words are needed. The road that led from non-violence to violence has been built by the rulers of South Africa since its pre-1948 stage, who did not have their ears to the ground. The Church has to speak and, as Clarke emphasises, it 'needs therefore to respect its prophets, even if it is sometimes unable to honour them because they speak uncomfortable words to the church' (Clark 2: 1100). Of course, *it also needs to speak with an undivided voice.*

ANALYSIS IN RETROSPECT AND PROSPECT

As has been stated earlier, religious symbols have a powerful social influence – negatively and positively. Nineteenth-century attitudes towards blacks still prevail in South Africa in a section of Afrikaner-dom and also among a section of the white English-speakers. Many of these people will establish some kind of relationship with illiterate and half-literate blacks but have difficulty with educated black people. In these circles there is strong resistance to any idea of equality between black and white. The Afrikaans Churches have done very little to remove this attitude. Prime Minister J. G. Strijdom could move from apartheid to 'baasskap' and Verwoerd from apartheid to white castles in the air. This means being imprisoned in the symbolic attitudes of the past. The contemporary situation calls for a reorientation of these symbolic attitudes and this is what the Nationalist Party is now trying to achieve, after enforcing on people for a quarter of a century their outdated attitudes in the form of legalised segregation. Only symbols which can motivate people in the contemporary situation to bring out the best in themselves and their environment will save South African race relationships from further deterioration. There is scope for Christianity here, with its symbols of service to God, of associating with and assisting the underdog and the downtrodden, with its symbols of love, empathy and warmth. It has had the opportunity in the past to help establish a much happier society. Unfortunately it became part of the problem, not only with regard to the race issue but also with regard to the selfish society South Africa has become. When a group accepts its preservation as of ultimate importance even at the expense of others; when all kinds of myths are built round this position and when its leaders become whipped up giants, then something radically destructive ensues. Afrikaners have been taught during the last half century and more that giants exist only in Afrikaner history – these are pictured as great men of faith who could hardly do any wrong. This gave them the power to act in certain circumstances in the historical context of South Africa in ways which are to the detriment of the future of this country and its peoples. These hero myths, of course, helped to subjugate what is human and the resultant, dehumanising, self-preservation psychosis reflected itself in the dubious methods and laws which were utilised to build up the imaginary haven of the future. South Africa has gone through a sordid history in this connection.

Christianity, which claims 77 per cent of the South African population, is more closely associated in this country with the polarisation of black and white than any other religion. The apartheid ideology has had its greatest support among those who claim to be Calvinists. The Church of Christ as a whole has deeply experienced the destructive force of racism. The conflict is severe even in the so-called integrated churches. White church leaders were questioned by blacks and white church members questioned their church leaders, accusing them of the betrayal of their churches in order to satisfy the 'unreasonable' demands especially of the black church leaders and members. A serious rift between white and coloured churches, between blacks and whites in the multiracial churches has ensued. The Churches were in the invidious position of maintaining the *status quo and* seeking change – some empathising with the former, others with the latter. The independent/indigenous churches did not experience this upheaval although they have their own convictions about change, injustices, deprivation and disenfranchisement and their own methods of approaching the situation.

The church's dividedness in its strategies has hampered its true witness and its tactics. Some reacted against unjust laws, though their own earlier racial attitudes helped in building up a climate for such laws, to the extent of calling apartheid a heresy; others supported the promulgation of these laws and even suggested their promulgation. Some Christians call for revolutionary methods for change, others have moved from *status quo* attitudes to the acceptance of gradual reform while yet others wish to retain the *status quo* at all cost. A paralysing dividedness has reigned through the years of political misery. Christians are fighting Christians. The type of Christianity which tries to satisfy the absolutist demands of a minority group loses prophetic insight into its situation. Social justice always suffers when this happens – no objective, in-depth analysis of the real situation is then possible. White Christianity, especially in its Calvinist form in this country, retards social change, while black people resist the *status quo*.

Religious Affiliation and Perceptions about Religion

While 77 per cent of the South African population classified themselves as Christian according to the 1980 census, 18 per cent were
indicated as belonging to no religion (of course, nearly all do belong to
a religion, mainly African traditional religion), 1.7 per cent were
Hindu; 1.1 per cent Muslim; 1.8 per cent indicated under the 'other'
category which includes Buddhists, Parsees, Jains, Confucians and the
new religious movements such as Scientology, Hare Krishna and
others. Christianity is the dominant religion among most of the groups
except the Indians: whites 91.8 per cent; coloureds 87.0 per cent;
Indians 12.5 per cent; blacks 74.1 per cent (Kritzinger, 7: 14).

In a multi-purpose survey conducted by the Human Sciences
Research Council during 1983 the highest proportion for whom
religion was important/very important was the so-called coloured
group (68.6 per cent) followed by Indians (62.6 per cent), then blacks
(59.5 per cent) and last of all whites (50.4 per cent). (Oosthuizen *et al.*
14: 28: also Addendum I, p. 117ff). According to Coetzee the low
importance religion has for whites relates to its position in their
personal lives, but they rate its socio-political influence highly (79.5
per cent). He sees this resulting from a white perception which regards
Western religion as an integral part of the Western structure of South
African society. For whites this is of course significant. On the other
hand the relatively low score of blacks (61.5 per cent) concerning the
social influence of religious movements may be due, according to
Coetzee, to the low degree of influence black religious movements
have on the South African scene (Coetzee 3). This is born out in the
research report *Religion and World Outlook* by P. Zulu and G. C.
Oosthuizen.

According to the South African Values Survey conducted by
Markinor in 1982, no less than 85 per cent of the respondents ask the
basic religious question, namely the meaning of life, and observe a
basic religious activity, namely praying or meditating; but low
percentages among blacks (52 per cent) and English-speaking whites
(48 per cent) were of the opinion that the church gives adequate
answers to the moral problems and needs of individuals. Only
Afrikaans-speaking whites contain a large proportion who find
satisfaction in their conventional Christianity. No less than 35 per cent,
41 per cent and 45 per cent respectively among black, coloured and
Indian groups felt that life may be meaningless in the society in which
they find themselves. The Markinor 1987 survey indicated that 35 per

cent of blacks are still pessimistic about the South African situation. No less than 63 per cent, of blacks agreed that religious movements are ineffective in solving social and economic problems (Coetzee 3: Data 3 and 4).

The differences between white responses and the rest widen dramatically on the question of whether a religious movement should take a stand against racial discrimination – only 31.4 per cent of the whites agreed that whites should so react compared with 66.9 per cent, 66.5 percent and 61.8 per cent of blacks, coloured and Indians respectively. Oppression is considered to be more severe than racial discrimination as far as whites are concerned; 52.5 per cent of whites, 66.5 per cent of blacks, 75.8 per cent of coloureds and 66.8 per cent of Indians maintained that religious movements should always take a stand against this evil (Coetzee 3: Addendum I, Data 19 and 20). Religious movements taking a stand against laws such as the race laws which harm the lives of adherents was agreed to by only 41 per cent of whites but by 61.4 per cent, 65.8 per cent and 59.7 per cent of blacks, coloureds and Indians respectively. For no less than 53.3 per cent of blacks, violence could be used when human rights are infringed (Coetzee 3: Addendum I, Data 12–14). In the above-mentioned report entitled *Religion and World Outlook*, fully 69 per cent of the respondents stated that blacks should 'fight' and 'struggle' for such rights as to have a vote and be allowed to work anywhere; among established church members this numbers 72 per cent and in the independent churches 66 per cent, with traditionalists at 67 per cent. Here 'fight' and 'struggle' were actually interpreted as hard bargaining. Only 17 per cent overall were for strikes and confrontation.

Empirical research – not abstract ecclesiastical waffle – indicates that on general statements the gaps between whites and the rest are smaller – statements such as taking a stand against all forms of oppression. But on the really contentious issues, the white proportions are low. There is a clear difference between the perceptions and expectations of those who are underprivileged and feel oppressed and those in positions of privilege in South Africa. Structural liberation and the promotion of justice should, for blacks, coloureds and Indians be on the agenda of religious movements, while the largest percentage of whites does not see the existing social structures as counteracting human rights. Over 70 per cent in the various groups except the whites (20.1 per cent) agreed that if allowed to mix freely South Africans would co-exist in peace (6: 56–9; 71–4). These deeply entrenched differences in perceptions retard the development of racial co-operation and harmony.

Confronting ideologies and theologies

In any multi-racial society potential conflict could become a disturbing issue; this applies also to a multi-religious situation. The difficulties in this connection are even more complex when racial groups adhering to the same religion discriminate against one another, as is the case in South Africa. Pseudo-theological arguments are utilised to rationalise segregated churches within the context of segregated political structures. White Christianity and racial prejudice have become practically synonymous in South Africa, especially in the South African brand of Calvinism. Afrikaner identity, which started to develop in the nineteenth century, developed in an atmosphere of incessant confrontation which culminated in the Anglo-Boer War of 1899–1902.

The Afrikaans Reformed Churches became very closely involved with the once down-trodden Boer nation and this accounts for the close relationship between their church and that nation. Civil religion developed using religious symbols to underpin the political stance of the Afrikaner (Moodie 11: 18ff). The type of Afrikaner leader who emphasised the destiny of the Afrikaner received prophetic and even messianic attributes. The psychological harm that the Anglo-Boer War did to Afrikaners has never been adequately assessed. Here lie the roots of their laager mentality, of their fear of being destroyed as a nation, and the reason for organisations such as the Broederbond. Here lies the psychological basis for their emphasis on the apartheid laws at all cost. Afrikaners thus compared themselves readily with the Old Testament Israel, and everyone and everything round them became loaded with the atmosphere of biblical Egypt and the Egyptians. All this complicated South Africa's intergroup relations.

The blacks responded relatively late with their emphasis on Black Consciousness and Black Theology. The independent church movement which, as indicated, started with Nehemiah Tile, had already helped to give expression to their feelings against English-speaking missionaries and an English-orientated government in the Cape Colony under Britain. They helped to establish the African Native National Congress in 1912 in reaction to an English-dominated political situation. The independent churches became quietistic however, and politically motivated blacks carried on the struggle. During the 'Stalinist' era of apartheid which started in 1949, African reaction became stronger. Then in 1960 the African National Congress and the Pan African Congress were banned. In 1970 the Black Power and Black Consciousness movements emerged, aimed at freeing blacks from the mental slavery into which they had deteriorated through years of subjugation. With the emergence of Black Theology, black Christian perspectives on the socio-political reality of South Africa were carried into the socio-political arena as never before. The church was now seen as the liberator of the underdog. Thus, three themes were prevalent in black Christian thought during the last century in response to white domination in the churches, namely to experience the Gospel message in their own idiom, culture, liturgy and worldview and to make it relevant in the socio-political struggle which had already started during the late nineteenth century; to recover black identity; and to achieve black liberation. Black ministers were once subtly forced by white colleagues to avoid the political sphere, but this has now become impossible (Maimela 9: 40).

The latest reaction of black Christians to racism relates to the declaration of apartheid as a heresy. Most churches agreed with this declaration, and the Anglican church's executive committee declared the entire social structure of South Africa irredeemably racist. Black theologians see the entire social structure of South Africa as riddled with injustice and in need of radical changes, but the Afrikaners in general (and latterly a large section of South Africa's English-speaking whites) see radical changes as a threat to their identity. Different approaches between black and white are also evident in the mainline English-language churches, and a definite leadership tension has arisen there. In the Pentecostal and Charismatic churches tremendous growth in the urban areas is being experienced. Here the religious component is stronger than the radical one. The charismatic churches attract people from all race groups. While many whites in them are from the lower middle class, which is politically conservative, they have no difficulty in freely worshipping together with people of other race groups who also flock to those churches. Religion is transcending race more and more in the urban areas in this way, which is indeed a hopeful sign.

Tension tends to start when multiracial marriages and schooling come to the fore. In a survey carried out in metropolitan Durban, ethnic identity was accepted by a large majority of respondents – but as something spontaneous, not legalised. The last few years nevertheless have seen a serious degree of polarisation arising in the socio-political situation – left against right, black (especially the youth) against white, and so on. There has developed a hostility against minorities as never before. This has become an issue also between the United Democratic Front and Inkatha. Minority domination as practised by whites, especially the Afrikaner, has been challenged as never before. The best solution to this polarisation is to transcend divisive group interests. To this end it is vital to *shape the perception of individuals and groups with a basic set of values agreed upon by all the people concerned.*

Human rights, proclamation by the church, and violence

Human rights are fundamental to human existence. Only on this basis can justice be done. Justice and human dignity involve more than merely the rights of the neighbour, but also emphasise love for his or her potentialities (Du Toit 4: 29). Justice is aimed at the full realisation of the humanity of every person and is thus community-orientated. A hopeful measure of consensus on basic issues in this regard exists among the churches. Through serious and continuing dialogue this could be utilised in building up a level of mutual understanding among the churches. The *practical* implementation of human rights is, however, the main issue, with political rights being the main problem. While only about half of the whites are in favour of equal rights for all groups under certain conditions, the overwhelming majority of blacks, coloureds and Indians accept such equal rights for all groups, according to an HSRC investigation into intergroup relations. The crux is how soon human rights in South Africa could be the inheritance of each and every person.

Most of the churches agree on what the core of the Christian understanding of human rights is, namely the right to life, the right to express one's humanity fully and the right to a life in community with fellow humans (Du Toit 4: 259–61). The term 'core rights' indicates a distinction between 'basic' or 'fundamental' rights and 'secondary' rights which are deduced from the basic ones. This brings them down to the practical world of working conditions, education, administration, equal treatment before the law, the right to pursue truth, the right to live in the place of one's choice and so on. To implement human rights effectively the churches have to proclaim the positive values which enhance good relationships. Openness to self-criticism and a commitment to constructive change are vital.

In a thorough research report on the proclamation of the main white churches in South Africa, Müller came to the conclusion that 'public preaching does not give clear guidance on the sensitive issues of intergroup relations and in fact seems to avoid these problems because of their controversial nature. Although there is a clear qualitative difference between the churches in the *mood* in which statements are made, the most common tendency is to speak in a very general way, to stick to hackneyed clichés which say very little and which leave ingrained convictions and values intact' (Oosthuizen *et al*. 14: 85; and Müller 12).

An issue which has come to the fore especially since the publication of the Kairos document is violence. Violence is part of the South African way of life and is symptomatic of the serious defects in this society since it presupposes power and the lack of power. The violence of injustice leads to violence in reaction. Augustine subscribed to a just war; John Knox rationalised a just revolution. How should the churches respond to violence? Some condemn it on the basis of Romans 13. Others propagate conscientious objection to military service but justify violent resistance to oppressive laws. The Programme to Combat Racism of the World Council of Churches and its support to various movements active in southern Africa led to the hardening of white attitudes. But institutional abuse of power cannot counteract revolutionary violence effectively. This can only come about by means of a thorough assessment of the situation and by means of concerted action. Here the prophetic voice and example of the Church is vital. Violence has indeed become a central issue in spite of the large percentages who say they are against it, namely 70.1 per cent of whites, coloureds 62.5 per cent and Indians 59.8 per cent. Significantly only 36.6 per cent of blacks are against the use of violence. Nearly half of the blacks are not against the use of violence (Oosthuizen *et al*. 14: 98).

CONCLUSION

South Africa has become rigidly categorised. Unfortunately the churches are themselves also deeply divided, politically and doctrinally. One could say that a 'sick' Christianity has no hope of changing this overwhelmingly difficult situation. Its conciliatory social role is hampered by the fact that it is part of the problem. This is why a large number of South Africans, especially blacks, doubt the capability of Christianity, especially white-orientated Christianity, to help solve the socio-economic problems and political tensions of the country.

The challenge is to integrate ethical values into the personal, social and political sphere. Those who emphasise only the personal aspect of religion do not make a contribution to the struggle for social justice; those who emphasise the social aspect often withdraw from the chaotic circumstances that others envisage and create.

The overwhelming role that a specific type of white Christianity in South Africa has played concerning race relations as a result of its close involvement with the identity struggle and the socio-economic and political interests of one specific group, is a root problem. The Christian symbols it has used to serve these narrow interests, and its tacit support of apartheid legislation, instead of taking a prophetic stance on this negative development, have had destructive consequences for intergroup relations. On the other hand, the mainline English-language churches also have racial skeletons in their cupboards. Fortunately, they did venture into self-searching and lifted their voices – not always wisely but nevertheless they did speak out – against the evils of apartheid. It will be a tragedy if black-orientated mainline churches and black theologians inspired by Black Consciousness decide to go their own way. Now that the DRC (NGK) has reached the stage of self-searching, declaring apartheid a sin at its General Synod in 1986; and now that some of its younger theologians have come out, some of them forcefully, against apartheid, the possibility exists of dialogue with black Christianity. The NGK policy statement *Church and Community* ('Kerk en samelewing') is a step in the right direction. It has already had to clarify its stand in contrast to *Faith and Protest* ('Geloof en Protes') issued by the new all-white Afrikaner Church. The few prophetic figures in the NGK and in the mainline English-language churches and the prophetic leaders in the black and coloured churches have helped to save this country from disaster. Those who have fought apartheid are not against South Africa; they are for a stable future based on principles without which no society has a future – mutual respect and mutual concern undergirded by faith, hope and love.

Christianity's impact on the race issue in South Africa has been extremely ambivalent but there are signs on the horizon of a definite coming break, which may lead to a healthy and balanced revival of what is basic in this great faith.

BIBLIOGRAPHY

1. Church of the Province Archive AB 191, Clayton Papers, Extracts from the Minutes of Episcopal Synod (1949).
2. Clarke, R. G., *For God or Caesar? An historical study of Christian resistance to apartheid by the Church of the Province of South Africa 1946–1957*, Vols. I and II, PhD Dissertation, University of Natal, 1983.
3. Coetzee, J., *Religie as inisieerder, begeleier en inhibeeder van sosiale verandering*, HSRC National Investigation of Intergroup Relations, 1984.
4. Du Toit, D. A., *Menseregte: 'n empiriese teoretiese ondersoek vanuit teologies-eties perspektief* (Report: HSRC Investigation into Intergroup Relations. Stellenbosch 1984).
5. Eiselen, W. M. M., *The meaning of apartheid*, South African Institute of Race Relations, 9 July 1948.
6. HSRC Surveys, MPS/OV/56–59 and MPS/OV/71–74.
7. Kritzinger, J. J., *'n Statistiese beskrywing van die godsdienstige verspreiding van die bevolking van Suid-Afrika* (Pretoria: University of Pretoria, ISWEN, 1984).
8. Lückhoff, A. H., *Cottesloe* (Cape Town: Tafelberg, 1978).
9. Maimela, S. S., 'Black power and black theology in Southern Africa', *Scriptura* 12, pp. 40–53, cf. Goba, B., 'The influence of three political movements on the church's role in the South African Liberation Struggle', *S.A. Outlook*, April 1987, pp. 45–6.
10. Marais, B. J., *Colour: The unsolved problem of the West* (Cape Town: Howard Timmins, 1953); Keet, B. B., (Fr. N. J. Marquard) *Whither South Africa* (Stellenbosch/Grahamstown: University Publishers, 1956); Pistorius, P.V. *No further trek* (Pretoria: CNA, 1957).
11. Moodie, T. D., *The rise of Afrikanerdom: power, apartheid and the Afrikaner civil religion* (Berkeley: University of California, 1975) p. 328. See also Bosch, D. J., 'The roots and fruits of Afrikaner civil religion' in *New faces of Africa* Hofmeyr, J. W. and Vorster, W. S. (eds), (Pretoria: Unisa) pp. 14–35. See also Kinghorn, J., 'DRC Theology: A theology of exploitation?' in *Journal of Theology for Southern Africa* 49, pp. 4–13.
12. Müller, B. A., 'Die openbare verkondiging van die kerk as medium van verbetering en verandering van tussengroepverhoudinge' (Report: HSRC Investigation into Intergroup Relations) (Stellenbosch: 1984).
13. Oosthuizen, G. C., 'Black theology in historical perspective', *The South African Journal of African Affairs*, Vol 3 (1973), pp. 77–94.
14. Oosthuizen, G. C., Coetzee, J. K., de Gruchy, J. W., Hofmeyr, J. H., Lategan, B. C., *Religion, Intergroup Relations and Social Change in South Africa* (Pretoria: Human Sciences Research Council, 1985).
15. *Pretoria News*, 1 April 1954.
16. SACBC, Pastoral Letters, Press Commission SACBC, Statement issued by the Plenary Session of the Conference held in Pretoria 2–6 July 1957.
17. Saunders, C. C., *Tile and the Thembu Church*. The Abe Bailey Institute of Interracial Studies, Reprint No. 3, 1971.
18. *The Leader*, 13 February 1949.

19. Union of South Africa Laws Amendment Bill (to be read a second time on Wednesday, 20 February 1957). Appendix G, p. 1133, Col. 1).

20. Verslag van die ad hoc kommissie van die Raad van Kerke 1956 in NGK, *Die NG Kerk in Suid-Afrika en Rasseverhoudinge*, appointed by the Federal Council of DR Churches in South Africa, Johannesburg, NGK (Transvaal) 1956, pp. 8–17.

21. Zulu, P., and Oosthuizen, G. C., *Religion and World Outlook*. Unpublished Research Report.

7 Implications of Apartheid for Christianity in South Africa*

Martin Prozesky

PRELIMINARY CONSIDERATIONS

Judging by New Testament material like the parable of the Good Samaritan, the heart of Christianity consists of the central religious vision and example of Jesus of Nazareth declaring that the world exists within the power of an everlastingly and perfectly loving God. With this to inspire and unite them, and numbering some three quarters of the total population of the country, South Africa's Christians could clearly be a significant and even vital factor in the search for a post-apartheid era providing equal rights, opportunities and safety for all. Among Afrikaans-speaking whites this factor could be especially significant because theirs has historically been an exceptionally devout culture, and because they are a majority among those who control power in South Africa.

But the road to such an eventuality can only be through a prior stage of self-criticism and self-transformation, because the apartheid experience demands a critique of everything that has aided it historically. Since Christians have unquestionably been prominent in the creation of this system, that critique must also be applied to them and the religion which helps shape their values and beliefs. And if such a critique brings to light problems within Christianity, problems which help explain why Christians could ever have had a hand in apartheid – an involvement which raises problems of credibility for their religion – then the situation demands something else as well: it demands action to liberate Christianity from those problems so that it can fulfil its potential as a truly humanising force in society, and do greater justice to the vision and example of its founder, Jesus of Nazareth.

The present essay offers just such a constructively critical perspective; it uncovers just such problems within the teachings of traditional Christianity; it proposes just such an inner transformation to reshape this ancient faith into greater conformity with the central message of its founder, and thus it also suggests avenues along which South Africa's Christians could contribute something decisive to the healing of their desperately injured country. As these people enter the second millennium of their contacts with and presence in that land, it is urgently necessary that they become a more effective, humanising force to the benefit of *all* people there, and earn a more favourable verdict than their deeds so far appear to warrant in the eyes of certain informed critics (for example, Majeke 10: 1986). I myself take up this topic not as a theologian or ecclesiastical leader but as a university scholar working in the history and philosophy of religion. I share with other progressive scholars in religious studies the view that legalised and enforced racial discrimination is a vicious denial of the message and example of universal love which Christians trace back to the founder of their faith, and believe that the creation of apartheid is the most problematical issue thus far in the story of Christianity in South Africa, whose full significance and seriousness have yet to be satisfactorily understood and faced.

My concern in this essay is thus to explore the enigma of apartheid in a country with strongly Christian characteristics, and I do this on the basis of the internal logic of the central Christian message as summarised at the start of the essay. For about two thirds of the world's population, this Christian vision of reality is either partly or even totally incorrect – the two thirds who follow the other religions or the various secular philosophies (Barrett 2). It is the duty of the student of world religions to know this sort of fact and acquaint others with it, especially those who have only known a world dominated by Christianity. But for the purposes of the present exploration it is necessary to enter as fully as possible into the world of Christian experience and belief, and accept, if only for the moment, their vision of reality in order to understand the creation of apartheid as a problem internal to the story of Christians in South Africa. The genuine healing of our society cannot happen unless we face the truth about its present and past condition, however unpleasant that may be, and academics have a special duty in this regard to discover and announce that truth. In attempting to discharge this duty in the form of a constructive evaluation of Christianity in South Africa and its apartheid connection, the scholar has an obligation to present the facts accurately, sensitively and frankly, and to evaluate them according to relevant and above all fair criteria. For example, the sincere intentions of those in the Dutch Reformed Churches who originally believed that racial segregation was the wisest policy for South Africa lest injustice to the black people get even worse, must be presented without caricature or distortion (Kinghorn 9: 86ff.). Similarly, the type of twisted picture of people like Archbishop Desmond Tutu which some of the mass media in South Africa paint must be countered in the interests of factual accuracy and fairness. To ensure such fairness, the basic criterion I shall apply when evaluating relevant aspects of Christianity is the one supplied by Christianity itself in its central message, namely that the supreme reality is love – in the life of God, in the example of Jesus, and in the path Christians commit themselves to walk when they throw in their lot with this faith. Using this criterion in conjuction with the principle of consistency (which nobody who values truth can find objectionable, because without it truth could not be distinguished from falsehood), I shall show that we have not yet heard the full truth about Christianity and apartheid, whose real nature is much more disturbing and far-reaching than, for example, the recent charge of heresy against the white Dutch Reformed Churches.

At the same time Christians in South Africa could yet help transform their country into a post-apartheid society with equality and well-being for all. If apartheid constitutes a dark and ominous cloud in the Christian sky for believers in South Africa (and beyond), then the opportunity to dispel the gloom and let in the bright, warm sunshine of total transformation constitutes an historic challenge to those selfsame believers. This in no way means ignoring the contribution that people of other faiths or of a secular outlook must also make. The work of Gandhi shows just how significant that has been in the past and could continue to be. But apartheid is not the creation of Jews, Hindus, Muslims or secularists. It is the creation of people from a Christian culture, and the present volume of essays focusses on the impact of *this* religion, not on all the religions of South Africa. Confining the topic to Christianity therefore involves no disrespect whatsoever towards people of other persuasions.

The remainder of this essay contains four main sections. The first one discusses apartheid. The second deals with the question of what apartheid reveals about Christianity, in view of the fact that significant numbers of our Christians have been involved in creating, legitimating and supporting it. In this crucial section of the essay I argue that the invention and implementation of apartheid by people within the direct influence of orthodox, mainline Christianity cannot be explained adequately merely as an aberration or departure from traditional Christian teaching considered as an historical whole. More is involved than that, the real explanation being that apartheid, considered as a system of unjust domination, exclusion and disadvantage, conflicts only with certain parts of the message of the church, but not with others. This means that the traditional teachings of Christianity must be seen as a complex in which some parts contradict others, and in which some parts are spiritually and morally superior to others. Declaring apartheid to be in conflict with the ethics of Christianity and pronouncing its attempted theological justification a heresy is valid in so far as it condemns a system which is morally offensive (Richardson 14: 1ff.; De Gruchy and Villa-Vicencio 5). But it sheds little light on the basic problem of why a group of people from an entirely orthodox religious background and with entirely orthodox personal convictions could have devised, implemented and justified to their own satisfaction an apparently glaring deviation from that orthodoxy. To put the point differently, the condemnation of apartheid as a heresy deals with the *effect* but does not identify the *cause* and is thus an incomplete strategy. Furthermore, it may also encourage Christians who rightly detest apartheid to remain unaware of serious contradictions *within* the orthodox church doctrines. This allows those problems to continue unremedied, undermining the work of sincere but often uncritical believers. And I believe, above all, that it prevents the authentic teaching of Jesus of Nazareth from exercising a more beneficial influence on South African society, in ways which people of other faiths and of a secular outlook would probably also be able to support because of their desirable ethical quality. The effect is a loss of credibility in this religion, with its own disturbing implications. These I explore later in the chapter, but let me state at once that at their most serious they involve a complete erosion of faith in the message or even desirability of Christianity, *killing off in some people the capacity to find God real.* If the symbolic notion of deicide has any use, this surely is it.

Section three of this chapter indicates some main items in the teaching and practice of the churches that require serious rethinking and reformulation because of the apartheid connection, while the final section proposes ways in which a transformed Christianity could help South Africa out of its apartheid nightmare into something lastingly better for all. I argue there that the genuine transformation of South African society into a place of peace, justice and benefit for all depends on our embracing and implementing a set of social and personal values unlike those which underlie the present system – *values which promote the greatest, egalitarian well-being of all our people*. Identifying and spreading them would be a greatly beneficial development as a non-violent contribution to real improvement in the country, and I see here a significant challenge to and opportunity for Christians – in partnership with others, lest they make the mistake of trying to combat political apartheid with religious apartheid – as they struggle to overcome the problem of diminished credibility caused by the support many influential members of their faith have hitherto given to a system which has resulted in so much suffering and injustice, no matter how good the intentions behind the system doubtless were.

APARTHEID REDEFINED

The first matter that needs attention in this main section of the essay is apartheid. By this I do not merely mean the policies pursued since the Nationalist government came to power in 1948. I mean the social, political and economic arrangements that have been in force in this country since Union in 1910, with roots going back much further (Cochrane 3: 55ff.), in which the position of black people has been legally and practically inferior to that of whites by every significant measure – access to economic power, the vote, citizenship, education, health care, life expectancy, work opportunities, income, freedom of movement, prospects of improvement and even places of worship and burial. I do not for a moment deny that some of these measures of imposed inferiority have improved, especially in the past few years. We must acknowledge these. But still the practical realities of black people's lives remain fundamentally inferior, for example, in disparities of education, housing, political and economic power, and civil rights. In this sense apartheid is still very much alive.

Thus the first truth that white South Africans, especially those who are Christians, must accept is that their society remains grossly incompatible with the commitment to love one's fellow human beings as oneself, because none of its basic features involves real equality and well-being for all South Africans, and real love cannot be content with anything less. As such it obviously contradicts what I have summarised as the central message of the founder of Christianity. But, as I shall show in due course, the larger body of teachings generally seen as orthodox Christian doctrine contains other tenets as well, and it is by no means clear that all of them are incompatible with apartheid and its discriminatory injustices.

This is still not enough as a description of apartheid. The fuller truth is that the long story of racial injustice has often been the work of Christians, of people shaped and nurtured in a biblically-orientated and mostly Protestant form of Christianity as orthodox as any other. The Houses of Parliament in Westminister where the original blueprint of unjust discrimination was passed in 1910 are the Parliament of a people with nearly one-and-a-half millennia of Christianity in their culture. Yet they legislated the constitutional basis of apartheid into existence. And here in South Africa there has been an even more intense Christian involvement in creating the conditions in which black people have been forced to exist since the beginnings of white domination and especially since 1910 and 1948.

Taking all this together I propose that the simplest valid definition that can be given of apartheid is this: *apartheid is a legalised injustice which whites who identify strongly with Christianity have imposed by force on blacks in South Africa, the majority of whom are their fellow Christians*. It is the iniquity of a people nurtured on bible-reading and prayer, church-going and sacrament. Thus it belies the Parable of the Good Samaritan which Christians ought of all people to exemplify.

I do not for a moment deny that good things have been done by these people. In fact it is essential that we recognise what has been done and give praise where it is due. That is not the point. Nor is it valid to say that without the Christian consciences of white South Africans things would have been far worse for the black people of the land, because only that conscience saved them from the kind of genocidal treatment meted out to the native peoples of the Americas and Australia by European settlers there, for precisely such a virtual genocide was in fact carried out against the San in Southern Africa (Van der Post 17; cf. Davenport 4: 124ff.). In any event, the point that must be faced is simply this: we whites, most of us Christians, have built up and still have a fundamentally inequitable social system for our black people, mostly fellow Christians, a system that does not even begin to measure up to the standards of loving one's neighbour as oneself. And it is a system that owes as much to the money of English-speaking whites as to the votes of the country's Afrikaners.

WHAT APARTHEID REVEALS ABOUT CHRISTIANITY

It would be very unfair to imply that Christian involvement in social evil is confined to white South Africa. Far from it! The deeply Christianised people of Germany gave the world the sickening horrors of the Holocaust; another Christian culture gave it Hiroshima, while a whole consortium of the world's most long-standing Christian nations gave humanity the two worst wars of all time within a single generation. But since the present subject relates only to South Africa, it is not relevant to deal further with those wider instances of massive social evil. The main point is that nationally and internationally a religion which sees itself as the sole or at least main doorway to salvation, and its scriptures as the true and living Word of God, has had a direct association with some of the worst evils of history. In South Africa, however, this association is especially disturbing. The systematic, genocidal savagery of Nazi Germany has no parallel in South Africa, though this must never be seen as a denial of the grotesquely sustained inhumanity associated with apartheid. But the political leadership in Nazi Germany was not Christian in the way it has been here, nor did the churches with the greatest political influence supply such crucially important biblical and theological reinforcement for the state as our have. *Therefore South Africa is religiously much more problematic because the agents of oppression have in many cases been active Christians themselves.*

Why has this happened? I do not think it is because the people concerned are inherently more wicked than any others in the world. Nor will it suffice to say that theirs is a perversion of the Christian position, for the agents of apartheid have studied the same bible, believed the same orthodox creeds and belonged to the same churches as the rest of the world's Christians. If anything, the evidence reveals a people, and I now have in mind especially the Afrikaans people, who are exceptionally devout and sincere about their faith, and who certainly belong to the main line of Protestantism.

The real answer seems to lie in a combination of factors, which come to light when we turn the critical spotlight on traditional Christianity itself, reviewing its social record and teachings as searchingly as we might indeed review apartheid. I shall identify six problems about Christianity, which go a long way towards explaining how some members of that religion could possibly have come up with a system as un-Christlike as apartheid when they devised their way to rule the country. And while this critical review is occasioned by developments in South Africa, much of it is applicable to Christianity in other countries as well.

An inadequate social impact

The first problem about Christianity is that its potential for good in society is extremely underdeveloped. This is a structural contention, not a personal one, and as such has nothing to do with the good intentions and social conscience of individual believers. But it does mean that the kind of total commitment to an existence governed by humane concern for all which the message of love surely implies, has not yet been translated into either a persuasive theology of politics and the economy, or into effective modes of organising these matters along adequately humanitarian lines. *Apartheid shows just how easily even devout believer in a heavily Christianised culture can unwittingly make their faith into an effective component of group self-interest in the forms of nationalist domination and economic exploitation.* This of course reveals that the latter are in practice the stronger social forces. Either that means that the foundations created by Jesus of Nazareth simply have not yet been adequately utilised by his followers in order to carry out his vision in the social realm (as I am proposing here), or his central vision has no real social power, a verdict Christians will surely be the very last people to want to reach. Therefore they must accept the other verdict and face up to a relative neglect of the social realm in the expression of their religion. One form this neglect has taken is the lack of critical realism about socio-political and economic structures. A recent high-level investigation into the social role of religion in South Africa has even found that thus far our religions have generally had a divisive influence, which would mean that, in this respect anyway, actual harm is done to our society by religion. No believer can rest content with such a situation, or try to sweep it under the carpet (Oosthuizen *et al.* 12: 104ff.).

Contradictions and defects within orthodox doctrine

The second problem brought to light by a critical examination of Christianity in virtue of its connection with apartheid (and, of course, with any other kind of discriminatory injustice) is the presence, within the compass of orthodox, traditional Christian teaching as it has evolved since the days of its founder, of some mostly undetected contradictions between its cardinal principle of universal love and certain other teachings. For example, large parts of Christianity do not, so far as I can see, set forth a *clear, egalitarian* view of human existence, at least when scripture is read at face value and without the benefit of sophisticated interpretations using the noblest religious and ethical themes as their key to what such an interpreter judges to be the true meaning of the bible – interpretations which scripture itself does not clearly advocate in its opening lines for the guidance of readers, and which were in any case not available to ordinary believers in South Africa when they first encountered the native peoples of the country. If the churches or the bible did contain a clear-cut, egalitarian social teaching, surely Christians would have opposed social inequalities, not to speak of slavery, from the start, but they have done no such thing. Thus believers who concluded from their history that survival depends on domination will not have been unambiguously challenged by the churches or the bible, and there is much to support the view that the latter in particular played a significant part in shaping the self-conception of many white South Africans, although this influence should also not be exaggerated (Adam and Giliomee 1: 17ff.).

We must also recognise that biblically fundamentalist forms of the Christian religion in particular include certain important orthodox characteristics which might actually encourage a domination model of society. These, too, are not what one would expect in an egalitarian message of universal love embracing all people alike. The history of ancient Israel from Moses to the fall of Jerusalem, read uncritically, is one example. What we find there is the repeated subjugation of nations that are perceived as Israel's enemies, from the Egyptians to the Canaanites, just as Israel itself repeatedly suffered oppression and subjugation at the hands of other nations. Since some forms of orthodox Christianity, including ones which have been prominent in South Africa, teach that the scriptures containing this material are divinely authored, we can hardly blame their followers if they take them seriously and use them as models for their own history.

Some Christians argue that the New Testament, or even parts of it, are the decisively authoritative scriptures, paying correspondingly less attention to others. Luther is a good example of this policy, with his famous emphasis on the writings of Paul and his reputedly less favourable view of books like Esther or James. But Calvinism has a different approach, deeming all of the bible to be authoritative (Kerr 8: 15ff.). Is it all that surprising, then, if believers of this kind take the whole bible as normative and start thinking in all sincerity that what they see as the plain meaning of scripture has a legitimating significance for them in their own struggle for survival – as they study the stories of ancient Israel defeating the Amalakites or the people of Jericho and taking forcible possession of their promised land, supposedly under God's guidance?

Moreover, it is not difficult for such believers to gain from their religion the impression that this history of subjugation, at times very brutal, is God's will. For example, to free his people Israel from slavery he is said in the book of Exodus to cause the death of the Egyptian first-born, some of whom must have been children. This, taken as historical fact about a pivotal part of the biblical tradition (as many Christians seem to do), is most unlikely to foster attitudes of universal, egalitarian benevolence. Nor is it the only scriptural passage in which things work out rather violently to Israel's advantage. Why then would people who believe this to be God's way of doing things, and hence the best possible model of all, want to adopt a totally different policy? And if there is any validity in the exploration of ideas above, does it not mean that the culprit behind the theology of apartheid is to be found at least partly in aspects of orthodoxy itself? Instead of merely deeming those who justify apartheid theologically to be guilty of heresy, are we not forced to conclude that the real position is much more complex than that, with factors like sincerity, a pre-critical approach to religion, faulty ways of interpreting the bible and problematical items within the body of orthodox Christian teachings being the causes of the apparent anomaly before us?

Thus, without even referring to biblical passages like the tower of Babel story or the supposedly divine command that Israel should never seek the welfare of its Ammonite enemies (Deut, 23: 6), it is easily possible to find some fairly prominent themes in traditional forms of Christianity which manifestly set forth what might be called a winners-and-losers view of humanity rather than egalitarianism.

This in no way denies the presence in scripture or doctrine of the latter, at least by strong implication, but it calls sharply in question those who think that traditional church teaching gives a clear-cut message of universal, egalitarian benevolence. Therefore it is valid to contend that people who in earnest simplicity relied on these teachings for their bearings in life will not have found there an unambiguous condemnation of the politics of dominance and exclusion. The simple truth is that there are various views in scripture and within orthodox doctrine, some incompatible with others, and the sooner Christians accept this fact the better, because once they do they will be able to start sifting the wheat from the chaff in their heritage. It may of course also be the case that forms of religion which place as much emphasis on acceptance of authority as the more traditionalist parts of Christianity, will thereby encourage in believers a mental conformity which would count very much against any effective critical awareness. Problems about the bible or anything else in one's religion are then unlikely to be detected, and the struggle for truth becomes even harder to conduct.

Nor are followers of a very strongly bible- or church-based religion likely to look to other sources for the truth, because they have been taught to believe that they already have the best.

And there is a further point to be made. It is one to which I turn with considerable apprehension because it raises extremely difficult problems, but I think they must be placed on the agenda, above all in South Africa with its rich diversity of faiths. In this way the matter can receive a full, sensitive and critical discussion, and if the perception I shall present is mistaken, it can be challenged and changed. If, on the other hand, there is a real problem here, then the way may open for Christians to rethink their position appropriately. At any rate, I have enough confidence in the mental resources of our Christians to believe that the last thing they would reject in this day and age is the desire to examine *everything* in their heritage that might involve serious problems, especially ones which our South African experience of apartheid, with all its cruel and unjust exclusions, shows to be particularly contrary to the spirit of universal love, justice and goodness. With these remarks in mind, let me broach this most serious of doctrinal problems associated with the link between some Christians and apartheid.

The problem is the traditional Christian view of salvation, at least if we take as our norm the central message set forth by Jesus in teaching about the perfect and universal love of God, and therefore find abhorrent the kind of loveless disadvantaging and exclusion that rightly stigmatise apartheid. I refer now to the doctrine that only the Christian message provides people with access to eternal life by connecting them with Christ, or (less severely) that no other religion does so as effectively. In its severer form, which nowadays is more likely to be held by Protestants than Catholics, especially evangelical Protestants, this teaching rests on two basic beliefs: firstly, that all people exist in a fundamental condition of guilt and condemnation before God and therefore face eternal damnation, but, secondly, that if they believe in Christ (understood as a conscious act of faith in him) they will be saved. Certainly this view is rejected by Christian pluralists, but they are a small minority, especially in South Africa. The majority view is either *élitist*, in the sense of believing that God's free gift of salvation is more effectively or richly channelled through the Christian church than anywhere else because it alone has Christ as its founder, or *exclusivist*, in the sense of believing that only Christianity can connect people with the source of salvation and that this requires a conscious act of faith in Christ. These majority views probably have much better biblical grounding than the *pluralist* idea that at least some of the other faiths are valid and effective paths to salvation in their own right.

The lesson that emerges from all of this is the likelihood that some people, deeply and uncritically immersed in the assumptions of traditional, salvationally élitist or exclusivist Christian teachings, will have in their personal belief systems important (but invariably implicit) discriminatory, non-egalitarian notions, and may also think of these as validated by God himself. They do not see that a God who really does exemplify perfectly the unconditional and universal love taught by Jesus of Nazareth is hardly likely to make salvation – the greatest conceivable benefit according to Christianity – available to only some people. Such a God would make this supreme gift equally available to all his children for the simple reason that he loves them equally. But this is not what traditional salvation theology implies, because it is perfectly obvious that enormous numbers of people down the centuries have never even heard of Jesus Christ or had the opportunity to commit themselves to him as their saviour in a conscious act of faith, through absolutely no fault of their own. Yet traditional doctrine tells us that God is indeed a perfect being whose nature is to love his creatures with an everlasting and perfect love. And here the contradictions in traditional orthodoxy are at their most acute. For does this one not amount to the impossible view that there exists a perfect parent with endless resources, whose four children *all* urgently need that parent's help – but that the help is made available by the parent in such a way that only one of the four children has effective access to it, while the others, through absolutely no fault of their own, do not? (Available statistics suggest that only about one quarter of the human race has had effective access to the gospel message.)

What thus emerges from a critique of traditional church teaching as distinct from the message of universal love, in the light of the apartheid experience, is that the church has not yet found adequate ways of enriching society with the humane vision of its founder, and harbours within its stock of traditional teachings some major elements which do not square with the implications of the core message of Christianity itself but are uncomfortably akin to precisely some of the most morally and spiritually unacceptable parts of apartheid, in so far as they too involve things like inequality of access to the greatest benefits. How can we condemn political apartheid but condone spiritual apartheid? And it cannot be emphasised enough that the critique which discloses these problems is not based on alien, secular norms but on a consistent application of the cardinal values and central vision found in the teachings of Christ himself. Apartheid certainly clashes with universal, egalitarian love – but not with some other tenets present in large parts of traditional, orthodox church teaching. Thus we can see at last why some devout Christians could find apartheid compatible with their faith; for in their case Christianity is understood primarily in terms of those other, non-egalitarian tenets.

I am well aware just how contentious a matter this is, and raise it not for some superficial love of controversy but because it presents itself much too pressingly to be swept aside, and needs to be discussed very fully by Christians in South Africa, (especially Protestants, among whom the theology of religious pluralism lags far behind that being developed elsewhere), despite the exceptional diversity of religions found here. That is why one of the chapters in this book is devoted to precisely this theme. What is not, however, a matter for debate but simply for acceptance is that in South Africa a long-standing and intensive exposure of very many people to the teachings of the church has not prevented the creation and maintenance of some of the worst kinds of discriminatory injustice found anywhere. Racism is a moral outrage because, like a few other highly pernicious kinds of discrimi-nation, it disadvantages people on the basis of a factor they are permanently powerless to change, namely their colour. Thus it elevates biological and cultural accident above moral and spiritual principle. That it should ever have formed part of the policies of Christian people is a tragedy for which both South Africa and Christianity on these shores are already paying dearly, as I shall now explain in turning to the third of the six problems which emerge when we consider Christianity and its apartheid connection. The question here is what damage this connection is doing to the church.

Erosion of Christian credibility

What is now apparent is that the moral credibility of at least some parts of orthodox, traditional Christianity has been seriously damaged by its involvement with apartheid in two ways: in the perception (by young black people in particular) that Christianity is inimical to their interests, and in the objective logical sense that contradictory teach-ings cannot all be true. Thus we either endorse the Christian teaching that love is supreme and reject everything which clashes with it, like the teachings identified above, or we retain those teachings and forfeit the logical right to uphold the central vision announced by Jesus.

People who spurn consistency might want to ignore this problem but for all serious-minded believers it demands a solution. What is at stake here is much too serious to be ignored, scorned or wished away by worried Christians in South Africa, because unless these problems are faced the loss of credibility will get worse, calling radically into question such basic Christian beliefs as the view that the churches and the bible are essentially rooted in an act of God, or that they have any significant connection any more with the Jesus whose teachings they in certain respects contradict. And what will remain of the prospects of the churches in a future South Africa if increasing numbers of black people repudiate the belief that there is a God who cares for them in their sufferings because this belief simply ceases to be credible to them – a conclusion already argued in the work of the black American religious humanist William R. Jones? (Jones 7). Thus the worst result of the whole tragic connection between Christians and apartheid, from the point of view of Christianity, is the complete erosion of any belief in a caring God or a relevant Christ. This is already happening in South Africa (Natal Witness 11). It may not be widespread yet, but from a Christian point of view even one such total erosion of credibility is surely critical. Apartheid then becomes the event in which this destruction of faith takes place. For such people it then has a deicidal significance because it is the historic reality which destroys Christian theism for them by means of a radical negation of its concept of God.

Let me explain now why this suggests, if not demands, the metaphor of deicide for its interpretation. Religions involve a matrix of ideas, customs and influences within which faith becomes possible (Sutherland 16). Without such a matrix a God cannot live in a person's life, because the only way in which people can find meaning is precisely on the basis of such a religious matrix. That is shown in the fact that the gods of any religion have no life for outsiders, whereas they definitely impart power, value and meaning to insiders. Faith is impossible without such a medium. Without it we would not even have a word like 'God'. The belief that God reveals the things he wishes us to know, or that he alone creates faith, in no way conflicts with or refutes what I am pointing out because such revelations necessarily make use of the existing conceptual and linguistic resources of those to whom they are believed to come. If they did not do so, they could not makes any sense and therefore could not *reveal* anything reliable or meaningful. Christianity involves one of many such matrices or contexts of meaning. It is the historical matrix within which faith in God through Jesus Christ has become possible for millions of people. But if that matrix should be severely enough damaged, so that it loses credibility completely, then the God who has lived through it in those people's lives will die for them, by *ceasing to be believable*. What happens is that a whole set of religious beliefs loses its ability to convince and activate the person concerned, because at one or other crucial point it suffers such serious damage, for example through powerful, contradictory experiences, that it collapses. Christianity has rightly taught that true religion requires faith. Loss of credibility means that in a given matrix faith has become impossible, and that, for all practical purposes, is the death of God for the person concerned. It has happened many times in the past, for example to Canaanite religion, and it nearly befell ancient Israel because of the fall of Jerusalem in 586. It also happens to individuals, as with Paul in relation to Judaism. An event happened to him (his experience of Christ) which permanently ended his erstwhile form of faith. What he had taken to be the purest truth then seemed to him to be an absolute blindness, and what he formerly hated he came to embrace. A particularly important example of this death of faith happened to Friedrich Engels, lifelong friend, financial supporter and co-worker of Karl Marx. As a young person he had been converted to Christ, but what he later saw of Christianity in relation to social distress completely disillusioned him (Hay 6: 33). With apartheid's emergence in a context where Christian influences have unquestionably been very strong a similar deicidal possibility has been created. The loss of credibility is that serious.

Insufficient critical realism

A further problem which church people generally need to address is their stance in a relation to the practice of self-criticism. In South Africa a rather conservative and often traditionalist orientation tends to prevail in the churches, very unlike some other countries, and one result is insufficient critical self-awareness. This is a natural tendency in any religion which thinks that it rests largely or wholly on divine foundations, because such a belief obviously implies that there isn't much need for critical attention to the faith itself.

But the evidence is strongly against such a view of the church, just as serious biblical scholarship has long since repudiated a parallel belief about how the bible came about. The discussion above surely makes it all too obvious that alongside the beautiful and noble elements in Christianity, which believers will want to see as the gift of a gracious God, there are others which look for all the world like typically imperfect human efforts. Had greater realism on this score been present from the beginning, we might have been spared the phenomenon of Christians giving biblical and theological legitimacy to apartheid, because the teachings which do mandate that type of thing would never have been seen as divine authorisations. Implicit in the point before us is of course a changed perception of religion in general and Christianity in particular, and that brings me to the fifth of the problems in this critical review.

An unrealistic concept of religion

Great problems tend to result when people come to believe that what they think and do are God's way of doing things, because their inevitable human failings are then apt to be concealed. And there can be no doubt that countless sincere Christians believe with all their hearts that their faith is no mere human contrivance, but comes essentially or even wholly from God. Infallibilist views of the bible are perhaps the most widespread form of this conviction in South Africa. But if the truth is different; if all religion involves at least some human creativity, then great potential for harm arises from believing otherwise. The story of Christian involvement in apartheid brings home very forcefully that precisely such a misperception of the nature of religion has been and remains prevalent here. Coupled with the absence of much critical self-awareness, far too many of our believers have clung tenaciously to a view of this matter which collapses when placed under the salutary light of a balanced, critical analysis in the interests of the greatest possible love of our fellow human beings and guided by the normative central message of Jesus. It is thus time for those of South Africa's Christians who have not already done so to turn a major corner here and embrace a more realistic understanding of their own faith and of other religions, by facing up to the elements of flawed, human contrivance in them. This is a complex matter and I cannot discuss it in detail here, but what must be emphasised is the inadequacy of the idea that the generally accepted body of traditional Christian doctrine is a coherent whole all, or at least most, of which comes to us unsullied from God and is thus beyond the scope of valid human criticism, let alone human transformation. Misled by this untenable idea, and seriously lacking in healthy self-criticality at least in matters religious, many sincere Christians in South Africa have done great though entirely unintended harm to the reputation of their religion and to millions of their fellow human beings through their involvement with apartheid. It is time this understandable but none the less serious misperception of the nature of religion be unmasked and disarmed once and for all, a complex task which I have discussed elsewhere (Prozesky 13).

Disunity

It hardly needs adding that the disunity of the churches and the sheer range of varying beliefs and practices among believers greatly reduces the persuasiveness of their witness in society. It is not even evident that Christians have a clear, widely shared sense of what is central and basic to their faith. The result is confusion about fundamentals within the churches, scepticism outside and a reason for politicians to ignore the attempts by religious leaders to influence national affairs. From the point of view of an empathetic scholar trying to review the position of Christianity in South Africa with more critical distance than is usually possible for people looking at things from an internal ecclesiastical standpoint, it seems that there has been a relative neglect in ecumenical discussions of the problem of defining Christian essentials. By this I mean the minimal, central, fundamental tenets which a love-centred religious philosophy deriving historically from Jesus of Nazareth logically entails, and no more. From the point of view of such a scholar, it seems that consensus at this most basic level is very much more important than the quest for agreement about questions of ministry, worship, doctrinal detail and other matters. Perhaps South Africa's Christians could set an important process in motion by launching an inclusive, participatory search for consensus about precisely these Christian essentials.

MAKING CHRISTIANITY MORE CHRISTLIKE

On the other hand, there are further implications in all of this which offer us real hope, because it is now surely clear that Christians themselves have a very real responsibility for shaping their religion and thus for eliminating anything that now disfigures and impoverishes their beliefs and practices. It is simply untenable to hold any longer that their founder's legacy to the world is a complete and perfect system of faith and action, requiring no more than acceptance and obedience from believers. What he inspires is a central, normative vision of reality as existing in the power of an infinite and everlastingly loving

God whose supreme wish is for *all* of humanity to grow freely and creatively into the joy of a reciprocal love towards him/her and one another. No other kind of God can plausibly be the ultimate reality, worthy of total devotion and service by people dedicated to the highest level of goodness and truth, because a God who did anything less than this would neither be perfect nor Christlike. If the theological meaning of apartheid is that it finally makes incredible any idea of perfect, divine authorship for the whole of that religion, or that the God whom it worships acts by unilateral interventions in our history which override human moral responsibility, then we must accept that Christianity is at least in part a human product, and then its flaws at once become intelligible. But in that case they also become corrigible, and therein lies an important source of hope. If Christians were to transform the problematic parts of this faith so effectively that it helped save and transform South African society, then its credibility could recover. What the creation of apartheid has destroyed, the destruction of apartheid would recreate. But nothing less than a doctrine of universal love for all alike, effectively channelled into new political and economic structures, and also issuing in a better view of the other religions and philosophies of the earth than our present élitist and especially our traditionally exclusivist views, will suffice to redress the damage, because what is needed here is something powerful enough to overcome the prejudice, fear, self-interest and greed that have proved so intractable in the past.

Christians would have to recreate, or rediscover, a purer view of God as the power of perfect, universal love effectively transforming the world; they would have to recentre Christology in a view of Jesus as one who personifies that generous and gentle power and invites all people into its blessings and responsibilities not in the manner of a dictatorial master but in the manner of an inspiring and enabling friend; they would have to develop a new stance in relation to the bible as a document that needs to be creatively filtered by the norms of such a love, and would need a new ecclesiology that both accepts rather than denies the critically important part we humans play in constructing our own faiths and also accepts the responsibility of embodying and realising in history the view of God it sets forth in its teachings. In short, what South Africa's Christians now need is a *radical rehumanising of their faith*. What else does the logic of incarnation mean? Nothing less will adequately minimise the evil in our country (and planet, for that matter) and release the kind of transforming powers we so urgently need.

So it would appear that to regain credibility and live once more, traditional Christianity must, paradoxically, die. But there is a double paradox here, in that it is precisely a central teaching of traditional Christianity that things must sometimes die in order to live. There are some strange ironies here. Traditional Christianity appears now as a prison from which the evil of apartheid frees us. A living God dies at the hands of some of his own most dedicated devotees, crucified not by unbelief but by faith, and a dead God issues a stronger call for love than when he lived in those people's hearts. But if death and evil and horror can be the seed from which come new life and hope, then a faith now without credibility for some begets faith anew, and there really is good news after all. Or do these ironies show us that in the end the idiom of traditional Christianity collapses into incoherence by asserting the absurd? We shall then have reached a situation, with apartheid, of conceptual collapse, of a religious matrix failing to make sense any more. Either way, we shall have come to the end of an ancient path. Yet the journey towards a fuller life for all must go on, and the parts of Christianity that absolutely contradict apartheid cry out for release.

There is here a powerful lesson touching the very foundations of our understanding of the Christian faith. It involves abandoning the old view of Christianity as embodying an undiluted infusion of divine power and goodness into human history for the salvation of the world, and its replacement by a more tenable view as a human amalgam of good and evil, created in a sincere but sometimes clumsy and confused responsiveness to Jesus of Nazareth, within which there takes place a painful, halting, sometimes heroic, sometimes regressive struggle for something purer and better, a struggle that will never be content with anything less than the highest reaches of truth, goodness, happiness and universality, seen by believers as, in the end, a journey towards divine reality, for others perhaps not, but always a self-sufficient embracing of the spirit of universal love at each step along the way. Within traditional Christianity in South Africa at least this human amalgam of good and evil is for the most part entirely unperceived because of the (human) doctrine of divine origins and guidance. This permits the harmful impulses to flourish unsuspected and undetected, giving Christianity its tragic but undeniable ability to inflict harm and suffering in all sincerity, as apartheid and other evils reveal. In fact, there is a double problem here. Evil is bad enough unsuspected, but it is made worse by being carried unawares on the powerful shoulders of high religious resolve, confident of its divine authorisation. And this in turn naturally blocks or at least reduces the flow of goodness and truth from Christian people. But the good is not destroyed, at least not yet, and provides a platform from which Christians can see through the traditional belief that their religion is necessarily a basically good thing in all respects because of its supposed wholly divine origins and guidance. A sense of profound dismay at the evil involved may then arise, joined with a determination to root it out and cultivate more effectively the potential for universal good. Thus the creation of a purified, new age Christianity that is spiritually defined by the universal, central vision going back to Jesus of Nazareth, and which, loving its God with all its mind, also cultivates a mature, sensitive, critical mentality, would have the potential to release great powers of good for all in our society, and maybe even for the whole world.

Theologically this would be the rediscovery that what Christianity at its best has seen as the true God stands in radical judgement not just over sin and evil, but also over faith, sincerity, bible, creed, church and anything else supposedly sacred when they fall short of the highest and most universal goodness and truth, but also offers them the opportunity for radical change and growth. That too is deeply embedded in this religion and contains a depth of spiritual wisdom of great value to South Africa's Christians at this critical stage of their history.

TRANSFORMING SOUTH AFRICA

What South Africa needs now is national political salvation through an unambiguous commitment to and peaceful, co-operative implementation of the goal of a society with equal rights, opportunities, benefits, security and responsibility for all its people. For this to happen, several requirements have to be met. Since whites control the political and economic power of the country, there will have to be a significant redirection of that power from group self-interest to the common interest, but without loss of security. A blueprint for a non-threatening egalitarian society is therefore also essential, but is at present not emerging. If it did, it would have to be effectively communicated to the electorate in ways that maximised its acceptability, and hence from a credible quarter. Also necessary is the ability to initiate the process of creating such a social blueprint on an inclusive, participatory basis, so that appropriate, nationally-transforming values and ideas can be reached democratically. Then there has to be a motivation among the white electorate strong enough to accept this kind of national transformation. I believe that a significant potential for this exists in the moral and religious earnestness of many Afrikaans people, especially when a realistic acceptance of the true nature of apartheid becomes widespread and gives rise to a determination to transform that ugly reality. And it is here above all that the commitment of a renewed and united Christianity could be decisive, but only if the necessary transformation of Christianity also takes place. There is no way a better South Africa, free of social apartheid, can be built on foundations already structurally cracked by spiritual apartheid. Above all, it is absolutely essential that white, Afrikaans-speaking Christians commit themselves on a large scale to this possibility and make it happen. Theirs has been the main hand in the creation of the present apartheid state since 1948; they must thus be prominent in its removal and replacement by something better. If Christianity is to regain credibility as a genuinely redeeming power, it must do so in the social vision of these people or it may not do so at all. Such is the magnificent, creative, historic opportunity that I see for contemporary Christians, in the white Dutch Reformed Churches in particular, but for all the others as well. But will they see it too?

What these requirements amount to in the first instance is the urgent need to identify the changed, *basic, social values* that are necessary if there is to be well-being and security for all without injustice to any. It is quite clear that the necessary vision and values are not emerging from any of our political parties. The South African Council of Churches might be seen as a potential agency for this task, but it suffers at present from the problem of having little credibility in the white Dutch Reformed Churches and not as much Roman Catholic involvement as that of English-speaking Protestants. Nor do any of the universities have the structures or funds that would be needed. The business community might have the funds, but it does not have either the information resources or the values. Our problem is therefore that in a situation where just about everybody senses that the old system of basic social values cannot be maintained, the means of articulating a really worthwhile replacement in a credible way simply do not exist.

It is here that a window of opportunity might exist for South Africa's Christians. Let me suggest some additional ways of grasping that opportunity while it lasts.

I have already emphasised that it will be essential for Afrikaners to contribute prominently to the creation of a post-apartheid society, otherwise it cannot happen without even worse violence than we have already. One opportunity that is available is for the Afrikaans language to show its power as an instrument of liberation for all South

Africans. Another is for creative and courageous use to be made of the ferment currently taking place in the white Dutch Reformed Churches. They could, for instance, set the political situation a crucial example by seeking an entirely non-racial structure. After all, if a common Christian faith, truly rooted in the vision and example of its founder, cannot be expressed non-racially by members of the same Reformed tradition, how much hope is there for society at large in South Africa? Or are these churches now completely behind the times, at best irrelevant and at worst even harmful to society? I do not think so; I think they could yet play a decisive part in our national salvation, but time is short.

Identifying the kind of basic social values without which real improvement for all South Africans will not take place might be helped by the existence of an independent, non-racial Centre for Social Transformation, with the resources and credibility to help us find the architects and contractors to build a just, participatory and sustainable future. Funds made available for this purpose by Christians could make such a centre possible very rapidly, perhaps in association with a well-placed university.

One of the worst problems about defective social systems is their lack of institutions capable of improving matters. Therefore those institutions have to be created. We need one now, which would fuse the highest values taught to us by religion and morality with the best intellectual resources of the academic world, and which, free of the crippling sectional obligations of a political party or of business, would be able to give the quest for national salvation that input of ideas, values and arrangements needed in order to bring it to fruition. Something effective along these lines could give credibility to a changed, new-age Christianity by tangibly helping South Africa to a better future. An opportunity as daunting but also as fertile as the exile was for ancient Israel now exists for Christians in South Africa to help create a new epoch of faith and social relevance. Let us give them all the help we can to take it.

I have concentrated these constructive proposals on white Christians in South Africa because the creation of apartheid is overwhelmingly their affair. Let me add, however, that black Christians have at least as much to contribute here, if not more, in allaying white fears, in generating precisely the kind of new values and vision that we need as the foundation for a better future, in forgiveness, perhaps also in self-criticism as searching as that which they expect from whites. But I do not think it is appropriate for a white like me to try to explore this further and define that role. All I am sure of is that Christianity can die in South Africa at their hands just as surely as at the hands of those who have inflicted apartheid upon them. What can appropriately be said here is that much will depend on how humane, sophisticated, convincing and especially effective a presentation of their faith they offer to a population part of which is retreating into its ethnic laager, thereby effectively repudiating the *universal* love proclaimed by Christianity, while another is discerning in the philosophy of historical materialism a superior worldview, thereby effectively denying the *transcendental* dimension of that religion.

CONCLUSION

Will there be such an act of Christian self-transformation to promote the path of peace, love and justice in South Africa, with profound implications for Christianity everywhere? Will what has died for some on our soil rise again? It is certainly possible. The Christian faith has important resources to offer, such as repentence, trust, forgiveness, love, ability to find victory in defeat and above all the strange operations of that benign power which Christians call grace. The Afrikaans people have qualities of determination and a religious and moral earnestness, which, if directed anew, could prove decisive. White Christians have plenty of money to offer. Black Christians have a richly life-affirming and communitarian outlook, among other things, with which to foster greater humanisation as a church contribution to the future. Above all, our Christians have a truly magnificent challenge to heal the wounds of apartheid, a challenge whose global and historic significance could generate its own great power of renewal. At stake is the future here of traditional Christianity, of our children and also the momentous question of whether significant moral progress can happen without violent revolution. Will Afrikaner Christianity prove or refute the Marxists on this issue? Did so much ever depend on the stirrings of conscience and goodwill now evident, however slight they may seem? Such a reality could breed its own power. So there are important grounds for hope. But there is another side to consider. Powerful conservative and negative forces are deeply entrenched in church and politics. Ecclesiastical life often seems to the observer to be governed by ritual rather than socio-ethical priorities. Many will resist change in the name of God, like Samuel in ancient Israel when the need for a monarchy became urgent. It is possible that we are carrying too many Samuels for change to come in and through Christianity, and their resistance to change will be so much harder to overcome for being based on a sincerely-held faith. But if the thought of a society held back unwittingly in its sufferings and turmoil by too many Christian Samuels seems depressing, perhaps South Africa's more progressive believers can draw encouragement in this dark night of the nation's soul from an old Russian proverb quoted by Alexander Solzhenitsyn in his Nobel Prize acceptance speech in 1970: 'One word of truth is of more weight than all the rest of the world' (Solzhenitsyn 15: 55).

REFERENCES

1. Adam, H. and Giliomee, H. *The Rise and Crisis of Afrikaner Power* (Cape Town: David Philip, 1979).
2. Barrett, David (ed.), *World Christian Encyclopedia* (Nairobi: Oxford University Press, 1982).
3. Cochrane, James, *Servants of Power: The Role of English-Speaking Churches 1903–1930* (Johannesburg: Ravan Press, 1987).
4. Davenport, T. R. H., *South Africa: A Modern History*, 3rd edn (Johannesburg: Macmillan, 1987).
5. De Gruchy, John, and Villa-Vicencio, Charles (eds), *Apartheid is a Heresy* (Cape Town: David Philip, 1983).
6. Hay, David, *Exploring Inner Space: Scientists and Religious Experience* (Harmondsworth: Penguin, 1982).
7. Jones, William R., *Is God a White Racist? A Preamble to Black Theology* (New York: Anchor Books, 1973).
8. Kerr, Hugh T., *A Compend of the Institutes of the Christian Religion by John Calvin* (Philadelphia: Westminster Press, 1964).
9. Kinghorn, Johann (ed.), *Die NG Kerk en Apartheid* (Johannesburg: Macmillan, 1986).
10. Majeke, Nosipho, *The Role of the Missionaries in Conquest* (Cumberwood: Apdusa, no date, [1986?].
11. *The Natal Witness (Echo)*: 'Jesus is the White Man's King' (Letter) 6 February 1986.
12. Oosthuizen, G. C. *et al.* (eds), *Religion, Intergroup Relations and Social Change in South Africa* (Pretoria: HSRC, 1985).
13. Prozesky, Martin, *Religion and Ultimate Well-Being: An Explanatory Theory* (London: Macmillan, and New York: St Martin's Press, 1984).
14. Richardson, Neville, 'Apartheid, Heresy and the Church in South Africa', *Journal of Religious Ethics*, 14(1), 1986, 1ff.
15. Solzhenitsyn, Alexander, *Nobel Prize Lecture* (London: Stenvalley Press, 1973).

16.   Sutherland, Stewart, *Jesus, God and Belief* (Oxford: Blackwell, 1984) and *Times Higher Education Supplement*, 12 October 1984, p. 21.

17.   Van der Post, L., *The Lost World of the Kalahari* (London: Hogarth, 1958).

* This essay is based on a paper with the title 'Christianity and Apartheid: From Christian Deicide to Socio-Political Salvation in South Africa' which was presented at a conference on Salvation and the Secular at the University of Natal, Pietermaritzburg, in June 1985.

Part III
Christianity and Social Issues

8 The Impact of Christianity on Socio-Economic Developments in South Africa

Klaus Nürnberger

INTRODUCTION

South Africa is the product of the colonial era – whether in terms of its social structures or its convictions. So our point of entry into the theme will have to be colonial history. The first question is whether the Christian faith had anything to do with the evolution of the historial dynamic which led to the domination of the world by a few European countries. The second question is what role it played in the evolution of a particular colonial entity, namely South Africa. Here we have to distinguish between the historical impact of Christian convictions on the colonisers, on the colonised and on the relation between them. Finally we shall consider a possible scenario for furture developments.

The scope of the theme is gigantic. What I offer is a tentative and impressionistic survey of the entire field. It is no substitute for detailed investigations. Moreover, the causal relation (if any) between a particular system of meaning and the evolution of a particular shape of social structures is a highly controversial issue. In a postscript I shall mention a few methodological considerations which should guide us in more serious research.

CHRISTIANITY AND IMPERIALISM

The emergence of the mentality which led to Western imperialism is an involved issue. Some scholars assume that its cradle is the merger of ancient Hebrew and Greek thought. The Greeks discovered the power of rational thinking and the existence of dependable principles which underlie experienced reality. By understanding and applying what

149

ultimately turned out to be the 'laws of nature' one could gain mastery over nature. The Hebrews contributed the awareness of a linear, goal-directed history and the belief that it is propelled by the will of a single God who is the Master of reality as a whole. The human being is meant to participate in God's mastery over the universe. Both world views progressively demythologised the universe. There was no place for uncanny forces, spirits, or demons. Eventually a secular mentality emerged in which the world was entirely at the disposal of humanity (Gogarten 1953). Other influences, Eastern, Roman, Germanic, contributed.

It took centuries before the potentially explosive dynamic of this merger of world views began to get off the ground and pick up speed. Static assumptions and authoritarian structures distintegrated only gradually. In modern times its rate of acceleation reached a breath-taking pace (Toffler 1971).

Originally the new mentality was embedded in metaphysics and religion but gradually the assumptions of both an ontological structure and an all-determining divine authority were jettisoned. The human being with its gifts of observation, rationality and willpower became the only fixture in the relativity of all that exists and the endless flow of history. A mechanistic, evolutionary, progress-oriented view of reality developed. Its ethic was geared to the systematic subjugation of reality and thus to world transformation. A missionary and pioneering spirit combined idealist zeal to help humankind solve its problems with the most ruthless pursuit of self-interest.

In liberalism it was the individual who was released from all authorities and fetters and a premium was placed on the development and utilisation of all available potentials for private gain. In national-ism this legitimation of self-interest as a supreme principle was applied to an ethnic collective. The vast discrepancies in power and privilege which resulted from both these forms, gave the age-old demand for justice and equality a political potency unparalleled in former history. This is the root of the modern struggle for democracy, socialist policies and human rights.

Diverse historical phenomena are but different dimensions of this new dynamic:

(1) the development of science and technology which led to possi-bilities unthinkable in earlier stages of history;

(2) the voyages of discovery and conquest which led to establishment of global empires and the subjugation of virtually the whole of humankind under the hegemony of a handful of European nations;

(3) the emergence of the capitalist system, built first on commerce, then on colonial exploitation, then on the industrial revolution and finally on information technology. The outcome of this development is the present world economic system dominated by a few industrialised nations. Marxist socialism formed a powerful counter-system; (4) a missionary movement of global proportions which combined religious with cultural aspects. It was followed by waves of secular thought that swept through the élites of the entire world. To these belong liberal humanism, socialist materialism and the ecological movement. In all these forms one detects global horizons, a goal-directed motivation and a strong sense of calling.

SOUTH AFRICA AS A COLONIAL PROTOTYPE

There are those who view the colonial era in a positive light. If they are Christians, they may be proud of the Christian contribution in this regard. There are others for whom colonialism lies at the roots of the present predicament of the Third World. They will be inclined to see Christian missions as part of the evils of Western imperialism (cf. Majeke 1952).

South Africa could provide the material for a particularly revealing case study. It is obvious that its present shape is the product of European colonialism. It is one of the few cases where the antagonism of two successive colonial empires (Dutch and British) made the formation of a dominant culture impossible. It is the only case where the colonists did not form the majority (in contrast to the USA or Brazil), yet were not rendered impotent with decolonisation (as in Algeria or Zimbabwe), but continued to dominate the scene as a powerful minority. As such they continue to represent the colonial age and to mirror its continuation in present neo-colonial arrangements the world over. Moreover, the white élite has strong affinities to world capitalism while the black majority develops powerful socialist leanings. So both the North-South, and the East-West conflicts find their expression within this one society.

It is also a country in which about three quarters of the population profess allegiance to the Christian faith in some form or another. These particular forms manifest an incredible variety. They are partly the heritage of Western traditions, partly the result of indigenous appropriations of this faith (Sundkler 1961). If anywhere in the world, it is here that we should be able to study the complexity of an evolving interplay between Christian convictions and social structures.

CHRISTIANITY AND THE DUTCH SETTLER POPULATION

The dominant Dutch section of the early colonisers subscribed to the Calvinist stream of Protestant thinking. It was reinforced by Huguenot settlers and later by Scottish influences. German and other elements were deliberately absorbed. The policy of religious and cultural assimilation was extended over the subservient Khoi-Khoi and over the slave population from the East. Developments in the Cape Colony in fact were set to follow the pattern of Brazil or similar countries in this respect (cf. the works on the emergence of Afrikaner thought in the bibliography).

Three forces reversed this trend. In the first place a second wave of colonialism, the British, superseded the first and followed its own assimilation policy. Secondly, the Cape Dutch migration reached the solid Bantu-speaking settlements in the East which were both too numerous and culturally too intact to be conquered and absorbed. And thirdly, in contrast with the Cape Dutch settlers, the British colonialists had gone through the Enlightenment and experienced the emergence of a liberal spirit. In the wake of these they often took sides with the underdog Hottentot and slave populations as well as with the Bantu-speaking neighbours on the volatile Eastern frontier against the settlers. The Cape Dutch cultural group was, therefore, under pressure from the West and the East, from above and below. In the half century between the first frontier war (1779) and the beginning of the 'Great Trek', when many settlers packed their belongings and moved inland in search of self-determination (1835), their typical 'laager' survival strategy and mentality were forged.

During the gradual migration of the settlers to the interior their Christian religion was practically the only sustaining and formative spiritual influence. Naturally it was affected by their particular historical experience. In this synthesis it played the role of:

(1) spiritual sustenance. The Biblical faith supplied the overall system of meaning, a system of values and norms as well as the assurance of one's right of existence;

(2) identity formation. The emerging Boer cultural group depended on the Bible for its clues concerning its self-interpretation and the interpretation of its historic experience. Constant reference to the

Bible helped to forge a new cultural tradition. Identification with the elect people of God (in a merger of the concepts of Israel and the church) served to form a particular group consciousness; (3) an educational medium. The Bible was, in many instances, the only book the family possessed. As such it helped to maintain the link of the 'fragment culture' in the Cape with its European heritage; (4) the legitimation of social, economic and political group interests had to be formulated against the background of Biblical presuppositions.

Regarding legitimation a number of stages can be distinguished. In the first stage the clear distinction between Christian and heathen served to legitimate the subjugation of the aboriginal Khoi Khoi (Hottentot) and the virtual eradication of the San (Bushmen). Similar attitudes were developed towards the black communities on the Eastern frontier. For a long time a converted non-settler was, however, regarded as part of the community, even if of a lower class (Kinghorn 1986).

During the Great Trek the image of the conquest of Canaan by Israel served to explain and legitimate the movement of the Boers into territory formally occupied by blacks but left relatively vacant by the Difaqane and Mfecane (a wave of wars beginning with the militancy of the Zulu empire of Chaka, in which black communities ousted their next neighbours after having been ousted themselves – Wilson and Thomson, I, 1969, 391ff.). It should be remembered, however, that this identification with Israel in its conquest of Canaan was common practice during the era of colonialism. The Spanish, Portuguese, British and other colonial powers used this legitimation (Norman 1981, Sandison 1967, Stokes 1960).

After the Anglo-Boer war great numbers of Afrikaners (as the Boers then called themselves) entered a period of social decline, economic impoverishment and political powerlessness. Now the impact of industrial society made itself felt on the previously rural population. During this period the Dutch Reformed Church, especially, played a key role in restoring self-respect, national pride and the will to regain self-determination and prosperity among the Afrikaners.

At this stage the interesting question arises whether the Calvinism of the Afrikaners lent itself to the legitimation of liberal-capitalist assumptions as Max Weber's famous thesis of the 'Protestant Ethic' might have suggested (Weber 1905, Tawney 1926). It is an involved issue. As long as they constituted the top layer of a rural feudal structure their superior position was legitimated religiously, but there is little to suggest the emergence of the restlessness, profit-motive and progress-orientation so typical of the capitalist mentality. Nor are there convincing signs of ascetic frugality and dedicated industriousness claimed by Weber to be the hallmarks of the 'Protestant spirit'.

When and as far as they became an urban proletariat their collective interests again precluded the formation of an ideology which legitimates liberal-capitalist assumptions. Rather, in a generally embittered mood, British capitalist imperialism was seen as the enemy of the people. The outcome was a merger between quasi-socialist principles, ethnic loyalties and a capitalist base which was called 'volkskapitalisme' (O'Meara 1983). It is only recently that the spirit of 'free enterprise' came into its own among the higher classes of Afrikaners. But by that time religious motivations had largely disappeared (cf. Bosch 1984, Stokes 1975, de Klerk 1975).

The mood of the first half of the century found its religious legitimation in a powerful ideology which combined ethnic romanticism with a particular Kuyperian interpretation of the Reformed tradition (Kinghorn 1986). During these formative years of the Apartheid ideology the Dutch Reformed church played its most prominent role as a supplier of meaning, legitimation and motivation. Through the Broederbond, 'Christian-national' ideals gained prominence in the entire educational system with widespread formative effects. 'Volkskapitalisme' led to state enterprises such as Iscor. Apartheid became the political slogan of the 'purified' National Party.

Once accepted as fundamental, this ideology was taken for granted to such an extent, however, that it gradually emancipated itself from theological legitimations, the latter stagnated in orthodoxy and the role of the church in political matters became more and more peripheral. The initiative passed to charismatic ideologues, such as Dr H. Verwoerd (Kinghorn 1986).

The vehement attacks on racial ideologies from liberal (humanist and Christian) quarters did not pass them by, however. As liberal values penetrated the Afrikaner community and as the wave of decolonisation rolled towards their life world, the legitimating ideology changed from *baasskap* (lordship), which assumed that blacks can never attain to the level of whites, to guardianship, which assumed that they are not yet ready for it, to separate (later plural) development, which ostensibly granted them equal opportunities to develop themselves according to their own criteria, to democratic and liberal reforms under the presupposition of state security. Technocratic arguments such as that white South Africa is a regional super power and the source of political stability and economic development in the subregion, play a role as well. It is clear that the basic political and economic interests have not changed. But the legitimating arguments have (Nürnberger 1984, 137–46).

A conservative wing was not able to go along with this ideological transformation and split off on the right. Recently the Dutch Reformed Church has adapted its own stance to developments in the National Party (witness the document *Church and Society*, 1986) with the result that it faces a similar split. With that the integrating power of the church seems to have broken up along with that of other Afrikaner ethnic organisations, notably the Broederbond (Bosch 1985).

On the other hand resistance against fundamental change demanded by the leadership of the restive black population is still legitimated by appeals to Christian motives alongside those of political ideology: God instituted and authorised the state to ward off not only the communist (= godless) threat, but with it revolution, anarchy, crime and chaos. No doubt the South African soldiers on the 'border' and in the townships are made to feel that they are fighting a holy war.

THE BRITISH SETTLERS

In contrast with the Afrikaner community settlers of British extraction displayed:
(1) denominational diversity. Christianity did not provide a very powerful basis for social or political cohesion in the English-speaking community. Also the attitude towards public affairs differed considerably between the different traditions. Anglicanism always had a strong affinity with the British state. It was, therefore, most closely identified with the Empire and its wars, whether against blacks or against Boers. At the opposite end of the spectrum we find evangelical and pentecostal groups whose faith is individualistic, private and spiritual, rather than social, public and down-to-earth. As such it provides legitimation by default for whatever happens in the political realm;
(2) a greater leaning towards economic liberalism and political tolerance. This was often combined with democratic ideals, human rights and humanist goodwill. By and large British Christianity legitimated the power game as much as Afrikaner Christianity did, but with shifted emphases (Cochrane 1987). There was no historical necessity among the British for the enclave mentality so typical of the

Afrikaners. Thus they found it much easier to attack ethnic and racial attitudes. In contrast, this economic élite was not too eager to attack the liberal assumptions on which its prosperity rested. Thus there was little critique of industrial capitalism and its effects. Only more recently, small but significant groups with radical convictions have challenged not only the conservative, but also the liberal stance. Often the concern for social justice was inextricably woven together with political enmity against the Afrikaner. Christianity, where it played a role at all, often served to underpin these differing sentiments. The result was that Christians could seldom speak with a united voice on public issues but found themselves on opposite sides of the political front lines (cf. de Gruchy 1979).

(3) a much higher level of secularisation. This is particularly true of the great number of adventurers and fortune seekers who streamed into the country after the discovery of gold and diamonds.

In the latter two respects the fact that the weaning of the English-speakers from their European cultural context took place much later and only very partially, made itself felt. One could argue that the difference between Afrikaner and British Christianity (both with Calvinist roots) is the difference between the Europe of the seventeenth, and the Europe of the nineteenth century.

Just in passing we have to mention that the Indians too belong to the settler population. In a way they are an appendix to the English-speaking white group, just as the 'coloureds' are to the Afrikaans-speaking group. The Indians were penetrated only marginally by Christian missions and by and large belong to Islam or to Hinduism. With the exception of such illustrious figures as Mahatma Gandhi, the minority status of the Indians gave them little leeway for socio-political impact. However, similar to the Jews, a minority of them played a considerable role in business.

THE IMPACT OF CHRISTIAN MISSIONS ON THE INDIGENOUS POPULATION

Apart from being driven out or killed by people professing the Christian faith, the San experienced virtually no impact of this faith. The Khoi-Khoi were gradually assimilated into the Cape Dutch culture together with Malay slaves and other elements if they did not change to Islam. We shall here concentrate on the Bantu-speaking population which was the prime target of the Christian missionary enterprise over the last two centuries.

Beginning with the impact of the Christian proclamation on their collective consciousness, we may distinguish three dimensions (Nürnberger 1975). In the first place the Western interpretation of the biblical faith undermined the dynamistic-magical world view of these pre-literary cultures. The mechanisms of this are quite involved. Dynamism assumes that reality is constituted by a pervasive fluidum of power which can be in equilibrium or turmoil and which can be channelled into profitable or detrimental avenues. The first is done by means of socially sanctioned rituals, the second through sorcery which is the most dreaded of all crimes in the African community.

The manipulation of these forces has its limits, however. The ancestors who are the source of the life force of the ongoing lineage, have left the living with detailed prescriptions and any deviation from the latter is considered to be precarious – not only because some counterproductive mechanism may be set in motion, but also because the ancestors themselves do not tolerate such deviations and punish the transgressors.

Moreover, the ancestors themselves are not almighty. There are occasions when all the rituals to appease them and restore the balance in the community have been performed, yet drought, disease or infertility continue. In this case nothing can be done. In the Sotho-Tswana religion, for instance, Modimo (the 'supreme being'), is a personification of the totality of these impersonal forces. He does not speak and he cannot be addressed. He does not act but things happen. The expression: *Modimo o gona, ga re kgone selo!* (It is Modimo, there is nothing we can do!) expresses the fatalistic attitudes towards this 'God' – or rather towards what we would call 'fate' and its inscrutable and impenetrable secrets.

In its biblical form the Christian faith itself has not reached the stage of the modern mechanistic and rational perception of reality. However, it subjects the whole of reality to the supreme will of a personal Creator God who can manipulate reality at will, who can be addressed and who invites human beings to share his creative authority over reality. Modimo is no longer an impersonal ocean of dynamistic power in which one drowns when one leaves the ship of the communal life stabilised by rituals, but one's powerful Father. If one's powers fail, this does not mean that the powers of one's God have reached their limits, nor that he could not again empower one in some way. Once this conviction penetrates into the deeper layers of conviction, the human being is no longer the helpless victim of an inscrutable fate. Reality has lost its sovereignty and fatalism makes way for self-confidence and assurance.

From here it is but one step to reach a mentality of scientific and technological mastery over the world. This attitude had already been fused with the biblical faith in the mindset of the missionaries. It opened the way of entry into the industrial civilisation within the collective consciousness of the African. Or vice versa, it opened the collective consciousness of the African to the 'imperialistic' penetration of Western cultural, scientific and technological assumptions. And this was the prerequisite for the integration of the African population into the capitalist urban-industrial system.

One has to take note of the fact, however, that where economic incentives presented themselves, tribal Africans were apparently able to develop considerable economic initiative in spite of what one would have expected on the basis of above considerations (Bundy 1979). One has to be careful, therefore, not to overestimate the relative role of religious presuppositions. The latter must be seen in the context of a greater whole in which complex relations between multiple factors prevail. And again any unqualified application of the Weberian thesis is put into question.

A second aspect is that the orientation towards the past – which is implied in a religious context determined by ancestor veneration and the absolutisation of tradition – gradually turns forward towards the future. Because missionaries mainly represented a pietistic, upward- rather than forward-orientated spirituality, this did not happen automatically. In fact, the Christianity of the missionaries may even have retarded the development of a this-worldly future consciousness. The infamous dictum pie-in-the-sky-when-you-die is a telling critique of this mentality. Africans have probably been forced into a historical future-orientation by the merciless march of social, economic and political transformations and their cataclysmic consequences rather than by the Christian gospel. But the biblical faith was able to underpin an urge forward towards regaining control over one's fate. That is the significance of Black Theology and Liberation Theology with their clear commitment to selfhood and social transformation.

A third aspect was the undermining influence of the Christian faith on the social cohesion and the social control of tribal society in its rigidly structured hierarchical network. At first this was more indirect than direct. Christian missions had a tough time penetrating the core of tribal society. But they did reach and pick up those who found themselves on its disintegrating fringes. Converts were often people who no longer had a stake in the traditional setup and who longed for freedom from it. The church provided an alternative system of meaning and an alternative community. The latter had its own laws but the primary severance of tribal ties was a decisive break out of traditional social controls.

Tribal distintegration was, however, also the result of deliberate colonial policies. This had a number of contrasting effects. On the one hand many who broke loose, ended up in disorientation and anomie. The emerging black churches by and large responded to this threat with the development of powerful patterns of authority and discipline, although the latter hardly match their traditional counterparts. The security of the church was, however, only available at the price of dependency on Western leadership, theology, expertise, finance, medical care and so on. Reaction against dependency and cultural alienation in the mainline churches again led to the phenomenal growth of the African Independent church movement. Here the victims of cultural breakdown and moral disorientation found their emotional stability and social protection in a more authentic African cultural atmosphere. One can hardly overestimate the importance of these little communities during the period of acculturation.

It also needs to be mentioned that in a time when the churches were virtually the only viable non-state and non-tribal organisations left in the black community, they played an inestimable role in structuring social relationships, providing social identity, leadership and cohesion and acting as a training ground for democratic procedures and financial administration.

On the other hand church and school led to a growing number of people who were able to offer their services to the evolving industrial and commercial economy on various levels of sophistication. In time they developed into an urban-industrial proletariat with gradually loosening ties to the traditional society. Most important was the rise of a new black élite which was soon able to outcompete traditional authorities and gain more and more influence, wealth and status in the black community (cf. Saunders 1969). Whatever leeway the white system left for the development of black leadership was immediately occupied by this Westernised group – in spite of the fact that the white system often favoured the chiefs as instruments of 'indirect rule'. The emergence of a modern leadership in Africa is quite unthinkable without the mission school, even if it has now been superseded by secular ideological influences.

The role played by these new élites has been an ambiguous one. Seen from the vantage point of traditional Africa, they were traitors and bridgeheads for the penetration of Western cultural and religious imperialism. They quite naturally developed into offshoots of the white controlled economic, social and political power structure – basically sharing the interest patterns of the latter and allowing themselves to be used as instruments of white domination.

However, these Westernised élites were, at the same time, the only serious challengers of white colonial and racial domination. The more acculturated they became, the more vehemently they claimed their rightful place in modern society and they were the only ones who could add weight to their demands. In this respect the impact of the Christian proclamation can again be discerned. Desmond Tutu, for instance, suggests that the power of the liberation movement is derived from the fact that blacks began to take the gospel which whites had brought, seriously and to claim their birth-right as children of God. Certainly the awareness of having an almighty, just and loving God on one's side must lead to the development of a healthy self-respect and self-confidence which will not easily be subdued.

This impact could move in various directions. In the early phases of the liberation struggle leaders longed for integration in the white, liberal society. There is still a powerful undercurrent of liberal motivations in the upper echelons of black society today. Here the struggle concentrates on racial barriers rather than on the class structure, on equality of dignity, political rights, judicial status and economic opportunity rather than on equal income. Even Black Theology historically was more aware of social and political, rather than economic power structures. In this respect there is a difference of emphasis between Black Theology and Latin American Liberation Theology. That South Africa, in contrast with Latin America, is not only a society based on class but also on race makes itself felt.

But the mood is changing. From early on socialist principles found a fertile ground among the disadvantaged and they are now gaining ground very rapidly. The contention that Christianity commends the socialist idea of sharing while it condemns the greed of capitalism is very widespread. Finally, cultural and racial self-assertion needs to be mentioned. Although it also fed on frustration and resentment, the Black Consciousness movement, for instance, has a strong spiritual main-spring (Leatt 1986 105ff.). The cyclical upsurge of the liberation struggle in the black community as a whole is largely underpinned by a mixture of Christian and humanist motifs.

On the other hand, there is also the phenomenon that blacks consider Christianity to be the religion of the white oppressor. The white God has not only given whites success, privilege and power but also effectively disempowered and subdued the black majority. This consideration can move in two opposite directions. To regain their strength and self-confidence, some feel that they have to turn to their own spiritual resources. Thus tribal traditions experience a renaissance, especially in rural areas. Secondly, this mood can easily be picked up by secular ideologies for which religion as such is nothing but a sedative administered by the oppressive powers in society which should be eradicated.

FUTURE PROSPECTS

The impact of the Christian faith on socio-economic developments in South Africa is likely to decline in the future. Increasing secularisation of perceptions and relationships, the functionalisation of social arrangements, pluralism, the concomitant privatisation of religion and the increasing power of ideological commitments will probably all contribute to this development.

As the conflict between the white power structure and the black revolutionary spirit escalates, the South African collective consciousness is driven apart into two worlds of perception and motivation precisely where the process of acculturation has brought the two main sections of the population nearest to each other. Deliberate isolation and self-immunisation, particularly of the white community but recently also of the black urban population, collective self-justification, propaganda and violent confrontation produce an emotional abyss which even the presuppositions of a common faith find increasingly difficult to bridge.

White interests will probably continue to work in the direction of conservatism in political affairs, and pietist fundamentalism in religious affairs. The nagging demand for social justice and open fellowship as well as the inability to maintain the plausibility of a Christian justification of the oppressive and racist system will probably have an ambiguous effect. On the one hand, they may keep at least some awareness of black misery and the legitimacy of black demands alive. Because of its ambiguous stance the Christian faith will probably lose further ground to the more determined liberal and radical world views in this regard. On the other hand, they may lead to a further abandonment of the Christian faith as a social determinant in favour of more ruthless survival attitudes by those inclined towards the right wing.

Black interests will forcefully push in the 'progressive' direction of a socialist revolution. The Christian faith will find it increasingly difficult to keep pace with the radicalisation of the mood in the black community and may find itself being ousted from its traditional role by its militant ideological counterpart, Marxism-Leninism. Black youth especially may find Christianity more and more repugnant as a soft option. Much will depend on whether moderate Christian leaders such as Tutu and Boesak will be able to maintain their credibility.

Where white and black Christians still meet, traitors interact with stooges. Even the word reconciliation raises antagonism on both extremes. White Christians are unable to meet both the white demand for the legitimation of oppression and the black demand for social justice, while black Christians are unable to meet both the white demand for moderation and the black demand for revolutionary change. Nevertheless, the stubborn continuation of these fragile contacts may maintain an infrastructure of human relationships which may gain in importance as the situation deteriorates and the system approaches breaking point. Without such a basis, prospects for a wholesome reconstruction will be dim. Also the continuing demythologisation of ideological absolutes and loyalties as well as the challenge to keep unpopular options open, will not be without its effect on the ongoing struggle.

CONCLUSION

A fully fledged belief system such as the Christian faith performs at least the following functions in society:
(1) it offers a foundational system of meaning and its concomitant set of definitions, values and norms which facilitate orientation in the universe, identity formation, moral guidance and assurance of one's right of existence;
(2) because of all this, it offers emotional security in primary groups and social cohesion in greater contexts. It is the hidden spiritual backbone of any viable community and, to some extent, of the social order as a whole;
(3) it provides the authority over against which the pursuit of individual and collective interests and the institutional means for their achievement have to be legitimised. In this regard serious distortions both of the system of meaning and of the perception and interpretation of reality may occur and often these are consciously manipulated by pressure groups to achieve the desired ends.

We have seen that the Christian faith has performed these three functions in various forms, on various levels and in vastly differing historical, cultural and social contexts. But it was not alone on the stage. African religio-cultural traditions on the one hand and secular humanism, both liberal and radical, on the other have entered into various relations of competition, syncretism or symbiosis with Christianity. Its influence varied according to places, times, groups and denominational forms. The interaction between these complex patterns of collective consciousness and the evolution of socio-structural structures and mechanisms presents an extremely confusing picture. Only penetrating analyses of delimited areas of interaction can produce relatively reliable results concerning the relative impact of Christianity on the formation of present-day South Africa and an assessment of its possible future role.

POSTSCRIPT: METHODOLOGICAL CONSIDERATIONS

1. I am a theologian. Theologians normally study a faith experience from within that experience. The advantage of this approach is that it offers the possibility of applying an authenticity critique to actual phenomena. Is a Christianity which legitimises racial discrimination, for instance, true to the fundamentals of the Christian faith? While questions such as these are not unimportant, I chose not to enter the discussion on this level, because it would have led to superficiality in a short essay. My approach, therefore, was not theological but phenomenological. That means that I tried to offer a disinterested presentation of the phenomena and withhold my own judgement.

2. Great controversy surrounds the relation between collective consciousness and social structures. Crude forms of idealism and materialism have been superseded by the more refined approaches of the sociology of knowledge (which believes that symbolic universes underlie the social order), and neo-marxism (which offers a critique of ideological legitimations of social power structures). My own position is that there is a complex reciprocal network of interaction between the two levels (Nürnberger 1984 113ff.). This means that social structures do not determine collective consciousness, and collective consciousness does not determine social structures in any unilateral and determinative way. The complex structure of causation can only be analysed in a given situation by means of a systems analytical approach which is able to integrate 'soft' (non-quantifiable), with 'hard' (quantifiable) factors (Checkland 1981).

3. On the consciousness level the interplay between faith and ideology is crucial (Leatt 1986 273ff.). I define ideology as the legitimation or concealment of group interests at the expense of the interests of other groups. Ideology has to operate within the context of given sysems of meaning and to utilise their symbols, values and norms. We have seen that the Christian faith has been used to legitimate completely contrary interests and action patterns. This ideological manipulation of a religion must be distinguished from the genuine motives of its content. But it is not always easy to unravel the tangle – particularly without a theological critique.

4. The phenomena are made even more complex by the fact that the Christian faith does not provide its own world view but incarnates itself in a great number of perceptions and interpretations of reality. These can be dynamistic, ontological or historical. They can be static or dynamic. They can be dualistic and heaven-oriented, or eschatological and future-oriented. They can concentrate on personal authenticity or social involvement. They can presuppose a feudal-patriarchal, a liberal-competitive or a collectivised social order. This does not mean that all these patterns of thought are equally appropriate to the essential content of the Christian faith. Yet one has to ask whether the impact of 'the' Christian faith in a given situation is due to its central thrust or to one of its accidental incarnations.

5. Moreover, there is no one Christianity but only a variety of forms of appropriation, each with its particular system of co-ordinates. For Catholics the authority of the ecclesial hierarchy is crucial; Calvinists structure everything around the sovereignty and glory of God; Lutherans distinguish between an achieved and a granted relationship (law and grace); anglo-saxon Evangelicals are concerned mainly with personal salvation; Pentecostals want to experience the impact of the divine Spirit; Liberation Theology is mainly concerned with social reconstruction. Obviously the social impact of Christianity will vary according to these particular denominational emphases. To do justice to our theme we would have had to consider the whole range – from Canterbury cathedral to the beating of the drums under a marula tree.

6. Finally, Christianity is not the only system of beliefs in South Africa. It competes, and gets mixed up, with African traditional views of reality, secular (liberal or radical) humanism, the mechanistic-utilitarian approach of the technological and commercial civilisation, and various other religions.

This then is the context in which our theme should be treated if one wanted to do justice to it. As I have said, the present essay is nothing but a tentative survey of the entire field.

BIBLIOGRAPHY

Adam, H. and Giliomee, H. (1979), *The rise and crisis of Afrikaner power* (Cape Town: David Philip).

Boesak, A. (1977), *Farewell to innocence: A social-ethical study of black theology and black power* (Johannesburg: Ravan).

Bosch, D. J. (1984), 'The roots and fruits of Afrikaner civil religion' in Hofmeyr, J. N. and Vorster, W. S. (eds), *New faces of Africa: Essays in honour of Ben Marais* (Pretoria: Unisa).

Bosch, D. (1985), 'The fragmentation of Afrikanerdom and the Afrikaner churches' in Villa-Vicencio, C. and de Gruchy, J. W. (eds), *Resistance and hope* (Cape Town: David Philip).

Brandel-Syrier, M. (1962), *Black women in search of God* (London: Lutterworth).

Bundy, C. (1979), *The rise and fall of the South African peasantry* (London: Heinemann).

Checkland, P. (1981), *Systems thinking, systems practice* (Chichester: Wiley).

Cochrane, J. (1987), *Servants of power: The role of the English-speaking churches 1903–1930* (Johannesburg: Ravan).

Davenport, T. R. H. (1977), *South Africa: A modern history* (Johannesburg: Macmillan, SA).

De Gruchy, J. W. (1979), *The church struggle in South Africa* (Grand Rapids: Eerdmans).

De Kiewiet, C. W. (1941), *A history of South Africa, social and economic* (London: Oxford University Press).

De Klerk, W. A. (1975), *The Puritans in Africa: A story of Afrikanerdom* (Harmondsworth: Penguin).

Degenaar, J. (1978), *Afrikaner nationalism* (Cape Town: University of Cape Town).

Du Plessis, J. (1911), *A history of Christian missions in South Africa* (London: Longmans, Green).

Du Toit A. and Giliomee, H. (1983), *Afrikaner political thought: Analysis and documents. Vol. I. 1780–1850* (Cape Town: David Philip).

Durant, J. J. F. (1970), *Swartman, stad en toekoms* (Cape Town: Tafelberg).

Elphick, R. and Giliomee, H. (eds), (1979), *The shaping of South African society 1652–1820* (Cape Town: Longman).

Gerhart, G. M. (1978), *Black power in SA: The evolution of an ideology* (Berkeley: University of California Press).

Gogarten, F. (1953), *Verhängnis und Hoffnung der Neuzeit* (Stuttgart: Vorwerk).

Hammond-Tooke, W. D. (ed.) (1974), *The Bantu-speaking peoples of Southern Africa* (London: Routledge & Kegan Paul, second edn).

Harrison, D. (1981), *The White tribe of Africa* (London: BBC).

Hastings, A. (1981), 'The Christian churches and liberation movements in Southern Africa', *African Affairs*, Vol. 80/1981.

Hexham, I. (1980), 'Dutch Calvinism and the development of Afrikaner nationalism', *African Affairs*, Vol. 79/80, pp. 195–208.

Hinchliff, P. (1968), *The church in South Africa* (London: SPCK).

Hunter, M. (1961) and (1936), *Reaction to conquest* (London: Oxford University Press).

Karis, T. G. and Carter, G. M. (1972ff), *From protest to challenge: A documentary history of African politics in SA 1882–19643* (Stanford, Cal.: Hoover Institute Press).

Kinghorn, J. (ed.) (1986), *Die NG Kerk en Apartheid* (Johannesburg: Macmillan).

Leatt, J., Kneifel, T. and Nürnberger, K. (eds), (1986), *Contending ideologies in South Africa* (Cape Town: David Philip).

Lodge, T. (1983), *Black politics in SA since 1945* (Johannesburg: Ravan).

Majeke, N. (1952) *The role of missionaries in conquest* (Johannesburg: Society of Young Africa).

Mayer, P. (1971) and (1961), *Townsmen or tribesmen* (Cape Town: Oxford University Press).

Moodie, T. D. (1975), *The rise of Afrikanerdom: Power, apartheid and the Afrikaner civil religion* (London: University of California Press).

Morris, C. T. and Adelman, I. (1980), 'The religious factor in development', *World Development*, Vol. 8/1980, pp. 491–501.

Motlhabi, M. (1984), *The theory and practice of Black resistance to Apartheid: A social-ethical analysis* (Johannesburg: Skotaville).

Norman, E. (1981), *Christianity in the Southern Hemisphere: The churches in Latin American and South Africa* (Oxford: Clarendon).

Nürnberger, K. (1975), 'The Sotho notion of the Supreme Being under the impact of the Christian Proclamation', *Journal of Religion in Africa*, Vol. VII/1975, pp. 174–200.

Nürnberger, K. (1984), *Power, beliefs and equity: Economic potency structures in SA and their interaction with patterns of conviction in the light of a Christian ethic* (Research Report No. 04/PO17 to the Human Sciences Research Council, Pretoria).

O'Meara, D. (1983), *Volkskapitalisme: Class, capital and ideology in the development of Afrikaner nationalism, 1934–1948* (Johannesburg: Ravan).

Odendal, A. (1985), *Vukani Bantu! The beginnings of Black protest politics in SA to 1912* (Cape Town: David Philips).

Paauw, B. A. (1960), *Religion in a Tswana Chiefdom* (London: Oxford University Press).

Paauw, B. A. (1973), *The Second Generation* (Cape Town: Oxford University Press, second edn).

Paauw, B. A. (1975), *Christianity and the Xhosa tradition: Belief and ritual among Xhosa-speaking Christians* (Cape Town: Oxford University Press).

Rich, P. B. (1984), *White power and the liberal conscience: racial segregation and South African liberalism* (Johannesburg: Ravan).

Sales, J. (1971), *The planting of the churches in South Africa* (Grand Rapids: Eerdmans).

Sandison, A. (1967), *The wheel of empire: a study of the imperial idea in some 19th and 20th century fiction* (London: Macmillan).

Saunders, C. C. (1969), *The new African elite in the Eastern Cape and some late 19th Century origins of African nationalism* (London: Institute for Commonwealth Studies).

Stokes, E. (1960), *The political ideas of English imperialism* (London: Oxford University Press).

Stokes, R. G. (1975), 'Afrikaner Calvinism and economic action: The

Weberian thesis in South Africa', *American Journal of Sociology*, Vol. 81, 1975–76.
Sundkler, B. G. M. (1961) and (1948), *Bantu prophets in South Africa* (London: Oxford University Press).
Tawney, R. H. (1926), *Religion and the rise of capitalism* (Harmondsworth: Penguin).
Toffler, A. (1971), *Future shock* (London: Pan Books).
Treurnicht, A. P. (1975), *Credo van 'n Afrikaner* (Cape Town: Tafelberg).
Turner, H. W. (1980), 'African Independent Churches and economic development', *World Development*, Vol. 81/1980.
Walshe, P. (1971), *The rise of African nationalism in SA: the African National Congress, 1912–1952* (Berkeley: University of California Press).
Weber, M. (1976) (1905), *The Protestant ethic and the spirit of capitalism.* (transl. T. Parsons) (London: Allen & Unwin).
Wilson, M. (1971), *Religion and the transformation of society* (Cambridge: Cambridge University Press).
Wilson, M. and Thompson, L. (eds), 1979 (part I), 1981 (part II), *The Oxford history of South Africa* (Oxford: Clarendon).

9 Christians and Education in South Africa
Calvin Cook

Dias' expedition was contemporaneous with three other developments that together opened new chapters in human potential. The Renaissance brought fresh appreciation of the distant past and offered substantially different models of human behaviour and thus the continuing alternatives of a choice between clerical and classical views of human nature and destiny. The flowering of spirituality extended the exploration of inner space, while the invention of printing provided the means to distribute widely the knowledge of explorers' experiences on these journeys. Each of these developments signified the possibility of transcending the limits set like the pillars of Hercules by ignorance. Knowledge was power, so education seemed crucial to such self-transcendence. Calvin and Loyola, in particular, agreed that the key to future spiritual supremacy lay in the education and training of a new generation of masters and saw to it that their disciples founded schools and colleges committed to the complete formation of their pupils. Faust, who also materialises in their shadow, also knows that knowledge is power. The reformers built their plans for effective living on strict obedience and self-discipline; Faust chose the alternative of self-indulgence and rebellion. In both cases there are some surprising ironies and ambiguities: obedience had its bitter moments and disillusionment; the other way could be, as Milton sang, occasionally heroic.

Education in Europe has vacillated ever since between obedience to discipline and rebellion against established usages. This vacillation tells its own story, particularly the imprudence of claiming finality for any explanation or scheme as well as the imprudence of rejecting the past completely. Further, in human behaviour, as in physics, fission releases energies as well as fusion, a point of significance for a society that has recently lived with the two seemingly contradictory mottos of 'unity is strength' and 'separate development'.

When Dias sailed, the universal sovereignty of the papacy which had allocated the East to Portugal and the West to Spain was about to be successfully challenged in the name of particular sovereignties. One result of this challenge as far as South Africa was concerned was that the chief European influences – Holland and Britain – represented not a universal loyalty, but two particular ones. The papal monopoly was either unable or unwilling to meet the requirements of European diversity and faced not simply a reform that might have preserved its claims, but rebellions that rejected its authority. The Dutch monopoly first and then the British met the same fate in South Africa. Now the Afrikaner faces a similar choice between reform and revolution. Of the three, the first monopoly was both geographically the most limited and also the most complete. The British monopoly was always shot through with exceptions, while the Afrikaner, because it has had to face the greatest diversity, has so far resorted to the most compulsion.

In the 500 years between Dias and the present, the continent of Europe accepted literacy as compulsory for its peoples. The conviction of the necessity for compulsory education for all was slow in coming, progressed unequally, and was never completed. Nevertheless, one consequence was the gradual extension of the franchise because those with the powers literacy created either directly or indirectly could not be prevented from being given some participation in determining their lives and destinies. While there could be mass movements without literacy, literacy provided the skills needed to raise standards of living through a real increase in wealth. At some point along the line, the decision to make secondary education compulsory became a take-off point in social development. In South Africa the caravels have been nudging their way down the skeleton coast trying to find the turn that leads into the new ocean of the future. Literacy always eventually produces political power-sharing because education generates wealth. Little wonder therefore that educational policy remains such a divisive issue.

The Netherlands had managed a successful rebellion against Spain. In the process they discovered that toleration could be profitable, but when the Dutch East India Company founded its refreshment station at the Cape it did so on current economic theory that favoured a monopoly. The company was constantly challenged by those who found the limitations of monopoly irksome, degrading or inhibiting. One challenge came early with the settling of Huguenots in 1688. As a great concession they were allowed to use French in worship, but their children were to be instructed in Dutch. It was assumed that those who had been persecuted out of France would have no objection to becoming Dutch, particularly given the common religion. So tight was the monopoly in religion that not till a century after the Huguenots were the Lutherans allowed to build their own church. Since it was taken for granted that the instruction of children was under the auspices of the church, permission for a church led to recognising a Lutheran way of life through instruction in school. Was this relaxation another sign of weakness in the Dutch East India Company as it slowly slipped into bankruptcy? The 'receivers' had long since come to believe in the profitability of toleration.

By this time, the American colonies had successfully applied Locke's justification of 'the glorious revolution' to their own cause and won their independence; the French Revolution was about to give teeth to the rationalist theories of the Enlightenment and demand that all local peculiarities ('liberties') based on traditional particularities appear before the universal bar of reason. The Dutch East India Company's monopoly was thus destroyed by trekkers who drifted beyond its rule until they found tribes willing and able to defend themselves and their ways; by military defeat and change of sovereignty and perhaps most disturbingly of all, by a rationalism that was not only anti-dogmatic but bent on disturbing the social order of master/servant within the colony. Just when circumstances seemed to dictate the need to recognise the plurality of societies in the Cape, Calvinism gave the Dutch colonists a creed that equipped them to do battle as their ancestors had done against overwhelming odds in the Netherlands and in France. God's call to His people was unique and constituted a covenant of grace that depended on God's choice alone and not upon any merit or lack of it on the part of those He called; an atonement limited in its effects if not in its intention absolved the elect from any responsibility towards clearly reprobate groups other than preserving their identity. If God's blessings were limited, it would be both prodigal and pointless to try to share them. Had Jesus not warned his disciples not to cast pearls before swine?

These powerful motives encouraged resistance. To succumb to anglicisation was to renounce language, identity and perhaps also faith. It was to bow not just to political bondage, but to alien ways and habits. During the wars of liberation later in the century, the issues became even more clearly defined: what besides greed threatened Boer independence? And who could claim that the uitlanders were godly? What sort of 'liberation' was it that to overthrow a godly government used corrupt and violent means? After the peace, Milner's proposal to run schools by means of a centralised bureaucracy had fatal flaws. It disregarded the church's part in religious instruction, deprived parents not only of their rights but of their duty; and in relinquishing mother-tongue instruction for English was asking Afrikaners to accept an educational handicap as well as to renounce their birthright.

The dogged resistance of the Boers and the willingness of British liberals to compromise won some of the basic contentions of *Christelike Nasionale Onderwys* (CNO). Schools in the OFS and in the Transvaal were organised differently from Milner's imperial design. The church and parents retained a place in the organisation and running of the schools so that they reflected for better or worse the outlook of the local community. From Scots, the most accessible source of pure reformed religion and educated capability, the Afrikaner learned a good deal about the role of education in upward mobility. Knowledge was power, and could enable anyone who possessed it to transcend social, political and economic limitations. In a society in which politics was almost exclusively confined to whites, and within which a wide-ranging franchise already existed, the Afrikaners' greater numbers largely offset their lack of economic power. In a couple of generations, the Hoggenheimers gave way to '*ware Afrikaners*' or true Afrikaners through largely mercantilist business practice which harnessed nationalist fervour to economic activity. When the new CNO manifesto was published in 1948, it was no longer a strategy for resistance, but looked forward to a republic about 'to come into its own again' with a fervour reminiscent of the 1660 House of Commons.

While some of the features of the Afrikaner experience were incorporated into the plans for Bantu Education (such as parental 'control' and contributions, and mother-tongue instruction), the whole framework had changed. Instead of being devised by masters of guerrilla strategy, Bantu Education was a parade book manual imposed from above by an authority determined to control the process of education at every point where it might upset the balance of a society already heavily weighted in favour of whites. Black education would not be compulsory; it would be financed not as was white from general revenue, but from black sources. Those who were to pay the piper were not permitted to call the tune and Dr Verwoerd made it clear that the place for which the black would be educated was not for full participation within 'white' society, but for whatever labour might be needed. Not unnaturally many Christians both white and black, as well as others, felt such a programme hardly helped the development of human potential. In this they may have erred. The gift of literacy, once given, has a way of moving beyond censorship and control.

Nevertheless, Verwoerd's vision had further implications: since black 'labour units' in white areas did not require higher education (though these very areas were where the most rapid changes were happening and where new skills were most needed), the new universities would be established in tribal areas (the least developed). Once the new universities had been established, black access to the white urban universities was limited still further.

Though they may not have fully realised what they were doing, the oppressed were once more on the way to becoming the oppressors. In making race a basis for discriminating between the different inhabitants of the land, and in using the position of trusteeship to benefit primarily the trustees, the nationalist regime drew to itself the opprobrium not merely of marxists but of a much broader spectrum of world opinion, appalled at the spectacle of the inexorable and irremediable inequity racial discrimination induces, regardless of what exoneration is offered for it. Race had become a world focus: while the defeated Axis powers had been 'racist', how was it that the wealthier nations of the world were still generally white and the poorer generally not? Again the most notable exception was Japan, which despite defeat and lack of physical resources had one of the world's highest literacy rates. Was this because what had previously been spent by the military was now available for education?

Black education had for the most part been the work of missionaries (even if a good percentage of its cost had been paid through government subsidies) whose primary concern was evangelisation and saw the school as one of the best means at their disposal. In their task, the missionaries had to face both black and white prejudice: from the former because the school portended breaches of custom by transferring authority to the literate, and from the latter because education seemed to give the blacks airs if not other powers. What was regarded as 'cheek' was often a masked accession of real moral, spiritual or intellectual power, the beginnings of independence. While the first stage of missionary education was directed at training 'native agents', that is, church workers, Sir George Grey was to make 'industrial' training part of his scheme for pacifying the border. We may note the ambiguity: pacification was clearly in the interests of the colonial government, but what about the interests of those being educated? Pacification really presumed joint participation as well, and about the terms of this, the colonists, if not the colonial government, were less sure. Later, another factor arose: as technology developed, mission institutions were generally unable to provide much more equipment than simply literacy required. Part of the growing differential which developed between expenditure on white children and expenditure on others was because gradually the more expensive forms of technical training were made available to the one, but not to the others.

No one knew for sure how far 'the natives' would advance or what they might demand as a result of their new capabilities. Experience elsewhere was beginning to show that once the door of educational opportunity was opened, it was impossible to control further advances: the balance of power might shift in unpredictable ways but always in the direction of greater participation. The wider the educational net was thrown, the more likely it was to bring up democracy. What if the 'black Scotsmen' that Lovedale was accused of producing became a series of Carnegies? What is more, as Feuerbach had pointed out, the beginning of all social criticism was the criticism of religion. Hence the training even of native agents might have formidable consequences. Many of the factors which produced the Afrikaner Bond were also operating to form the ANC.

If most black hopes of advancement through education were frustrated, and people like Colenso who believed in them were rejected, at least some pressed forward. The establishment of the South African Native College (later Fort Hare University) was an example of persevering co-operation, and building on foundations already laid. Within two generations of its founding, the College had provided a number of leaders prominent in decolonisation throughout Africa. The often insufficiently examined assumption behind most Protestant missionary effort was that education would bring out the full potential of the individual and thus increase the real wealth of the community. Evangelisation detached individuals from their cultural background, and missionary opinion differed as to whether such individuals should find their new places in the life of a new community or return to their own people. The healed demoniac might hope for a future with his new-found companions; yet his final healing required his being sent back to his own city which in its respectable madness had rejected the saviour for a few thousand pigs. Missionary opinion began by thinking of an agent returning to his own people. Gradually it came to lay emphasis upon the contribution to a common society. In a way therefore missionary opinion and the dominant settler opinion moved in opposite directions.

Making the contribution to a common society raised the question of justice between the members of such a society. On what basis could differentiation be made either on the grounds of race or of sex, for the latter was in many ways the shadow of the former? Both black education and female education raised for a common society similar issues, incentives, differentials, and discrimination. Most important of all, the accession to personal and economic power of those who had been discriminated against brought with it the question of access to political power. If participation was right for economic reasons (and white entrepreneurs dreamed about the possibilities of a more developed black market) how could it be denied for political?

The slogan 'liberation before education' put the issue sharply; it was not merely a demand for political self-determination but a claim to total determination. The kind of education that would eventuate after political liberation would depend largely on the real wealth represented by the attainments of the country's people. A people's education that had not taught skills as well as awareness of disadvantages would be unable to fulfil what it had promised. If the missionaries had taught skills without being able to ensure participation and exercise of what had been learned, the comrades' programme seemed likely to offer participation frustrated by lack of skills.

First came the grand design of Bantu education the Nationalists devised and were determined to implement. The practical effect of the Bantu Education Act was to sever official links between churches and schools in everything but hostels. As Verwoerdian apartheid began to take shape with its resettlements into 'homelands' and attempts to limit black participation in white areas to labour requirements, criticism of the whole scheme became international. A government that professed itself Christian and claimed that its actions were based on scripture found itself under almost universal condemnation not only from fellow Christians throughout the world, but from most of world opinion whether Christian or not. The fact that this criticism was nearly unanimous proved nothing except that it was a league of the godless: the convenanting tradition had never been upset by being in a minority. At this point (1968) the Christian Institute and the South African Council of Churches which had set up a working group of theologians issued 'A Message to the people of South Africa'. The call was addressed to Christians and in terms of Christian scriptures and Christian tradition denounced apartheid as a sin. The two dominant Christian traditions in the country were thus at loggerheads about Christian responsibilities towards the society in which they lived. As long as Christians could not agree about those responsibilities, how could there be agreement about the appropriate kinds of education to be offered? Nearly all of the misgivings that had been voiced at the time the Bantu Education Act was passed had been confirmed in the experience of the next 13 years.

Predictably the Nationalist government was incensed and regarded the 'Message' as the latest of a long series of local clerics playing to an international gallery. This view ignored a crucial issue: the Message was directed by Christian citizens to their fellow Christians within South Africa. The authors (who had the franchise) were carrying out their rights as voters, expressing convictions that had been formed through experience and fellowship with other Christians, some franchised, others disfranchised. More, they were also addressing their fellow members in the churches, summoning them to a common repentance. Since repentance depends on the existence of an alternative way, they were frequently asked 'what alternative is there to apartheid?' Thus challenged, the churches undertook 'The Study project of Christianity in an Apartheid Society' (SPROCAS),[1] aimed at working out alternatives to apartheid in such fields as church life, economics, the law, education and politics. All concerned in this project found it a major exercise in their own education, since the various commissions were charged not just with making statements of principle, but with producing practical recommendations.

The report of the education commission set out a programme that continued the liberal and missionary traditions. It assumed a common society since even apartheid maintained a complex network of interconnections and apparently found it impossible to make the final breaks its theory required. The task therefore was to consider the educational structures the country would need as the spring-tide of apartheid ebbed. Such structures would depend upon a more equitable apportionment of resources. The commission also proposed various timetables for implementation of stages, stressed the role of private initiatives that could begin at once as well as those that might have to wait for the attitude of government to change. The one possibly utopian point was that on which the rest of the report was based: the assumption that the leopard of government might change its spots. Along with this, the report made two basic points: first, that enforced integration would be as detrimental both to education and to society as forced segregation had been: whoever coerced would err. Second, the authoritarian attitudes that had characterised so many South African educational structures and procedures were also inimical to education, because inappropriate for a pluralistic society. South Africans needed to face this pluralism frankly. Whatever the customs within a cultural group might be (and many of the South African sub-cultures were frankly paternalistic or authoritarian) the existing social structure in which one group dominated the others was no longer tolerable. *Kragdadigheid* (or vigorous political domination) generated not peace but strife. The whole country needed both a new style of politics based on power-sharing, and intergroup relationships based on dialogue and negotiation: in short, education should work for an ethos that characterised a democratic society instead of a house divided against itself.

The report then listed unacceptable principles and unacceptable practices. Among the latter 'in order of urgency' were the allocation of resources, access to educational opportunities, and the aims and content of education. Behind the first of these lay the unwillingness to accept the principle of compulsory education for all, which had been a take-off point for Western nations. The failure of a still all-white government to accept this principle for its black subjects was responsible for its continuing failure to make adequate provision for education. The commission was realistic enough to recognise that such a policy might not be able to be implemented overnight, but looked for some kind of acceptance of the principle. The report listed 11 further defects arising from the failure to allocate adequate resources, such as the appalling drop-out rates, vastly disproportionate expenditures per pupil and discrepancies in the qualifications and service conditions of teachers.

These discrepancies compounded troubles: blacks found access to educational opportunities much more difficult than their counterparts. Sometimes the obstacle was physical, like the distance from school and lack of transport; at others, the trouble lay in the cumulative effects of malnutrition, inferiorities of training, books, facilities, opportunities and other resources.

Finally, as to the aims and content, the first criticism was directed at the language burden imposed on the black teacher and child: to teach and learn in a second and third language merely multiplied difficulties and led to uncertainty in the child's mind about the ultimate value of the whole exercise. What was the use of learning if the learner had no confidence in putting what he had learned into practice?

The report listed 49 recommendations for an alternative to the way of apartheid. Most of these recommendations were practical and gradual, given the acceptance of the basic change of direction. At the same time, these recommendations exposed the central requirement: the need for a change of political will. Those who had won their dominant position largely through numbers and education were being asked to contemplate and provide an education for those whose numbers and powers generated by education would lead at least to participation and perhaps even to senior partnership in a new society. Thus the debate in South Africa over education has generally been first and foremost a debate about the sharing of and participation in power. Fifteen years after the SPROCAS report, the government made its first chameleon-like movements towards allowing political participation. By the time it did this, it had a new problem on its hands: finding credible leaders in the black community to participate in the strictly limited forms of power sharing it was prepared to offer. Those who for political reasons had been willing to burn their schools were ready to burn collaborators and their homes as well.

Since SPROCAS, education has been continuousy in the news because the debate about education is a debate about the nature of South African society and in particular a debate about the direction and pace of change. Black power has until the present been largely harnessed to white economic goals but pressures have been building because other kinds of power have been created, demographic, cultural and political, all directed towards conscious participation in a much wider range of activities. The advance has been evident particularly in the trade union movements, in tertiary education, and in the political apprenticeship the homelands have afforded in all levels of government. All this has been part of the wider education of South Africa in the arts of negotiation and less destructive management of conflict.

At the same time, the continuing unrest within the country and the wars on its borders are still reminders of how much remains to be done while propagandists on both sides are squandering the resources of grace and truth that have been given to the community as it has worshipped the Word made flesh dwelling among us. The crucial question remains whether those who call themselves Christians are going to be willing first to allow their Lord and Master, the source of the authority that directs their powers, to cleanse those powers and then to use them cleanly, or whether they are going to resist what he needs to do and alone can do for all. Otherwise whatever name or authorisation they claim, these powers will be exercised in the self-seeking and corrupting ways of all who refuse his basin and towel.

*   *   *

For half a century before Dias' great voyage, the Portuguese explorers had been inching their way along the African coastline and had planted their padraos as they went. They did not perceive any ambiguity or conflict of interest between the crown of Portugal, the search for gold or the search for slaves and the cross of Christ. The venture into the interior from the Cape also had its ironies and ambiguities unperceived at the time but increasingly and painfully obvious to succeeding generations.

The voyages of exploration to find a truly Christian kingdom have had their own measures of ambiguity and irony as have the various attempts to find a way of educating and training people to live in such a kingdom whilst at the same time living in the chieftainships, colonies, empires, unions, dominions and republics that have been the political forms of South African society. These political schemes have been like medieval maps, combinations of fact and fancy with insufficient exploration to establish which was which. Even when the headlands and rivers have been accurately charted, what of the interior?

At the time the SPROCAS reports began to appear, they seemed to be fanciful in the context of Nationalist policy and the proposal, common to most of the reports, for a move towards greater equality and liberty, seemed not to be a political possibility.

Yet since SPROCAS, and the turmoil in education that erupted in Soweto and elsewhere in 1976, there has been a growing consensus that no other way will prove acceptable in either the short or long term. The de Lange commission[2] (1981) signalled some changes in the direction of greater flexibility and variety and the Human Sciences Research Council report[3] on intergroup relations (1985) carried further a similar insistence on the need for a just and therefore flexible treatment of each of the country's many groups. However much more than politics justice may be, it always has an irreducible political component which if treated one-sidedly inevitably produces injustice.

Tired of headwinds and the unendingly hostile Namibian coast, Diaz turned southwest into the Atlantic. By the time he headed east again, he had passed the Cape and landed instead at Mossel Bay. The same headlands have been called both the Cape of Storms and the Cape of Good Hope. The name does not change either the weather or the rocks themselves; yet it reflects different perceptions of what is possible. The training of right perceptions is one goal of education, another is when one has learned to perceive correctly, how truly to act. After all, it was 'the continuing in my word' that would lead to true freedom. Not to learn that lesson is to forget that what distinguishes the true Child of Abraham from the false is a divine deliverance from bondage and a persistance in the strange new way of life to which it leads, a life in which every past experience, even the memory of an enjoyable life based on garlic and melon evaporates in an apparently waterless plain. To reject such a quest as unfitting is not merely to refuse a destiny and identity but to manifest another from which we might have been delivered: a descent from the father of lies who was a murderer from the beginning. Imagine this, when in fact we have been called to learn together how to live together with the glorious liberty of the children of God.

NOTES

1. SPROCAS 1 related to publications arising out of the various commissions established for the project. Four occasional papers contained short papers from a wide variety of contributors: (1) Anatomy of Apartheid; (2) South African Priorities; (3) Directions of change in South African politics; (4) Some implications of inequality.

    Next came six volumes of commission's reports and a summary volume: (1) Education beyond apartheid; (2) Towards social change; (3) Power, Privilege and Poverty; (4) Apartheid and the Church; (5) Towards Political Justice; (6) Law and Justice; (7) Co-ordinated Sprocas report.

    SPROCAS 2 produced two publications: (1) R. Turner, *The eye of the needle*; (2) F. Wilson, *Migrant Labour in South Africa*.

    Sprocas 2 was primarily concerned with implementing the suggestions made in the commissions' report as and when the opportunities arose. It was intended to deal both tactically and strategically with opportunities for social change. As this army of 'irregular' volunteers began to move into action, it came up against both the serried ranks of apartheid law and order and their would-be surrogates. Dr Rick Turner was murdered; Peter Randall, who had directed the whole project, was banned. Nevertheless, ironically when the government at last turned its attention to constitutional reform, it found itself having to proceed in many instances along directions already mapped by its critics, who had encountered the realities of negotiation as they debated with one another in the work of the various commissions.

    On the completion of each report, the members of the commission involved were invited to sign the report, and their names were recorded as signatories. Thus each report had no authority except the intrinsic merit of its work. Given the range and qualifications of the signatories, this weight was considerable.

    Ravan Press, Johannesburg, published the volumes between 1971 and 1973.

2. *Provision of Education in the RSA* (Pretoria: HSRC, 1981).

3. *The South African Society: Realities and Future Prospects* (Pretoria: HSRC, 1985).

10 Christianity, Evangelisation and the Social Factor in South Africa
Denis Hurley OMI

When James Watt developed his steam engine in 1765 he created an enormous problem for the Church. He set in motion a process that was to cry out for a radical change in the Church's methods of evangelisation, which the Church by and large has found difficult to put into effect. I use the term 'evangelisation' here in the sense recently given to it in the Roman Catholic Church. Prior to the Second Vatican Council of 1962–65 and, even more precisely, prior to a 1974 assembly of the Synod of Bishops of the Catholic Church and the document that flowed from it, Pope Paul VI's *Evangelisation in the Modern World*, the term 'evangelisation' meant preaching the Gospel where it was not known, planting the Church in a place where it did not exist. Now 'evangelisation' in the Roman Catholic Church embraces every activity of the Church: proclamation of the word, catechetical instruction, Christian adult education, prayer, worship, promotion of Christian family life, community building, works of mercy and concern for development, justice and peace. Everything that promotes the reign of God in and through Jesus Christ is evangelisation.

The problem that James Watt created by perfecting the steam engine was the immense and intense growth of socialisation caused by the industrial revolution. Industry became socialised. The establishment of factories resulted in vast numbers of people coming together in single enterprises. Urbanisation expanded rapidly. Peasants became city slum dwellers. New social classes emerged – owners and workers, divided in interest and mutually hostile – exploiters and exploited. New social ideologies were formulated: capitalism and socialism. Capitalism joined hands with colonialism and gave added impetus to the enrichment of the colonisers and the oppression of the colonised.

The new human conglomerations, when not blocked by colonialism, became a fertile field for the democracy that eighteenth-century philosophers had called for and American colonists and French citizens had fought for and that would soon be favoured by the growth of popular education and of science and technology. Socialisation was on the march and the Church was getting left behind. It was becoming extremely difficult for the Church to cope with the eruption of social development and its institutions. The organisation and methods that had been more or less successful in little towns and villages and rural areas were often swamped and stifled in the great industrial complexes. Among the few who managed to cope to some extent were John Wesley and his Methodists and the Quakers.

Sheer numbers were part of the problem, new sociological developments another, but also the fact that before socialisation became so intensive the Church was hardly aware that social factors played such a large part in the way people received and lived the Christian faith. One does not recall very much concern in former times with social factors either in theoretical theology or pastoral practice. It has been given to our epoch to face this issue squarely.

The Church in South Africa comes late into the field. For half a century or so, it is true, we have had our declarations and denunciations, our prophets and confessors: clergy, religious and laity; imprisoned, detained and deported. But we have had little success in translating proclamation of principles and spasmodic acts of Christian witness into a sustained process of evangelisation profoundly affecting the social body of the Church either in its black or white membership. A social gospel applicable to South Africa has shown little tendency to blossom from pulpit or bible class, religious instruction or study group. From time to time, from place to place, religious attention has been given to South Africa's agonising problem, but never in a measure calculated to involve significant numbers of people. There has been no organised Church effort, only a take-it-or-leave-it approach. We have not really faced up to the issue that deep-rooted social factors need a lot more than that to be evangelised. The South African Council of Churches annually reels off resolutions by the score, scarcely giving a thought to whether the member churches for which they are intended will do anything about them. The leadership structures of the major anti-apartheid churches have become disenchanted with resounding declarations of intent. They are asking themselves how a Christian vision of justice can be communicated to their membership. It is time this happened – late though it be.

Three churches that are involving themselves in more vigorous efforts of communication are the Province of Southern Africa of the Anglican Church, the Methodist Church of Southern Africa and the Roman Catholic Church. Their programmes are entitled respectively Partners in Mission,[1] Ubulungisa,[2] and Pastoral Planning.[3]

Partners in Mission concentrates, as its name implies, on the doctrine and practice of mission, of 'being sent'. This programme or process has grown out of an Anglican congress held in Toronto in 1963 which aimed to promote mutual responsibility and interdependence between the provinces, 28 in all, that make up the world-wide Anglican communion. Mission is described in these terms: 'to proclaim the Good News of the Kingdom; to teach, baptise and nurture new believers; to respond to human needs by loving service; and to seek to transform structures of society'. The mission of the Church is the mission of Jesus who came both preaching and serving.

Partners in Mission is a highly organised and deeply spiritual and apostolic effort to intensify mission and its dimension of partnership. It is a prolonged process of consultation and discernment aimed at identifying and formulating priorities for mission. It involves the bishops, the other clergy and a significant number of laity. It is undertaken every few years. The latest effort in the Province of Southern Africa was announced in October 1984, discussed in parish councils in mid-1985 and then went through a variety of steps to its culmination in a consultation at provincial (that is, countrywide) level in November 1987 and a report back to the parishes at the end of the year.

The steps between mid-1985 and December 1987 involved the launching of the programme at a provincial synod in July 1985, followed by training events in dioceses and parishes, planning meetings of parish councils that were required to formulate practical steps, a Lenten programme in 1986, the holding of Partners in Mission parish assemblies to prepare suggestions for diocesan and provincial consultations, and regional review sessions. Diocesan consultations and conferences were held in the first half of 1987 and these culminated, as indicated earlier, in a provincial consultation in November 1987 in which delegates from other provinces of the Anglican community participated. Finally a report back is going to parishes which are expected to act on priorities agreed upon for the Province as a whole.

Inevitably in South Africa the identification and formulation of priorities in mission has led to a great deal of concern with the problems of apartheid and the steps that should be taken by Christians to deal with them. Anyone involved in the process would have been subjected to a deep and practical spiritual and social education. This is the most effective way in which the Church of the Province of Southern Africa is at present evangelising its members in social justice.

The Methodist Church of Southern Africa at its 1987 annual conference published a programme under the Xhosa title *Ubulungisa* (Justice) with the goal of enabling Methodists to participate in the process of political transformation in Southern Africa. The programme will involve the creation in local congregations of groups committed to struggling for justice, peace and reconciliation. The methods used will include promotion of awareness, reflection on and analysis of situations, response to conflict, action on Conference resolutions, partnership with community, civil, trade and political organisations, co-operation with like-minded denominational and ecumenical groups, participation in non-violent resistance and challenging local congregations on these issues. Resources will be provided and district co-ordinators will be appointed.

Ubulungisa will work in close association with other programmes like Zikhulise, which promotes development, and Initiatives for Reconciliation and Justice in the Methodist Church of Southern Africa, and inevitably it will have an even more significant educational role should a matter at present under debate culminate in the Methodist Church declaring itself a peace church.

The approach of the Roman Catholic Church resembles that of the Anglicans in that it forms part, a very important part, of a broad comprehensive programme of practical Christian education. This programme is still being developed and is called Pastoral Planning. It is a project of the Southern African Catholic Bishops' Conference and has grown out of the conviction that the great social problem of South Africa must be dealt with in a vigorous and systematic fashion and that the effort must flow from an intensified spiritual life of the Church, from a life that draws its vision and strength from the life and mission of Jesus present in the Church and from his Holy Spirit as its soul.

It began with a Pastoral Planning Working paper published in June 1984, to which dioceses, parishes and all interested persons and groups were invited to respond. A committee sifted and analysed the replies and recommended that a second working paper be compiled under the title 'Community serving Humanity' and that an endeavour be made to secure support for a pastoral plan based on that theme, in which the community is the Church. The Bishops' Conference accepted the theme and instructed a steering committee to bring out two publications: a Theme Paper with a simple and clear presentation and a

Workbook for use in parish and diocesan consultations. It is hoped that the consultations will reveal sufficient support for the Pastoral Plan to enable the Bishops' Conference to launch it shortly. The key concepts of the envisaged plan are community and evangelisation.

Evangelisation in terms of the description given earlier is the specific task of the Church. It is the fulfilment of the mission given by Jesus and is a sharing in his own mission. 'As the Father has sent me, so I send you' (Jn. 20: 21). There are, so to speak, four dimensions of totality in evangelisation. It must involve the whole message of Jesus. It must involve the whole Church, laity as well as clergy and religious. It must reach out to the whole of the human family. It must be concerned with the whole of humanity: the person, the family, society and, in regard to society with culture, politics and economics. Not that the Church has a mandate to promote directly culture, politics and economics, but inasmuch as it is mandated to transform them according to the values of the Kingdom.

Evangelisation seen in these terms is such an immense task that it requires the deployment of the full potential of the Church and this can be achieved only if the Church gives full play to its sense of community, derived from the teaching, example, practice, presence and power of Christ and his Spirit of love. Only in experienced community can the law of love be realised and lived and be given due witness.

The theme 'Community serving Humanity' is intended to express the two fundamental commitments: to community and evangelisation – evangelisation being the service in all its dimensions that the Church renders humanity.

As regards methods of translating the theme into practical reality, the Pastoral Plan looks to the example of Latin America which has achieved so much through its base communities, designated in their African dress 'small Christian communities'. These are groups of people varying in size and composition that meet regularly for bible sharing, prayer, reflection and concern with local issues. The bringing together of faith and life experience has been of immense importance in the Church of Latin America and the development of liberation theology and has also played an important role in the recent political experience of the Philippines.

In the United States a highly organised programme known as 'Renew'[4] applies the benefit of the small Christian community approach to the American scene and has been taken up in several other countries as well. The Catholic Church in South Africa is studying its possibilities for this country.

These exciting developments in three major churches in Southern Africa should be a source of hope. Please God there will be time for the churches to implement them and to find common ground in so doing. The Anglican and Catholic programmes bear a particular resemblance to each other arising out of their overriding concern with a comprehensive vision termed 'mission' by the Anglicans and 'evangelisation' by the Catholics and the importance given to education for social responsibility in the practical implementation of the vision.

Whatever programme these churches or others adopt will be difficult to implement. We dare not entertain illusions in that regard. Social factors are not easy things to deal with. It may be our God-given privilege in the twentieth century to be made aware of what social factors mean in evangelisation but it is a costly privilege. It demands a lot of hard work, a Copernican revolution in the process of evangelisation.

The reason is that social factors are rooted in social attitudes and social attitudes are the steel structure of human society. They give society shape, cohesion, endurance. They are the bones and sinews of a society's culture. They reproduce themselves in the children born into and brought up in it, socialised and inculturated into it. They provide the community context within which people see, perceive, understand, relate and reject, work and relax, love and hate. The community instinct is probably the strongest one in human nature. People can be induced to do practically anything for their community, especially their ethnic community.

An ethnic community and particularly one with a religious dimension is a very tough proposition indeed, as witness the dominant group in Northern Ireland and Iran and to a certain extent the Afrikaner nation. Here you have a complex of social attitudes held together by two of humanity's deepest and most powerful bonds. It is not easy for the individual to step out of that tangle of steel wires and look at his or her society through other eyes.

My dear friend Archbishop Desmond Tutu says he cannot understand why white Christians are so slow to throw out apartheid. The explanation, I would say, lies in social attitudes and our failure as churches to evangelise them. Because of that failure religion is often part of the problem and not of the solution.

It has been impressed upon us by the Kairos Document (1: 11) that the time is past when whites, whether Christian or not, can dictate the process of social change in South Africa. That we have to accept. But we also have to accept that black South Africans cannot dictate it either. They have taken the initiative and will continue to pursue that initiative. But to press it through to a successful conclusion looks like being a long, frustrating and bloody procedure. Scenarios are the order of the day in South Africa and about South Africa. The most hair-raising that I have read is that of Conor Cruise O'Brien (2: 67): a long drawn out civil war of terrorism and counter terrorism heading for total collapse and chaos, unless halted by a possible intervention of the two superpowers. Can the Christian churches stand back helplessly and allow that to happen? They may not be able to prevent it, but at least they should try.

Trying means concentrating a great deal of their potential for evangelisation on the social factors that seem to make the long drawn out struggle in South Africa inevitable. This is a huge undertaking and involves the development of appropriate methods like the ones mentioned in the reference to Partners in Mission, Ubulungisa and Pastoral Planning. Experience will most probably prove that these methods have to be constantly reviewed and amended or replaced. Monitoring and evaluating must be built into the process. In this context three considerations are of great importance.

First, the over-all plan must be geared to the whole Church that embarks on it. This does not mean that it will be acceptable to all its members. At least the plan should be drawn up for all and effectively communicated to all, not just to the tiny number of the converted; not just the in-group.

Second, since social factors differ so much between the black and the white societies (the former suffering oppression and the latter, whether consciously or not, enjoying privileges that are often oppressive in their very nature) methods of evangelisation addressed to the social factors involved may end up by differing quite considerably, if not in principle at least in practice. In principle for instance in both societies much emphasis may be placed on the group, the small Christian community, of Scripture sharing, prayer, reflection on life and appropriate action, but in practice the reflection and the action will tend to differ in the two societies.

Third, the promotion of such forms of evangelisation will demand an organised effort. It is not something that can be launched in a Church and left to the good will of the clergy, lay workers and members. The organised effort it demands includes education, both theoretical and practical; the preparation, promotion and maintenance of programmes and the selection and training of leaders, with special emphasis on the clergy. The effort must become a major, if not the most important, evangelising concern of the Church.

All this supposes an outlook, a theology. Along with the practical promotion a relevant theology must be developed and communicated. A relevant theology is a theology serving its true purpose: evangelisation. Theology, like any other discipline that achieves a certain success, incurs the danger of forgetting what it is for. It goes off on its own. Theology all too often has become an academic exercise, little concerned about evangelisation and spiritual growth. The kind of theology we are advocating here must be real, designed to fuel and focus evangelisation. With this in mind the Latin Americans developed liberation theoogy and the United States produced black theology which is also coming into its own in South Africa. Both endeavour to apply God's word to a situation of oppression and to inspire liberating activity.

The situation of oppression has to be examined and this is a form of social analysis. The word of God provides the criteria of a Christian assessment of the social factors and suggests the action that Christians should take to correct whatever needs to be corrected. Nor must we forget that the Christians in question may be members both of the oppressed and dominant societies. While this needs to be done at the professional level by persons with the requisite expertise, it must also be done at the level of day-to-day Christian experience and involvement; which is what has happened in the small Christian communities of Latin America and the Philippines and perhaps with less dramatic effect in parts of Africa and other areas of the world. People refer to this as 'doing theology', for in this context the development of religious conviction is intensely associated with the cultivation of social awareness and involvement in action. In any country with a burning social problem like our South African one it would appear inexcusable to omit from the curriculum of theological faculties and seminaries a significant exposure to such forms of social theology.

Nor need urgent social theology be confined to such countries. What of Western Europe with its growing and grievous problem of secularisation? Has this yet become the object of serious concerted study and of the development of methods calculated to revitalise the self-evangelisation of the Church and its overflow into dechristianised society? Western Europe might take a leaf out of Latin America's book and go all out for a theology of revitalisation.

Reverting to our main concern, a social theology accompanying and motivating a Christian social praxis in South Africa, no doubt different churches will be inclined to go about the theology and the praxis in different ways consistent with their various traditions. This would be understandable, yet what a magnificent opportunity South Africa in crisis offers for an ecumenical approach. What a wonderful opportunity too for the South African Council of Churches to refrain for a while from resounding resolutions that no church implements and get down to the hard work of facing up to the social factors in all their unyielding durability and attempting to formulate a broad programme of theology and evangelisation that different churches in close collaboration with one another could take up and adopt and apply to their common needs and various practices.

In any formulation of a social theology and praxis for South Africa, the issue of violence must figure high on the agenda. The issue of counter violence to neutralise the violence of the state has come up for a great deal of discussion. It would be difficult not to assume that great numbers of politicised blacks, especially young people, are convinced that there is no other answer. The Kairos Document came very close to saying that churches must align themselves with the liberation forces that resort to this solution.

An earnest appeal not to yield to this temptation was published recently (Wink: 3). It argues that non-violence holds out a greater hope than violence and that non-violence is already being put into effect in a very large measure though without understanding, training or organisation. In the end this could be the direction taken by the kind of ecumenical effort envisaged here. It would not be without opposition, without risk and pain, but, as the author of the appeal explains, the risk and the pain would be far less than if the country were allowed to drift into the chaos and collapse depicted in other scenarios.

NOTES

1.　Literature on Partners in Mission is obtainable from the Church of the Province of Southern Africa (Anglican) Khotso House, 42 de Villiers Street, Johannesburg, 2000. P.O. Box 4849, Johannesburg.

2.　Literature obtainable from Christian Citizenship Department, Methodist Church of Southern Africa, P.O. Box 27615, Bertsham 2013.

3.　Literature on Pastoral Planning is obtainable from the General Secretariate, SACBC, Khanya House, 140 Visagie Street, Pretoria 0002, P.O. Box 941, Pretoria 0001.

4.　Literature on Renew is obtainable from the Catholic Archdiocese of Durban, 154 Gordon Road, Durban 4001, P.O. Box 47489 Greyville, 4023.

REFERENCES

1. *The Kairos Document*, 2nd edn (Johannesburg: Skotaville Publishers, 1986).
2. O'Brien, Conor Cruise, 'What can become of South Africa?' *The Atlantic Monthly*, March 1986.
3. Wink, Walter, *Jesus' Third Way* (Philadelphia: New Society Publishers, 1987).

Part IV
Contemporary Challenges

11   When Violence Begets Violence: Is the Armed Struggle Justified?

Charles Villa-Vicencio

'Violence' is a key word in South African state propaganda. And in an insidious way 'violence' has come to exercise a similar function in news media not only in South Africa but throughout the Western world. News reports, for example, tell us: 'Police were compelled to use force to restrain violent youths who were throwing stones . . .' 'Police were forced to use teargas and birdshot to restrain student violence at the University of Cape Town'. 'The police used rubber bullets to restrain further outbreaks of township violence . . .'.

For this reason the *Kairos Document*, written by a group of Christians responding to the intensification of civil war in South Africa, rejects the 'blanket condemnation of all that is *called* violence'.

> The problem . . . is the way the word violence is being used in the propaganda of the State. The State and the media have chosen to call violence what some people do in the townships as they struggle for their liberation, that is, throwing stones, burning cars and buildings and sometimes killing collaborators. But this *excludes* the structural, institutional and unrepentant violence of the State and especially the oppressive and naked violence of the police and army. These things are not counted as violence. And even when they are acknowledged to be 'excessive', they are called 'misconduct' or even 'atrocities' but never violence. Thus the phrase 'violence in the townships' comes to mean what the young people are doing and not what the police are doing or what apartheid is doing to people.[1]

Violent clashes between protesting students or township dwellers and the police are frequently portrayed as having been initiated by the former. Revolutionary violence is blamed for repressive violence, and ironically the oppressed are held responsible for the brutality they suffer at the hands of the police and army.

Not all violence by oppressed people is revolutionary violence.

Sporadic, unco-ordinated and criminal violence is just below the surface among oppressed people in perhaps a more obvious way than among dominant classes. *Revolutionary* violence is, however, invariably a response to state and institutional violence.

THE CRIMINALISATION OF POLITICAL PROTEST

The politics of resistance in South Africa and the generation of propaganda concerning revolutionary violence cannot be understood apart from a consideration of the process of the criminalisation of normal political activity by successive acts of parliament.

In 1957, 156 people were arrested on charges of treason, with all of them being acquitted after a trial lasting four years. What the state could not do in court it then accomplished through parliament. The Unlawful Organisations Act became law in 1960, banning the African National Congress (established in 1912) and the breakaway Pan African Congress. The '90 days detention act' under the guise of the General Law Amendment Act followed in 1963, the '180 days detention act' was added to the Criminal Procedure Act in 1969, and the Terrorism Act of 1967 allowed for the indefinite detention without trial of political suspects. Since then the Internal Security Amendment Act of 1976 allowed for 'preventive detention'. An avalanche of legislation has excluded the possibility of all forms of viable protest and criminalised virtually all forms of normative democratic protest.

A consequence is an extraordinary high number of 'criminal' and 'political' prisoners and/or detainees – and it is often difficult to distinguish between them. Since the declaration of the present State of Emergency over 30 000 political detainees have seen the inside of South African prisons, with between 30 per cent and 40 per cent of these being children between the ages of 10 and 18. Others have been found guilty of public violence and related 'criminal' charges directly related to the prevailing political situation, while 36 people are on death row awaiting execution.

Legal repression of resistance to oppression is the ultimate form of state tyranny. It is not only the most sophisticated form of institutional violence but also a direct cause of revolutionary violence. Indeed, where normal democratic options of protest are prevented people do not remain passive. They resort to other forms of protest and resistance.

REVOLUTION AS A RESPONSE TO STATE TYRANNY

History seems to suggest that the will to political liberation is almost as inherent to what it means to be human as the will to life itself. Sustained oppression and imposed servitude have inevitably given rise to protest, resistance and revolution. The story of South African history is no exception.

When normal democratic channels are denied to people in quest of freedom, the armed struggle is regarded as the next costly but logical, necessary and justified step. It is a position which can be questioned by only the most dedicated of pacifists, and history is cluttered with those who have resorted to arms for less noble causes. Either way, violence has become an inevitable part of the political process. The story of Afrikaner history portrayed through the murals of the Voortrekker Monument in Pretoria, where the Boer soldier with his Martini Henry, horse and Bible are revered, and the memory of two wars of independence against the British, supports this claim. The presence of blood-stained battle colours, the Union Jack and the Cross in 'English' churches throughout the eastern Cape commemorating soldiers who fought and died for God, Queen and country, substantiates it.

The resort of blacks to revolution in this country has, however, been slow and reluctant. In 1952 Chief Albert Luthuli assessed the results of the moderate approach of the ANC at the time:

Who will deny that thirty years of my life have been spent knocking in vain, patiently, moderately and modestly at a closed and barred door? What has been the fruits of my years of moderation? Has there been any reciprocal tolerance or moderation from the Government, be it Nationalist or United Party? No! On the contrary, the past thirty years have seen the greatest number of laws restricting our rights . . . In short, we have witnessed in these years an intensification of our subjection to ensure and protect white supremacy.[2]

Ten years later Nelson Mandela, at his trial in 1962, identified a new phase within the struggle for liberation.

They [the white government] set the scene for violence by relying exclusively on violence to meet our people and their demands . . . We have warned repeatedly that the government by resorting continuously to violence, will breed, in this country, counter-violence amongst the people, till ultimately, the dispute between the government and my people will finish up being settled in violence and by force.[3]

Two years later his words were even more decisive:

The time comes in the life of any nation when there remain only two choices – submit or fight. That time has now come to South Africa. We shall not submit and we have no choice but to hit back by all means in our power in defence of our people, our future and our freedom. . . .[4]

The state had created the conditions of revolution. The oppressed people responded. This is how oppressed people perceive the struggle and it is important that *this* perception be emphasised in a situation where the dominant view of the present conflict is shaped by state propaganda. The dominant or ruling ideas of any society are inevitably the ideas of the dominant or ruling class, and these are the ideas that make the headlines. There is, however, always another side of the story. To tell that side of the story can in a small way contribute towards resolving the conflict – and in this situation towards addressing the *cause* of the violence.

SOME THEOLOGICAL ASPECTS OF THE VIOLENCE DEBATE

In situations of sustained repression revolution is perhaps historically inevitable, in which case debate on the morality of revolution is about as pointless as it is to discuss the morality of a natural disaster. The church has nevertheless from its earliest days grappled with such questions and insisted on ethical rules for war, no less than it has demanded such rules for other aspects of social behaviour.

Each age raises its own questions on violence in response to the different demands and crises of the time.[5] The early Church, for example, expected God's kingdom to dawn imminently amidst the affairs of humankind, while it faced a hostile government determined to eradicate Christianity as a subversive influence in the Empire. For them the pertinent question was whether Christians were justified in taking up arms, either in self defence or in the service of the state. In the post-Constantinian medieval era, on the other hand, Christians readily fought for the Empire under the insignia of Christ. For the Church of the time a crucial question was what constituted a just war.

During this same period and indeed on many occasions when Christians found themselves victims of tyrannical rulers, they were compelled to ask what was the nature of their responsibility regarding such tyrants.

The Church in South Africa today faces all of these issues anew. White conscripts to the army ask whether it is theologically legitimate for them to fight in the South African Defence Force. The military occupation of Namibia, cross border raids and war in the townships are weighed in terms of traditional just war theory, the legitimacy of the South African regime is called into question, and its rulers judged to be tyrants.

In order for the violence debate in South Africa to be contextually located, it is to be considered in relation to each of these issues.

Just war

The dominant teaching of the mainline churches concerning war and violence is today still traditional just war theory, the classic form of which can be traced back to the Roman orator and statesman Cicero (d. 43 BCE). Ambrose of Milan (c. 339–397 CE) introduced his ideas into Christian theology, subsequent church fathers like Augustine and Thomas Aquinas entrenched the theory as a part of the Christian ethos, and Luther and Calvin carried it into the Protestant Reformation. Each of these writers and several others gave the doctrine of just war different emphases. These are important variations to be considered in relation to the ongoing encounter between the different traditions of the Church – at times firmly in the service of the rulers and at other times struggling to distance itself in the affirmation of an alternative liberative tradition.[6] What follows is no more than the essential emphases of the doctrine.[7]

1. There must be a *just cause*.
Augustine thought that 'a just war is justified only by the injustice of an aggressor'.[8] This suggests that a just war is essentially a defensive war. He went further, however, to allow that a just war could also be an aggressive war, arguing that a just cause for war could include the restoration of 'what was taken unjustly'.[9] Childress, in developing this tradition further, has suggested that a just cause could therefore be reasonably argued to involve the protection of the innocent from unjust attack, the restoration of rights wrongly denied a people or the re-establishment of a just order.[10] Briefly stated, a just cause has come to be regarded as directly related to the redressing of a situation that is unjust.

2. There must be a *just end*.

Closely related to the concept of a 'just cause', the object of war should be the restoration of a just and lasting peace. For this reason it has been argued, by some, that those waging war are required to assess the chances of success – the implication being that such wars which merely generate further misery and suffering for the indefinite future ought not to be engaged in. Others, Karl Barth among them, tend to disagree, arguing that should a person believe before God that a war needs to be fought its cost ought not to be regarded as a decisive factor.[11] The assessment of cost and the possibility of further misery is, however, always relative to a given situation. And the tragedy is that the suffering of the oppressed is sometimes such that they cannot imagine a future suffering worse than their present ordeal. Indeed history suggests that some prefer anarchy to continued oppression. The point of this particular criterion is simply that a just end involves peace and justice as a goal, rather than mere vengeance or the lust for power.

3. *Just means* ought to be used.

This criterion has often been understood to involve some relationship between means and end. It requires restraint in the choice of weapons with a view to minimising suffering and death, and the exclusion of the atrocities of war. The Geneva Convention (1949) and two subsequent 1977 Geneva Protocols are, for example, in accordance with this criterion in seeking to prohibit 'direct intentional attacks on non-combatant and non-military targets', arguing for the banning of nuclear arms, and seeking to prohibit the use of torture.[12]

4. War must be a *last resort*.

All other means are to be tried and exploited before the resort to force can be regarded as justifiable. For many it is this criterion which constitutes the most important emphasis of a just war theory. It is a dominant criterion. If war be anything other than a last resort, even if all other criteria apply, it is generally regarded as neither justified nor is it just.

5. War must be declared by a *legitimate authority*.

Theologians of the dominant tradition of the Church have consistently shown a bias in favour of the *de facto* rulers. Fearing the possibility of anarchy and chaos, they have resisted armed revolution. It is also clear, however, that if all *de facto* governments are to be regarded as synonymous with legitimate authority, resistance to tyranny could never be accepted. Yet both Augustine and Thomas Aquinas as the major proponents of just war theory, and Luther and Calvin as their

Protestant counterparts all argue that the tyrant should not be obeyed. They further agree that in one way or another, if it be the will of God, the tyrant will be removed from ruling over them. Precisely who is responsible for this removal and by what means is a question to which we shall return.

Debate on the just war theory continues and clearly it can be used and abused (as it has been throughout history) to legitimate wars of both oppression and anarchy. When honestly employed, however, it can provide a useful framework for analysing situations of potential war. It is a theory of reluctant violence, but also one which allows that war is sometimes not only inevitable but perhaps necessary.

It is within this framework that Pope Paul VI in *Populorum Progressio* (1967) discouraged revolutionary uprisings, while allowing for an exception. 'Everyone knows', he said, 'that revolutionary uprisings – except where there is manifest, longstanding tyranny which would do great damage to fundamental personal rights and dangerous harm to the common good of a country – engender new injustices, introduce new inequities and bring new disasters'.[13] A year later, with the same reserve, Pope Paul VI told the Latin American bishops meeting in Medellin that while a 'revolution is an unacceptable remedy for injustice because it gives rise to worse evils', there might be exceptions to this general guideline. Reflecting the revolutionary milieu of the Latin American continent, the findings of the Medellin Conference were also within the framework of just war theory. Having reversed the papal statement, the Medellin Document stated that revolutionary insurrection can sometimes be legitimate, while recognising that revolution often gives rise to its own injustices.[14] The 1986 Vatican *Instruction*, in turn, warns against the 'mystique of violence' in condemning what it regards as the destructive illusion of 'systematic violence put forward as a necessary path to liberation'. It nevertheless allows that 'in the extreme case' armed struggle is allowed for in the Church's Magisterium as a means 'to put an end to an obvious and prolonged tyranny'.[15]

Speaking from within a just war tradition, Kenneth Kaunda captures the limits to what violence can achieve politically in a poignant way by arguing that violence is at best a *first step* in the process of building a just order. But as a *last resort* it may be an unavoidable step towards the pursuit of this order.[16]

Briefly stated, the dominant tradition of the Church from at least post-Constantinian times to the present regards the resort to violence as legitimate under certain circumstances. And in more recent times, due to the challenge presented by situations of oppression in different parts of the world, together with theological insights gained within these situations, the bias which allowed only the *de facto* rulers to legitimately take up arms has been broadened to allow for the common people to resort to arms against longstanding tyranny. The very concept of 'legitimate authority' is under new consideration at present and just war theory has come to provide a theoretical understanding of the concept of a just revolution.

The World Council of Churches as early as 1970 concluded that since the oppressed people of Southern Africa had themselves concluded that the last resort had been reached in their decision to take up arms, Christians not directly involved in that struggle were in no position to suggest that some alternative strategy for liberation be adopted.[17] More recently some Christians went a step further in the *Lusaka Statement* of May 1987 to state:

> While remaining committed to peaceful change we recognise that the nature of the South African regime which wages war against its own inhabitants and neighbours compels the movements to use force along with other means to end oppression. We call upon the churches and the international community to seek ways to give this affirmation practical effect in the struggle for liberation in the region and to strengthen their contacts with the liberation movements.

Cautiously phrased, this statement is the closest Christians have come in a formal statement to legitimating the armed revolutionary struggle in South Africa. It does not explicitly employ just war theory in support of the armed struggle; it does, however, come close to doing so.

In reopening the theological debate on violence, and in challenging the churches to move beyond the naive rejection of all violence in a country that is already engulfed in violence, the theology of such documents as the *Lusaka Statement* and the *Kairos Document* is in continuity with a long theological tradition and a broad alliance of Christians around the world. It is a theology which challenges Christians to ask which form of violence is less evil, violence as a means of oppression or violence employed as a counter strategy of liberation.

Tyranny

'An empire without justice', said Augustine, 'is little more than a band of robbers. Peace is more than the absence of hostilities; it is the ordered harmony of its citizens'. A legitimate state is for Augustine 'an assemblage of reasonable beings bound together by a common agreement as to the objects of their love'.[18] Thomas Aquinas, in turn, provided a simple definition of tyranny: 'A tyrannical government is unjust because it is not directed to the common good'. 'Disturbing such a government', he said, 'has not the nature of sedition. . . .'[19] Martin Luther, who worked in close league with the princes, never doubted that every Christian had the right to disobey civil authority as part of his or her political responsibility.[20] Calvin was adamant that if a civil authority should command what is in contradiction to the declared purposes of God it should simply be ignored.[21] It is not necessary to provide further evidence of this tradition of resistance which has not been suppressed by a long heritage of collaboration between church and state.[22] Christian teaching concerning tyrants is unequivocal, they should not be obeyed. The only question is whether it is legitimate for Christians to remove them by violence.

Augustine never doubted that a state without justice and sustained by violence could not survive the exigencies of history. This, he argued in the *City of God*, was the reason for the fall of the Roman Empire. Thomas Aquinas rejected the possibility of ordinary citizens involving themselves in armed rebellion against the tyrant, while granting that in their obedience to God they may well find themselves martyred by the state. He also, however, allowed that while God might require that individuals suffer under the tyrant, God might also see fit to remove the tyrant. Luther's teaching showed a similar emphasis to that of Thomas. Should the tyrant command what is contrary to the will of God he should be disobeyed, with the expectation that such a ruler would be dealt with according to the will of God. Calvin went a little further than his predecessors, allowing that God would use people both of good and bad motives to remove unjust rulers, although he too counselled his followers not to involve themselves in the violent overthrow of the tyrant. (A rather strange situation prevailed in which Christians were taught not to involve themselves in violent revolution against a tyrannical government, while theologians accepted that other members of the community could apparently be relied on to do so!) After Calvin, however, the possibility of direct theological support for armed rebellion increased.[23] Calvin's successor, Theodore Beza, came close to allowing for violent revolution.[24] And during the history of religious wars that followed much of the caution of earlier ages was thrown to the wind, but ultimately what was happening was that the perceived hierarchical structure of the *ancien regime*, within which the ruler finds a location under God, was beginning to crumble. And in time as the shift towards participatory democracy occurred so the fundamental right of individuals to participate in their own government intensified. A natural consequence being that if suitable structures were not available for the removal of the tyrannical government by peaceful means then the only feasible alternative was the resort to violence.

It is in relation to this eventuality that just war theory is used to assess the legitimacy of rebellion. The alternative theology of the poor and the oppressed concerning the right to violent revolution is a natural consequence of this process. But all the restraints together with the realism shown within just war theory must apply with equal weight to any revolution if such theology is to be taken seriously.

Pacifism

The promotion of violence by the Church through the period of the Crusades remains a hideous scar on the history of Christianity. The doctrine of just war was an attempt on the part of the great theologians of the Church to *limit* war, but there remains a narrow line between the concept of a just war and a holy war. Against this background the challenge of pacifism and non-violent resistance remains a challenge which the world cannot afford to ignore. Given its minimal support within the history of Christianity, theological non-violent resistance must be regarded as part of an alternative theology for the Church. It was the 'normative' position of the pre-Constantinian church, and a tradition which is kept alive still today as the history of the early Church and the radical reformation is re-read.[25]

Like other aspects of the alternative liberative tradition of the Church, theological pacifism continues to haunt those who seek to be both relevant to the problems of the present and in continuity with the earliest tradition of the Church. Some find it difficult to affirm pacifism *in principle*, not wanting to rule out the possibility of resorting to arms in certain extreme circumstances while honouring non-violence as normative practice for the Christian. Others who *are* convinced pacifists know that the early Church was also a church of the poor and oppressed, and that until such time as the present-day Church becomes *this* kind of church it is (given its legitimisation of the *status quo*) presumably in no position to instruct oppressed people on how to respond to sustained violence and tyranny. It is the early Church tradition which convinces at least this adherent of the Christian faith that if the Church recognises any form of war or revolution as anything but a desperate last resort after all else has been tried, what Barth called a *Grenzfall* situation, the spiral of violence can only escalate until all that is worth living for no longer exists. An honest reading of history tells us, however, that such moments do come for oppressed people. And it may be that Christians are ultimately required to judge violence less harshly than indifference, if only because the latter can never be an instance of love.

Is a Revolutionary Armed Struggle in South Africa Justified?

Reference has already been made to the 1987 Lusaka Statement and its location within the just war tradition of the Church. The statement has been adopted by the South African Council of Churches and subsequently by the Church of the Province of Southern Africa, and 'received' by the Methodists, United Congregationalists and Presbyterian Church of Southern Africa for 'further study'.

It presupposes a position close to that taken by Archbishop Desmond Tutu on a visit to Mozambique later in the same year:

We regard all violence as evil. . . . This does not mean, however, that the mainstream tradition of the church does not reluctantly allow that violence may in certain situations be necessary. The just war theory makes this point clearly.

. . . The allies argued that it was justifiable, indeed obligatory to go to war to stop Hitler's madness, and the Church concurred with that decision. Most people (apart from the purest pacifists) knew in their bones that it was right to fight against Nazism.

This is a situation which causes much puzzlement in the black community. Not only did the allies go to war against Hitler with the approval of the church, but the church aided underground resistance movements which operated in Nazi-occupied countries. . . . More than this, most western countries have their independence written in blood. The USA became independent after thirteen colonies had fought the American War of Independence. But when it comes to the matter of black liberation the West and most of its church suddenly begins to show pacifist tendencies.[26]

South Africa seems poised to experience an intensification of revolutionary violence – and only a fool would doubt that this will unleash an escalation of repressive violence. President P. W. Botha, Defence Minister Magnus Malan and Minister of Police Adrian Vlok have repeatedly warned the oppressed people who resist and rebel against apartheid that they have only experienced the beginning of what the South Africa police and military are capable. The truth of the matter is that *Umkhonto We Sizwe* (the armed wing of the ANC) has itself been restrained. John Vorster (the former Prime Minister and State President) suggested that the very thought of total war is too ghastly to contemplate.

Can the Spiral of Violence be Broken?

The elimination of violence is directly related to the elimination of state and institutional oppression. This is seen no where more clearly than in the exchange of views between P. W. Botha and Nelson Mandela in 1985. Botha offered Mandela his freedom on condition that he reject violence as a political instrument. 'I am surprised at the conditions that the government wants to impose on me', Mandela replied:

> It was only when all other forms of resistance were no longer open to us that we turned to armed struggle.
> Let Botha show that he is different to Malan, Strijdom and Verwoerd. Let him say he will dismantle apartheid. . . . Let him guarantee free political activity so that the people may decide who will govern them.[27]

General Coetzee, the former head of the South African Police, seemed to miss this point when, in an affidavit to the Supreme Court designed to vilify alleged ANC supporters, he quoted Oliver Tambo's speech at the 75th anniversary celebrations of the African National Congress:

> The need to take up arms will never transform us into prisoners of the idea of violence, slaves of the goddess of war. And yet, if the opponents of democracy have their way, we will have to wade through rivers of blood to reach the goal of liberation, justice and peace.[28]

There is an alternative to the armed struggle. It involves the democratic process, and is essential that the South African rulers allow this to be the alternative to an armed struggle. The question is how democratic forces inside South Africa and the international community can combine to ensure that the present regime is brought to an end. It is this situation which is addressed by Bishop Tutu in a speech to which reference has already been made:

International action and international pressure are among the few non-violent options left. And yet how strident is the opposition to economic sanctions. Blacks cannot vote. We are driven therefore to invoke a non-violent method which we believe is likely to produce the desired result. If this option is denied us, what then is left? If sanctions should fail there is no other way but to fight.[29]

A pertinent question is, however, what is expected of the institutional Church in the event that it decides that the moment to fight has come? Does the Archbishop become a General? Hopefully not! This suggests that the question concerning the 'last resort' is important but (*in terms of practical institutional Church options*) misplaced. The nervous energy spent by the institutional churches on the question whether oppressed people have a right to resort to an armed struggle (with few taking ecclesial verdicts on such matters too seriously!) can perhaps better be spent in devising programmes of direct non-violent opposition to the existing order. The tragedy is, however, that the space for such options is consistently decreasing – and police action against black students and township dwellers shows that for some it no longer exists.

South Africa is presently living through a period within which, to quote Antonio Gramsci, 'the old is dying and the new cannot be born'. This, suggests Gramsci, is an 'interrugnum [in which] a great variety of morbid symptoms appear'.[30] For birth to occur something has got to 'give'. What will be born in South Africa will partly be determined by the kind of response which the churches and democratic forces inside the country offer in this interim period.

History will probably not judge the churches for failing to provide theological legitimation for the armed struggle. Future generations will, however, be justified in asking what serious alternatives were engaged in by the Church to bring the present regime to an end.

BEYOND THEOLOGY

The debate on violence is ultimately a debate which takes place beyond theology. Responsible ministry requires that the church analyse and understand the situation which presently prevails in South Africa. The 1986 Vatican *Instruction* is clear, 'the concrete appplication of . . . [the right to an armed struggle] cannot be contemplated until there has been a *very rigorous analysis of the situation*'. The major division within the Church occurs in relation to this analysis. The

Church does not have a common mind on whether it is dealing with a tyrannical government, described by the *Concise Oxford Dictionary* as one given to 'exercising power or authority arbitrarily or cruelly'. Kairos theologians and Church theologians disagree on this point. Oppressed and oppressors obviously disagree on this matter. There is, however, also little agreement on the matter between those who suffer most in the situation and those who benefit from it while exercising their own brand of liberal protest against the excesses of 'both sides'.

Socio-economic divisions within the Church render it incapable of a common diagnosis of the problem. This ultimately makes it impossible for the Church to commit itself with a single mind to any one strategy to bring about radical change in South Africa. There are also many within the churches, including those who have condemned apartheid most strongly, who have good reason not to support the demise of the present order. This enfeebling of the corporate witness of the Church contributes to an increasing number of oppressed Christians resorting to armed struggle, as 'the only option left'. Bluntly put, if the Church is opposed to the armed struggle it has an obligation to provide an alternative means to set the oppressed people free. This it has not yet done.

NOTES

1. *The Kairos Document: Challenge to the Churches.* (Braamfontein: Skotaville, 1986) p. 13.
2. A. Luthuli, *Let My People Go* (Johannesburg: Collins, 1962) p. 235f.
3. T. Karis and G. Carter (eds), *From Protest to Challenge*, Vol. 3 (Stanford: Hoover Institution Publications, 1977) p. 740.
4. *Ibid.*, p. 777.
5. For a consideration of the history of the Church's response to the problem of violence see: C. Villa-Vicencio (ed.), *Theology and Violence: The South African Debate* (Johannesburg: Skotaville, 1987). A significant part of this essay is based on the research undertaken by several contributors to this book.
6. See Douglas Bax, 'From Constantine to Calvin: The Doctrine of the Just War', Ibid.
7. See also Albert Nolan and Mary Armour, 'Armed Struggle as a last resort: The Roman Catholic Position', Ibid.
8. St Augustine, *The City of God*, XV, 4 (Garden City: Image Books, 1958).

9. St Augustine, *Quaestiones et Locutiones in Heptateachum*, V1, X. Quoted in W. O'Brien, *The Conduct of Just and Limited War* (New York: Praeger, 1981).

10. James Childress, 'Just War Criteria', in T. A. Shannon (ed.), *War or Peace* (Maryknoll: Orbis, 1980) p. 40.

11. See John H. Yoder, *Karl Barth and the Problem of War* (Nashville: Abingdon Press, 1970) p. 41.

12. O'Brien, p. 14.

13. Pope Paul VI, *Populorum Progressio*, in M. Walsh and B. Davies (eds), *Proclaiming Justice and Peace* (London: Collins, 1984) p. 141.

14. Donal Dorr, *Option for the Poor: A Hundred Years of Vatican Social Teaching* (Maryknoll: Orbis, 1983) p. 161.

15. Society for the Propagation of the Faith, *Instruction on Christian Freedom and Liberation* (Vatican City, 1986) pp. 46–7.

16. Kenneth Kaunda, *Kaunda on Violence*, edited by Colin M. Morris (London: Collins, 1980) p. 107.

17. For a discussion on the attitude of the WCC to the South African liberation movements' resort to violence see my 'Ecumenical Debate: Violent Revolution and Military Disarmament', in *Theology and Violence*.

18. St Augustine, *City of God*, XIX, 24.

19. Thomas Aquinas, *Summa Theologica* (London: Blackfriars, 1964) 2a2ae 42, 2.

20. Martin Luther, *Authority: To What Extent It Should Be Obeyed?* in *Works* (Philadelphia: Muhlenberg Press, 1959) Vol. 45.

21. John Calvin, *Institutes of the Christian Religion*, edited by J. T. McNeill (Philadelphia: Westminster Press, 1960) IV, xx, 32.

22. See my study of the moment of resistance within the history of the church in *Between Christ and Caesar: Classic and Contemporary Texts on Church and State* (Grand Rapids: Eerdmans. Cape Town: David Philip, 1986).

23. J. G. Davies, *Christians, Politics and Violent Revolution* (Maryknoll: Orbis, 1976) pp. 50f.

24. Theodore Beza, *Concerning the Rights of Rulers Over Their Subjects and the Duty of Subjects Towards Their Rulers* (Cape Town: HAUM, 1956).

25. See, for example, the essay by Sigqibo Dwane, 'Early Christians and the Problem of War', and that by John de Gruchy, 'Radical Peace-Making: The Challenge of Some Anabaptists', in *Theology and Violence*.

26. Desmond Tutu, 'Freedom Fighters or Terrorists?' Ibid., pp. 76–7.

27. *Weekly Mail*, 15 February 1985.

28. *The Argus*, 25 April 1987.

29. Tutu in *Theology and Violence*, p. 77.

30. Antonio Gramsci, *Selections from the Prison Notebooks*, edited by Q. Hoare (London: G. Nowell Smith, 1971) p. 276.

12 Religious Pluralism and Christianity in South Africa
Gerrie Lubbe

'Our first task in approaching another people, another culture, another religion is to take off our shoes, for the place we are approaching is holy. Else we may find ourselves treading on men's dreams. More serious still, we may forget that God was here before our arrival.'

Max Warren, 1983: 3

SOME BASIC FACTS

It is not reported whether Bartolomeu Dias de Novaes took off his shoes when on 12 March 1488 he raised a padráo, dedicated to St Gregory, at Kwaaihoek on the East Coast and just west of the mouth of the Bushman's River. He most probably did not. Even if he did encounter indigenous people, his task in performing the first known Christian act on our shores was not to look for the footprints of God in Africa. If he, as a civil servant loyal to the throne of Portugal, were ever to have theologised about his pioneering mission, he would most likely have seen in it the opportunity of bringing God to the 'dark, unknown' continent of Africa. In terms of the reigning attitude of the Western Church during the fifteenth century, other religions, such as Islam, Hinduism and Buddhism, were regarded as the enemies of Christ and were to be destroyed with the sword. The chances were therefore indeed negligible that an encounter with the traditional religions of Africa would have elicited any other response than to acquaint the 'pagan' African with the one 'true faith'. And yet it is clear that when Dias arrived at our shores, religion was indeed practised, and always had been, on the southern sub-continent. The Khoikhoi, the San and other people have observed their own religious beliefs and practices. It can therefore safely be stated that religious pluralism has always been a feature of society in southern Africa.

208

With the arrival of Christian settlers on the one hand and of Muslim slaves and political exiles in the middle of the seventeenth century, on the other, religious pluralism became more pronounced. Adherents of Hinduism who arrived here in the second half of the nineteenth century and East European Jews who made their way to South Africa at the turn of the century added even more facets to the local religious scene. The reality of religious pluralism, as portrayed by the presence of many different religious traditions, is of course backed up by population statistics.[1] (However, one is also inclined, with Chidester, to be rather curious about the substantial figure of 5 810 940 South Africans, or 18.9 per cent of the total population, who are grouped together according to the 1980 census data, in the categories of 'no religion', 'object to state' and 'unspecified'. 'Whoever these people may be, they form one of the largest religious constituencies in South Africa' [Chidester 1987: 10]). Be this as it may, religious pluralism is a social reality in South Africa, which is reinforced, as Chidester points out, by the fact that Christianity itself is plural: 'The existence of multiple Christianities is certainly obvious in South Africa' (1987: 10).

THE CHURCHES AND RELIGIOUS PLURALISM

Whether religious pluralism in South Africa is emotionally accepted and acknowledged by the dominant religious group is, however, another question, to which we need to turn now. Whilst Dias's act of planting a limestone pillar five centuries ago strongly reflected features of the Catholic tradition, it was Calvinist Christianity which first rooted itself on South African soil. This tradition was so strongly protected by the occupying Dutch East Indian Company that it was not until 1780 that Lutherans were given freedom of worship. Before that, they – and Catholics at all times in the Company period – had to rely on chaplains and priests on visiting foreign ships for the ministration of the sacraments. If the authorities displayed such bias against other traditions within Christianity, it is not surprising that the so-called Statutes of India were in force at the Cape until religious freedom was granted in 1804 under the reforms of Janssens and de Mist. In terms of these statutes Muslims were forbidden to practise their religion in public or to propagate Islam, transgression of which was punishable by death. What is in this regard indeed significant, though, is the fact that this particular clause is phrased as follows: 'Offenders to be punished with death, but should there be amongst them those who had been

drawn by God to become Christians, they were not to be prevented
or hindered from joining Christian churches' (quoted by Davids
1978: 33). By expressing respect for the dignity and freedom of
Muslims only in as far as they represented potential converts to the
Christian religion, government policy therefore exerted a decisive
influence on the attitude of the Church with regard to people of other
religious traditions. However, in view of the basic intolerance which
Calvin himself expressed towards other religions, one must concede
that the Church was certainly not forced into such a position, since the
sentiments expressed by the authorities at the Cape certainly corre-
sponded with the prevailing outlook in Church circles. Even when
freedom of religion was eventually granted, adherents of other faiths
were regarded only as objects of mission work, whilst any increase in
their own numerical strength was viewed as a threat to the position of
Christianity.

The most unique aspect of religious pluralism in South Africa is that,
with the exception of the relatively small number of Jews, white
Muslims and white Buddhists, all the adherents of religions other than
Christianity are black, that is, African, coloured or Indian. When
Christianity, and in particular white Christianity, therefore over a
period of three hundred years had to come to terms with the otherness
of people of other faiths, it was an otherness comprising both colour
and creed. The challenge that had to be faced was at the same time
religious and political. In order to assess the ensuing response, it will
be helpful to apply four orientations towards other religions which
Chidester has formulated as 'possible dispositions toward otherness
that might be adopted as religio-political strategies' (1987: 13).

Chidester firstly talks about the strategy of exclusion 'which is based
on violent methods of elimination'. It would seem that the Church in
South Africa by and large has not engaged in dialogue with other
religions. Having perhaps had neither the necessary experience and
theological expertise, nor the political freedom, the church regarded
adherents of other faiths as nothing but objects of mission. Whilst large
numbers of the adherents of those other faiths remained unas-
similated, spiritual exclusion took place in the sense that no known
attempt was made by Christians to come to terms with these believers
and to articulate a vision of one nation and one country in which there
are many faiths. If white Christianity had not already isolated those
other faiths as 'foreign', or was still agonising over the theological
significance of their presence, both of which assumptions seem to be
rather doubtful, then the formal introduction of the ideology of

apartheid in 1948 was certainly decisive. In terms of a policy which was based on 'the violent exclusion of otherness from a shared social space' (Chidester 1987: 13), black Traditionalists, Muslims, Hindus and Buddhists were no longer only spiritually but now also physically pushed into oblivion. The only evidence of religious pluralism which remained within the field of vision of white Christianity was, of course, the Jewish presence, in which otherness was only constituted by creed and not colour, but even here no dialogue was forthcoming. That political rather than religious considerations dominated in this process of exclusion is borne out by the fact that the largest component of Christianity in South Africa, namely black Christians, remained, due to their colour, excluded. In spite of the fact that they were the products of missionary efforts, black Christians were abandoned to the ruthless consequences of exclusion. It is therefore evident that Chidester's hypothesis of exclusion finds adequate validity in the South African context. With the promulgation of the Group Areas Act and related apartheid measures, the elimination of any real awareness of religious pluralism and the preclusion of any meaningful theological reflection in this regard were achieved, although perhaps not deliberately sought. Missionary efforts did, of course, continue amongst the excluded, but took the shape of peripheral exercises.

In considering Chidester's second possible disposition, namely the strategy of hegemony, it needs to be stated that he does not present his fourfold hypothesis in terms of stages but rather seems to regard them as alternatives. In the South African context these dispositions, or at least the first three, seem to represent different aspects of one overarching strategy. Under this strategy is then understood, *inter alia*, the 'hegemonic explanations of otherness by which plural religious beliefs, practices, and experiences are forcibly re-explained in terms enforced by the singular ideology of a dominant group' (Chidester 1987: 13). One need not look further than the constitution of the Republic of South Africa to grasp the applicability of Chidester's thesis. In very hopeful tenor, as far as religious pluralism is concerned, it commences as follows: 'In humble submission to Almighty God who controls the destinies of peoples and nations . . .' However, when it continues by stating, as the first of its national goals, that it intends 'to uphold Christian values and civilised norms, with the recognition and protection of freedom of faith and worship', it becomes clear that what has taken place is, in the words of Chidester, 'the conquest of the realm of sacred symbols by one particular religiopolitical coalition' (1987: 13). By quoting, as another example, only one statement taken from a teacher-training manual which is used by the South African Department for Education and Training, it becomes clear that not too much is being read into the above clause of the constitution: 'A child who follows the Christian faith is more likely to behave in a moral way than a non-Christian or an unreligious child' (Kitshoff and van Wyk 1983: 4).

When Chidester further states that hegemony is established by 'explaining and thereby absorbing, other religious symbols in order to diffuse whatever inherent political power they might otherwise activate, mobilise and support', another and rather recent example from the South African context is called to mind. The year 1985 saw hundreds of Muslims taking to the streets of Cape Town to join blacks in protests against the apartheid regime. The level of political awareness within the Muslim community rose sharply and several prominent Muslims found themselves in detention. Then scarcely one year later the general synod of the Dutch Reformed Church warned Muslims against involvement in revolutionary action, and in the same breath on 23 October 1986 resolved that Islam was a false religion and a great threat to Christianity in South Africa, Africa and the world at large. Notably it was the Chaplain-General of the Police, the Rev. Stoffel Colyn, who moved the controversial resolution.

The strategy of toleration, as the third of Chidester's dispositions towards otherness, may also apply to South Africa although perhaps rather as perceived tolerance than deliberately intended toleration. Chidester's supposition is that this strategy 'arises in a particular religiopolitical situation in which no single group is powerful enough to establish hegemony over all others' (1987: 13). As an example of an apparently tolerant attitude towards other faiths, we have already met with the intention of Christian-nationalism in the Constitution to recognise and protect freedom of faith and worship. The question whether there is indeed *freedom* of religion in South Africa is, however, not an easy one to answer, since any answer will largely be determined by one's own position in this society.

It can be argued that there are no restrictions placed on believers as far as worship and practice are concerned. All religious groups are allowed to erect buildings of worship and are accorded the right to gather for worship and other religious activities, as well as to instruct their own adherents in their particular faith. There are, furthermore, in principle, no objections against the missionary or proselytising efforts of different religions in the country. This would more or less constitute the official viewpoint. It becomes a different story, however, when one views the situation from the side of minority religions.

They generally conceive themselves as being tolerated but not free. The reason for this viewpoint is the fact that religion and racism are so closely connected in theory and practice in South Africa. Most minority religions find themselves so closely linked to racial issues that virtually every experience of racial prejudice is also understood and interpreted as an experience of religious prejudice. The general feeling among adherents of these religions is that as long as they are not free racially and politically they are not free religiously. The fact alluded to above that the majority of adherents of other faiths in South Africa are black and therefore at the receiving end of apartheid reinforces such feelings. To return then to the constitution, it would seem that the attitude of the State towards people of other faiths can be described as religious tolerance rather than religious freedom. In terms of South African realities, the strategy of toleration, if this is understood as allowing differences in religious opinion *without discrimination*, does not really feature in this context. Religious tolerance in South Africa should thus really be regarded as a particular mode of exclusion rather than as a genuinely alternative mode of positively relating to other religions.

THE FUTURE

Religious pluralism is a social fact in South Africa. That, in spite of this fact, the dominating religious group attempts, by its strategies of exclusion, hegemony and tolerance, to uphold the myth of a mono-religious society has also been pointed out. Saayman convincingly shows that religious pluralism, far from being fiction, is a fact in our society which is increasingly demanding attention (1981: 114–16). He mentions *inter alia* our increasingly pluralistic world in which Christians are a minority, the general renaissance of the traditional 'non-Christian' religions of the world and the growing influence of secularism as factors pointing towards the inescapable reality of religious pluralism in South Africa and elsewhere. It is therefore imperative that this important facet of societal life should, for the sake of the present and in particular the future, be thoroughly comprehended and reflected upon in terms of Christian theology. With this in mind, attention can now be given to the fourth and final strategy proposed by Chidester, namely integration.

When stating that 'the strategy of integration represents a disposition towards otherness that respects the integrity of the other as a matter of principle' (1987: 14), Chidester describes a situation where religious pluralism has been accepted sociologically as a feature of society, and theologically come to terms with. Instead of dismissing the strategy of integration as an unachievable ideal, it should be remembered that South African society represents an interwoven scene of religious and political factors. The strategy of integration as a disposition towards religious pluralism therefore runs concurrently with the dream and the demand for political liberation and justice, since both are aimed at the destruction of institutionalised exclusion and elimination. Realism compels one to accept that the vision of one nation with many faiths will not materialise until and unless political liberation is achieved. On the other hand it should be realised that a post-apartheid South Africa will be incomplete if a real awareness of religious pluralism does not replace the present exclusive appropriation of sacred symbols. In this regard Christian theology is facing an enormous challenge in terms of reflection and education.

It is the impression of the present author that white Christianity is not at present in a position to deal adequately and justly with religious pluralism. A number of reasons can be advanced for this opinion. In the first place the majority of white Christians are still aligning themselves with the strategies of exclusion and hegemony which they perceive as their only means of survival. Even if these views are shed, it is doubtful whether a tradition of complicity with apartheid will generate enough trust to create an atmosphere conducive to meaningful interreligious dialogue. Secondly, the basic psychological insecurities from which whites in this country are at present suffering may preclude the required theological reflection. For the latter to take place there must be meaningful contact and dialogue across religious boundaries. Such close encounters may cause white Christian participants to feel even more threatened about their position and future. Thirdly, the present growth which evangelical and charismatic movements are experiencing within white society will most likely militate against serious attempts to come to grips with religious pluralism. Having had no experience of natural daily contact with people of other faiths, such an exercise will most probably be seen either as flirting with syncretism or entering the domain of the demonic.

If theological reflection on religious pluralism and meaningful interfaith dialogue in South Africa are to take place, the necessity of which has, I hope, been convincingly outlined above, an important contribution could come from the black Christian community and black theological circles. To substantiate this view, the counterparts of the above arguments can be advanced. In the first place, then, black

Christians are, and always have been, living in the community of the oppressed and the deprived; perhaps even more so than the adherents of other faiths. Having shared with them the position of the underdog in society, black Christians should at least in principle be able to hear and understand the cry of minority religions for full integration into South African society. Secondly, the insecurities which blacks are suffering from at present are due to the current political system. In a more just political dispensation, and even right now, the presence of people of different religious persuasions would harbour no visible threat to black Christians. In the third place it is exactly the much-feared concept of syncretism which qualifies black Christians for the challenge under discussion. In discussing syncretism among black Christians, Maimela asserts that 'the reality of syncretistic tendencies proclaims loudly that African religious views have not been fully discarded by Africans and that, to understand the emergent African Christianity resulting from cross-fertilization between the Christian and African ethos, the church needs to acknowledge the viability of African religions and to enter into dialogue with them' (1981: 125). Coming from a tradition of religious pluralism, black Christians will then certainly have the necessary tolerance required for interreligious dialogue. They will furthermore be able to display realism towards the idea of syncretism as an issue which has to be faced rather than feared.

In resisting the ideology of apartheid and its resulting injustices, black Christians and the adherents of other faiths are increasingly discovering one another as comrades in the political struggle. That such discoveries will promote understanding and acceptance is obvious. However, if black Christians fail to give a theological content to such encounters, even when these occur within a religious frame-work, that failure may go down as pure political expediency and a chance of coming to terms with religious pluralism will be lost. It is essential, for the sake of proper dialogue, that Christians and people of other faiths should not only strive and struggle together for political rights but that within the realm of this struggle they will allow the other to witness to them concerning the perspectives his or her particular religion has to contribute towards contemporary reality. Against their will, black Christians have been made accomplices in the hegemony of Christianity in this country. The increasing reality of religious pluralism is at present challenging them to break their forced alliance with Christian nationalism and to adopt the strategy of integration towards people of other faiths. Black theologians certainly have both the theological expertise and tolerance to come to terms with religious pluralism in a contextualised way. By doing so they will not only prepare a post-apartheid South Africa for the reality of daily contact with people of other faiths, but will also avert the danger of interreligious conflict as a secondary, but very potent source of trouble.

NOTES

1. According to the figures of the 1980 census the religious affiliation of the South African population is to be broken down as follows:

Christians	22 603 000
Hindus	519 380
Muslims	328 440
Jews	125 000
Buddhists	10 780
Other or none	5 810 940

BIBLIOGRAPHY

Chidester, D. (1987), 'Religious Studies as Political Practice', *Journal of Theology for Southern Africa*, No. 58 (March) p. 10.

Davids, A. (1978) 'A Social History of the Bo-Kaap', *Arabic Studies*, Vol. 2, pp. 21–7.

Kitshoff, M. C. and van Wyk, W. B. (1983), *Method of Religious Education and Biblical Studies* (Cape Town: Maskew Miller Longman).

Maimela, S. S. (1981), 'Response to religious pluralism in South Africa' by W. A. Saayman, in Vorster, W. S. (ed.), *Christianity among the religions* (Pretoria: University of South Africa).

Saayman, W. A. (1981), 'Religious pluralism in South Africa', in Vorster, W. S. (ed.), *Christianity among the religions* (Pretoria: University of South Africa).

Warren, M. (1983), *Christians and religious pluralism* (ed. A. Race) (London: SCM).

Part V
Christianity and the Future in South Africa

13 The Church and the Struggle for a Democratic South Africa

John De Gruchy

More than 70 per cent of the people of South Africa claim membership of the Christian Church. It is not surprising then that the Church plays an important role in the social and political life of the country. The Church is not, however, a monolithic institution but a very diverse set of denominations and groups which differ in their interpretation of Christianity and include within their membership a wide spectrum of cultural background and political opinion. The divisions and interests which divide our society also permeate and divide the Church. Indeed, in the present conflict in South Africa Christians find themselves on radically different sides, and thus in heated controversy and conflict with each other.

As a result of these divisions, the responses of the Church and Christians to the issues that face us are contradictory and ambiguous. Parts of the Church are in the vanguard of the struggle for a democratic future for all; other parts are defenders of white power and privilege; and many are uncertain as to where they stand. The confusion is compounded by the fact that those to the right tend to regard Christianity as the basis for 'free world democracy' and therefore as anti-communist in principle, whilst those to the left see Christianity as consonant with the 'Freedom Charter' or some form of socialism. A vast ideological gulf, thus, separates one group from another, a gulf created and reinforced by different social perceptions, theological traditions, and material interests.

The debate about democracy in South Africa is not primarily about its value. With some exceptions on the political extremes, everybody, it would appear, wants to be known as the true democrat. The conflict is about the nature of democracy, and, more specifically about who constitutes 'the people'. To be sure, the people shall govern; the burning question is which people. That is the dividing line between the

219

advocates of apartheid and its opponents, between the policy of separate development or a racially based constitution on the one hand, and democratic government within a unitary state, on the other.

Even amongst those who would affirm the latter, there is a difference between those whose vision of democracy is essentially liberal and those for whom democracy implies a form of socialism. Related to this is the debate about means and ends, the question of the nature of representation and negotiation, and, looming behind everything else at the present time, the role of the military in shaping the future. Some people are even suggesting that a short-term military dictatorship may be necessary in order to achieve a longer-term democratic goal. This is the confusing and critical context within which the Church has to fulfil its task in helping to shape a democratic future for South Africa.

REFLECTIONS ON CHRISTIANITY AND DEMOCRACY

Democratic forms of government are a relatively recent phenomenon dating from the sixteenth century. For most of its two-thousand years of history the Christian Church has existed within political systems which have been hierarchical and authoritarian. The dominant established churches have generally supported such government and mirrored it in their own life and structures. Nevertheless, the egalitarian emphasis within the Hebrew prophetic tradition, Jesus' proclamation of the Kingdom of God, and the vision of Christian community we find in the Acts of the Apostles, have continually created ferment within the Church, leading to protest and reform movements. Some of these movements have resulted in the formation of more democratic forms of the Church, and also contributed to the rise of democracy, particularly in the Western world.

One of these reform movements, which has had particular significance in South Africa, was the Calvinist Reformation in the sixteenth century, a movement closely related to the rise of democratic aspirations within the emerging middle class. While John Calvin did not advocate a fully democratic form of church or state government, he did take some important steps in that direction. The event which turned Calvinists decisively towards democracy, however, was the St Bartholomew's Night massacre in 1572 when the Catholic authorities in France killed many of their Protestant, Calvinist compatriots, the Huguenots. This nightmare experience of repression raised several urgent questions, and in response led Calvinist theologians and lawyers to develop a democratic political theory which provided the basis for representative and constitutional government. For example, Calvin's successor in Geneva, Theodore Beza, in his important treatise *The Rights of Rulers and the Duties of Subjects*, published in 1574, declared that 'peoples were not created for the sake of rulers, but on the contrary the rulers for the sake of the people'. Beza also insisted that 'those who possess authority to elect a king will also have the right to dethrone him' (Beza 2: 30, 64).

Part of the irony and tragedy of the church of South Africa is that the heirs of the Huguenot and Calvinist democratic tradition within the Dutch Reformed churches, have become captive to the sectional interests of Afrikaner nationalism. Illustrative of the resultant racial and sectional democracy is the fact that in the old Transvaal Republic, democratic rights were virtually limited to Afrikaner Calvinists, a position supported by the Dutch Reformed Church in the Transvaal at the time. Thus, whatever democratic impulse there has been within these churches has been limited and determined by Afrikaner interests, and, more generally, by those of the white community. Hence support for rule by the wishes of some but not of all the people. This sectional racial democracy has proved so strong that it has, in turn, shaped the theology of the Church in its support for apartheid. Apartheid theology is a people's theology, but a theology serving the interests of only a section of the people.

The irony of the Dutch Reformed Church is, however, not so strange when we recall that the democratic vision of the Huguenots and other Calvinists was what we would now call a bourgeois or liberal form of democracy. It was formed in the middle and mercantile class struggle against the aristocracy and the established Church; it was not related to the grievances of the peasants and their struggle for recognition and rights, a struggle which eventually erupted in revolution and socialist forms of government as well as in the alienation from the Church of many within the working class.

This is the context in which we must also understand the role of the so-called English-speaking churches in South Africa with regard to democracy. For most of their history these churches have opposed racial discrimination in principle, but they have not generally followed that through with a clear commitment to a democratic form of government involving all the people of the country. Where they have, their understanding of democracy has been paternalistic, qualified by such concepts as trusteeship, and by such criteria as education.

Officially in their synodical statements these churches have now generally gone beyond such earlier positions, but their understanding of democracy, especially amongst the white membership, remains middle class and liberal. With a few exceptions, they would not, for example, see themselves as participating in the workers' struggle for a social democracy (See Cochrane 6: 174) even though they may see themselves as part of the struggle against apartheid and racism. Thus the tension between liberals and radicals of various kinds, which is present in the political arena as such, is equally present within the English-speaking churches.

Until fairly recently, many black political leaders in South Africa had their education in the more liberal missionary institutions belonging to the English-speaking churches. As a result many of the early leaders of the African National Congress were members of these churches, indeed, some were leaders and ministers within them. It can, therefore, be argued that the democratic aspirations expressed within such documents as the Freedom Charter, have a connection with the kind of Christianity taught at such missionary institutions. Of course, the traditional African emphasis upon communalism was deeply embedded within the experience of such leaders. But at least it was also clear to them that Christianity supported this, that it had within it democratic impulses, such as the idea that all people are equal in the sight of God. Thus, whatever the final role played by Christians in its production, there are close parallels between Christian teaching and the Freedom Charter (Suttner 10: 227f.).

None of this means that Christianity can be equated with democracy, nor does it mean that Christianity can only support democratic governments, or exist within democratic societies. That is patently not the case. Thus, writing within the North American context, Stanley Hauerwas rightly cautions:

> As Christians we should be particularly sensitive to the misleading assumption that democracies are intrinsically more just because they provide more freedom than other kinds of societies. Freedom is an abstraction that can easily draw our attention away from faithfully serving as the church in democratic social orders. The crucial question is what kind of freedom and what we wish to do with it. (Hauerwas 7: 111)

The fact that the Christian faith does not prescribe any particular form of government does not mean, however, that Christians or the Church should be indifferent to the form of government under which they live, or, to put it differently, the way in which political power is exercised. On the contrary, precisely because the Church should be concerned about the welfare of all people it has to be concerned about the way in which they are governed, the conditions under which they live, and therefore the kind of freedom which they have. 'There is justification for asking', wrote Dietrich Bonhoeffer, 'which form of the state offers the best guarantee for the fulfilment of the mission of government and should, therefore, be promoted by the church' (Bonhoeffer, Ethics 3: 352). Granted that the Kingdom of God cannot be realised by human hands in some kind of utopia, we can nevertheless prefer one kind of government to another because it more closely approximates and points towards the coming of God's kingdom.

My conviction is that democracy properly understood is that form of government which generally enables society to flourish best, even though it has problems and weaknesses, and is often fragile. Indeed, while we cannot equate Christianity and democracy, I would concur with Karl Barth who claimed that the 'democratic conception of the state' is 'a justifiable expansion of the thought of the New Testament' (Barth 1: 145). Similarly, Pope John XXIII, in his Encyclical Letter, *Pacem in Terris*, having set out the Catholic principles of good government in the modern world, expressly stated that this teaching was 'consonant with any genuinely democratic form of government' (Walsh 11: 56). But what precisely is that 'genuine democracy' which Christians and the Church should support? What kind of democratic future should the Church in South Africa struggle for?

The form of democracy which the Church may support as most consonant with its commitment to the Kingdom of God will inevitably vary from one historical context to another depending upon a variety of factors. What might enable a society to flourish in one situation may not in another. In other words, the Church's primary focus of concern is not democracy but good government, however that might be constitutionally embodied in a particular time and place. Thus, instead of defining democracy, and then defending our version of it, we should rather begin by considering what, from a Christian perspective, constitutes good government.

GROUND RULES FOR GOOD GOVERNMENT

There is consensus amongst Christian social ethicists, whether

Catholic or Protestant, that the moral basis for good government is justice and equity. Indeed, the primary reason for the existence of the state is to ensure that justice is pursued, for without justice there can be no law and order in society, only anarchy even if it is suppressed by force. It is therefore a travesty of good government when law and order, rather than justice, become the norm as is so often the case in South Africa today. From a biblical and Christian perspective, law and order can only exist on the basis of justice.

From the same perspective, however, justice requires equity. Unless all people are treated equally there can be no justice, so that laws which are discriminating on the basis of race, or class, or gender, are unjust. 'Hence', states *Pacem in Terris*, 'every civil authority must strive to promote the common good in the interest of all, without favouring any individual citizen or category of citizen' (Walsh 11: 56). The only exception to this rule is that 'considerations of justice and equity can at times demand that those in power pay more attention to the weaker members of society, since these are at a disadvantage when it comes to defending their own rights and asserting their legitimate interests' (Walsh 11: 56). This concern for the disadvantaged is of particular importance in seeking to establish a genuinely democratic society.

Throughout the Bible, for example, God is described as one who identifies particularly with the interests and struggles of the disadvantaged, the widows and orphans, the poor and needy, the rejected and oppressed. Good government cannot allow personal freedom to become rampant individualism at the expense of the disadvantaged. On the contrary, it shows a 'preferential option for the poor', or, to use the North American phrase, it encourages 'affirmative action' on behalf of the disadvantaged. This is not altruism; it is justice as the Hebrew prophets understood it. So much is this the case, that the Old Testament vision of society includes a Year of Jubilee every 50 years during which a redistribution of land and wealth is required. This 'year of the Lord's favour' is part of Jesus' own proclamation of the coming of the Kingdom of God (cf. Luke 4: 19). As I have already intimated, there is an egalitarian impulse which runs throughout the prophetic literature of the Old Testament, an impulse which is clearly a central part of the vision of God's kingdom or reign on earth (Brueggemann 5: 308ff.).

Rampant capitalism is certainly not consonant with this vision of the Kingdom of God, and therefore the notion that Christianity implies unrestrained 'free enterprise', and that this is the essence of democracy, is far from the mark. True democracy certainly implies human rights and freedoms, such as the freedom of the press, but it cannot be equated with an individual freedom which disregards social responsibility. Precisely for this reason, many theologians argue that social democracy is the form of democracy most consonant with biblical teaching. Jürgen Moltmann, for example, speaks of socialism as 'the symbol of liberation from the vicious cycle of poverty', and democracy as 'the symbol of liberation from the vicious cycle of force' (Moltmann 9: 332f.). Thus he insists that true socialism is impossible without democracy, and genuine democracy is impossible without true socialism. Individual human rights are vitally important, but they can only be defined and maintained within the context of social well-being and never at the expense of the weak or disadvantaged. A government of the people does not ensure that it is a good government any more than the will of the people is the will of God. But social well-being requires that power is subject to appropriate democratic checks and balances. A good government is one which does not abuse power, and one which serves the interests of the whole community, especially the most disadvantaged.

If the pursuit of justice with equity is the essence of good government, it follows, then, that no government is an end in itself, nor can any government claim absolute authority or power. This applies equally to a government of the people as it does to any hierarchical government. From a Christian perspective, the state derives its authority from God. This does not give the state or a particular government ultimate authority as some claim on the basis of Romans 13; precisely the opposite – the state is under the authority of God. The authority of the state is therefore derived, and is dependent upon properly fulfilling its task. The question is how the state and a particular government is to be held accountable, and how, if and when it is deemed to have failed, it can be replaced by another.

Questions such as these have, as we have seen, exercised the minds of Christians, theologians and jurists through the centuries. Those within the Calvinist tradition have often developed their theories on the basis of the idea of a covenant. By this is meant that the people, both rulers and those ruled, commit themselves under God to certain responsibilities and rights. Implicit in this theory is the acceptance of some common values and loyalties, as well as a moral and spiritual commitment. In our modern secular and religiously plural world such a covenantal understanding of government is problematic. Moreover, the very notion of a covenant is unacceptable to many in South Africa because of its association with the Battle of Blood River. There is also an understandable scepticism about including reference to God in a constitution because of the way in which this has been misused in our context. Nevertheless, certain elements derived from the idea of a covenant made by people under God remain essential if any democratic constitution is going to work, and, let it be acknowledged, democracies do not work without a great deal of effort even in the best of circumstances.

The first of these elements is that the constitution should have the consent of the majority of those governed, and that those who are elected to govern should honour the spirit and letter of the constitution; the second, and the foundation of all else, is that all involved should accept and be committed to common human and social values which transcend sectional interests, values such as justice, mercy, a concern for the weak and a commitment to human rights; the third is the need for there to be ways and means to check the abuse of power and the rise of totalitarianism. Hence the importance of independent courts of law. When power is abused those who govern have not just broken the constitution but undermined its ethical basis, its foundation in justice. From a Christian perspective, they have denied the God-given character and obligation of government. Relating this to human rights, *Pacem in Terris* declared that 'any government which refused to recognise human rights or acted in violation of them, would not only fail in its duty; its decrees would be wholly lacking in binding force' (Walsh 11: 57). For reasons such as this, both Protestant and Catholic theologians in the past and today have developed theories which justify resistance to tyranny, and even revolt. We turn, then, to the question of the Church's role in enabling the birth and flourishing of a truly democratic South Africa.

THE TASK OF THE CHURCH

Some parts of the Church are already deeply involved in the struggle for a truly democratic society in South Africa, but clearly the full potential of the Church in this regard has not been realised. In saying this I am mindful, for example, of the immense resources which the Church has in terms of people, leadership skills, property, and, in particular, its access to the various communities of our divided society. This potential is very significant given the fact that Christianity embraces every segment of our divided society, from poor peasants to the economically advantaged, from radical blacks to conservative whites, from those in exile to those in power. And, somehow, in a truly democratic society all these presently divided groups have to be reconciled and find a place, for otherwise violent conflict in our society will never cease.

Those who know the Church well from the inside are often the most sceptical about its ability to realise its potential. But this scepticism does not belie the fact that within these churches there are people of faith struggling for justice, nor does it deny that within them there is an even greater potential waiting to be released. Commitment to the Church is an expression of faith, a living and working in hope and expectation that the Church can fulfil its promise.

The main contribution of the Church to the well-being of any society is always that of proclaiming the gospel of the Kingdom of God. The more faithfully the Church does this, the better it serves society. This is its unique contribution, its main reason for existence, and everything else is derived from it. If the Church relinquishes this task, it might become another political organisation or social welfare agency amongst others, but it would no longer be the Church of Jesus Christ. But let us see what it means to proclaim the gospel of the Kingdom of God *faithfully* in the context of contemporary South Africa.

First of all, the faithful proclamation of the gospel implies a prophetic ministry in the tradition of the ancient Hebrew prophets. It is the Church's responsibility to proclaim God's demand of justice and equality to those in power. It is the Church's responsibility to affirm the God-given rights of every person, and especially the rights of those who are powerless and oppressed. In this way the proclamation of the gospel encourages the development of just and equitable government, and it also acts as a break or check on the misuse of power. By virtue of its calling, the Church must be a moral pressure group in society irrespective of who is in power, or who is struggling for power. An illustration of this is the role which some Catholic leaders played in the liberation struggle in Zimbabwe. Bishop Lamont, it will be recalled, was a strong critic of Ian Smith's UDI government, and an equally ardent advocate of the struggle for liberation. But after liberation he continued to exercise his prophetic ministry, this time against abuses of power in the new government. The Church's prophetic ministry is a de-absolutising task which must insist on the need 'to obey God rather than man' when there is a conflict of interests. Hence the need to oppose tyranny when it occurs.

In order to exercise this prophetic ministry the Church has to exercise its freedom. In many places, notably the United States but also here in South Africa, the concept of the 'freedom of the Church' is often misunderstood and misused (Bonhoeffer 4: 104). The freedom of the Church means its freedom to be the Church, to fulfil its task in society, to address society in terms of the gospel of the reign of God. In some situations where religious freedom is curtailed, the freedom of the Church may be expressed in its claiming the right to worship. Such a claim may well be a costly and profound prophetic statement because it challenges the basic assumptions and values of society. In other situations where there is religious tolerance, and freedom to worship is taken for granted, the freedom of the Church may need to be expressed in prophetic words and acts addressed to injustice in society. This freedom is not given to the Church by the state, it is a freedom which the Church claims for itself by virtue of the Word of God which it proclaims. The freedom of the Church is, therefore, not something which has to do in the first instance with the place given to the Church by the state or a constitution. It is of the essence of the Church. The fact that the Church may exist in a communist state does not mean that it is not free any more than its existence in a democratic state ensures that it is free. What is true, however, is that it is of the essence of a true democracy that such freedom be allowed for the sake of democracy itself. And this applies equally to religious freedom for people of all faiths.

Directly related to the prophetic task of the Church is the Church's awareness of human fallibility and sin. None of us is free from selfish material interests and the will to power and privilege, and all of us succumb to irrational fears, bad judgement, and self-righteousness. Precisely for this reason it has been argued that democracy cannot work, that rule by the people must end up as mob rule and a reign of terror. Certainly the Church cannot take a naive view of democracy, a view which assumes that people will elect the best representatives, or that those elected to rule will put selfish interests and the will to power aside. But the alternative to democracy is even more prone to the misuse of power because the further you move away from democracy the fewer the checks and balances, and the less do those in power become accountable. Thus the prophets direct their sharpest words to the kings and rulers of Israel and the nations.

Undoubtedly it is easier in one sense to rule by dictate and military force, but this can never create a society which is at peace with itself and able to develop its full potential. Indeed, you cannot have a responsible society unless all the citizens have a sense of belonging, of equal worth and dignity, of a shared future. For this reason democracy both engenders and requires responsibility and commitment, it nurtures and yet requires certain virtues and values. Amongst these, for example, is a sense of responsibility for the environment and thus a concern for future generations, as well as a special concern in the present for the weak, the defenceless, the poor, the oppressed, children and the aged.

Fundamental to the social responsibility of the Church, though not exclusive to it, is the enabling of the development of such virtues, values, and responsibilities, that is, to help overcome self-interest and help build a moral base upon which democracy becomes possible in the long term. Indeed, if the churches, together with synagogues, mosques and other religious institutions, are not developing people of moral integrity and virtue, where else can this happen on a socially significant scale, given the extremely high level of religious affiliation in South Africa? And if it does not happen, how can democracy flourish? The Church in South Africa is in a unique position to do this because of its resources and the fact that it embraces all sections of the population. As such it can provide the context within which such training in moral virtue can take place. But it is also important for Christians to be present and exert their moral influence within and in solidarity with other organisations which are struggling for social justice and equity. Indeed, for the sake of the future of South Africa it is imperative that a network of relationships be formed and sustained between people engaged in different ways in the struggle for justice. Only in this way can a basis for trust and communication be laid which will survive the difficult times ahead of us. Without this a democratic future will be impossible.

Closely related to this is the need for people to learn how to think and act democratically, and here, once again, the Church can provide a context of learning just as it has in the past. In this respect one thinks, for example, of the role which the non-conformist churches played in England in developing democratic leadership and skills in the nineteenth century. A similar process, I believe, is taking place within sections of the Church in South Africa today, not least amongst the African indigenous churches. This presents a particular challenge to those churches which are hierarchical in structure, or for those which are male dominated and even less democratic than society at large. It is difficult to see how the church can provide a model for a democratic society if it runs its own affairs in an autocratic way. By this I do not mean that the Church has to be run democratically in the sense that the will of the people is the will of God. We have to be careful of the concept of a 'people's church' or 'volkskerk'. Even the most democratic of churches would insist that a minority might be right in expressing God's will for the Church, as, indeed, is often the case in respect of those prophets who take a stand against the stream of popular opinion. The Church stands under the authority of Jesus Christ its Lord, as witnessed to in the Scriptures. But this does not deny the need for the Church to be involved in a process of communal discernment, of reaching out for consensus, of participation and sharing in decision-making, and in that way being a church of the people, a church which shares in the struggles and hears the cry of those who suffer.

At the outset I insisted that the Church's main task in society is the proclamation of the gospel of the Kingdom of God. That led us to consider the prophetic dimension of that task. But gospel means good news of redemption, and it is the proclamation and embodiment of that message that must finally be the focus of the Church's task. In its preaching task and pastoral care of all the people, the Church has to enable people to accept each other as God accepts us, to overcome fears and hatred, and to live creatively through the crises that inevitably accompany the birthpangs of a new society.

Three key interelated words sum up this focus. The first is that of repentance, then forgiveness, and finally hope. *The Kairos Document* rightly warns us against cheap reconciliation, and insists on the need for repentance before reconciliation can become a reality. With this in mind, the Church has to enable those with power and privilege to see and acknowledge their guilt for the injustice and oppression of our apartheid society. Perhaps the only way in which the Church can do this is by acknowledging not only its own share of the guilt for the situation, but by also acting vicariously on behalf of the nation. In other words, the Church itself has to take responsibility for the failure of the nation, and, more specifically, in our situation, the injustice, dehumanisation and violence of apartheid (see Bonhoeffer 3: 110f.). This would require two things: firstly, an actual statement, as concrete and specific as possible, in which the Church acknowledges its guilt and that of the nation; secondly, *metanoia*, that is, a change of mind and heart which is demonstrated in action on behalf of and in solidarity with those who have been the victims of apartheid.

At this time it is exceptionally difficult for some to forgive others because of the incredible violence that has been perpetrated in our society. Peter Hinchliff speaks to this when, in *Holiness and Politics* he writes:

I am convinced that a theology of forgiveness is the only thing that makes political (or any other kind of) morality possible. But I have to recognize that there is one area in which forgiveness seems to lose its power . . . One cannot do other people's forgiveness for them. One cannot say to a party of Jews on the way to the Nazi gas chamber, or to the relatives of South African blacks who have 'fallen' from a fourth-storey window while being questioned by the police. 'The way to solve this problem is for you to forgive those who persecute.'

(Hinchliff 8: 198f.)

This in no way detracts from the point that Hinchliff is making about the political significance of forgiveness. He is, rather, questioning the right or presumption of the guilty to tell the victims that they should and must forgive them. He therefore rightly continues,

. . . if it is presumptuous to decide that the oppressed must forgive the oppressors, it is equally presumptuous to decide, on behalf of the oppressed, that the moment has come when no forgiveness is possible and that they ought to kill and be killed in the class struggle.

The remarkable fact is that the capacity of the victims to forgive, in our situation as elsewhere, despite deep and degrading hurts, oppressive suffering and justifiable anger, is far in excess of the oppressor's willingness to acknowledge guilt and repent. And forgiveness is something that can only be a response to such confession. What is clear, however, and here we are talking about the Church's task in laying the foundations for a new society, is that a new society cannot be born or sustained if we are not finally able to overcome the hatreds of the past. Jesus' teaching about 'loving our enemies' and learning how to forgive them, has enormous social and political relevance. Indeed, without it there is no real way to move into a new future. Hence the abiding political significance of the gospel and its proclamation in word and action, and therefore as central to the social mandate of the Church.

In proclaiming the political power of confessing guilt and forgiveness, the Church also keeps hope alive because it witnesses to possibilities which fly in the face of reality. This is not a false or naive optimism, but a refusal to surrender to fate or what people perceive to be the historically inevitable. A fatalistic acceptance of what is regarded as inevitable is the ultimate denial of the reality of God even if we clothe it in religious jargon. Insofar as the church believes in God it lives in hope, it anticipates surprises, and therefore it never ceases to look for and attempt new ways of breaking through the logjam of historical forces and human folly. It believes that something new must emerge which can transform the existing alternatives which breed violence and fear, and enable the birth of a society which is socially responsible and truly liberated.

BIBLIOGRAPHY

1. Barth, Karl, *Community, State and Church* (New York: Doubleday, 1960).
2. Beza, Theodore, *Concerning the Rights of Rulers over their Subjects and the Duty of Subjects towards their Rulers*, trans. by H.-L. Gonin, ed. by A. H. Murray (Cape Town: HAUM, 1956).
3. Bonhoeffer, Dietrich, *Ethics* (New York: Macmillan, 1976).
4. Bonhoeffer, Dietrich, 'Protestantism without Reformation' in *Gesammelte Schriften*, III (Munchen: Chr. Kaiser Verlag, 1966).
5. Brueggemann, Walter, 'Trajectories in Old Testament Literature and the Sociology of Ancient Israel', in *The Bible and Liberation: Political and Social Hermeneutics*, ed. Norman K. Gottwald (New York: Orbis, 1984).
6. Cochrane, James, 'The Churches and the Trade Unions' in Charles Villa-Vicencio and John De Gruchy, *Resistance and Hope* (Cape Town: David Philip, 1985).
7. Hauerwas, Stanley, *The Peaceable Kingdom* (Notre Dame: University of Notre Dame Press, 1983).
8. Hinchliff, Peter, *Holiness and Politics* (Grand Rapids: Wm. Eerdmans, 1982).
9. Moltmann, Jürgen, *The Crucified God* (London: SCM, 1974).
10. Suttner, Raymond and Cronin, Jeremy, *Thirty Years of the Freedom Charter* (Johannesburg: Ravan, 1986).
11. Michael Walsh and Brian Davies, *Proclaiming Justice and Peace* (London: Collins, 1984).

14 Afterword: A Christian Vision of the Future of South Africa
Desmond Tutu

I want to start with a few stories. Once, when I was still General Secretary of the South African Council of Churches, with a number of other church leaders I went to a little village 70 miles to the west of Johannesburg called Mogopa. The Africans had owned the land there since the beginning of the century when they had bought it. They were now a stable and settled community who had developed the whole area – building schools, clinics and churches as well as shops. They had decent homes. They had cultivated the land and had laid on a good supply of clean water. No mean achievement in a rural area in South Africa which was subject to outbreaks of cholera, very odd in a country that has pioneered highly sophisticated techniques such as heart transplants, and yet is not able to ensure that every South African has a regular supply of clean water.

And then like a bolt from the blue the people of Mogopa were told that they must move. They were that unforgivable phenomenon, a black spot in an area that had come to be proclaimed for white occupancy. If they were moved, they would become part of the doleful statistics of apartheid, that vicious policy of successive white minority South African governments. They would go to swell the horrendous figures of over three million people who have become the victims of that government's forced population removal policies, when to satisfy a racist obsession, people, God's children, have been uprooted and dumped in poverty-stricken bantustan homeland resettlement camps, dumped as if they were rubbish or just things in a place where there was little work and even less food. The result was that the father would be forced to leave his family there eking out a miserable existence whilst he, if he were fortunate, would become a migrant worker in the white man's town. Living an unnatural life in a single-sex hostel, prey to prostitution, homosexuality and drunkenness. Black family life was being undermined not accidentally but by deliberate government policy through the iniquitous migratory labour system long ago

233

condemned by the Cape Synod of the white Dutch Reformed Church as a cancer in our society. The policy of forced population removals means that children were often starving not because there was no food but because of deliberate government policy.

And so Mogopa was to be yet another casualty of apartheid. We church leaders went to Mogopa to hold an all night vigil with the people of the village on the eve of their threatened forced removal. One of the few methods left to persuade the government to abandon its intentions was providing adverse publicity in this country but more especially overseas and we were accompanied by a number of TV crews and a significant contingent of journalists. There are really very few non-violent options left for helping to dismantle apartheid.

In Mogopa over a period the authorities had been doing certain things as 'gentle persuaders' to the villagers, to get them to move 'voluntarily' as the authorities put it. For instance, they had already demolished their schools, clinics, shops and churches. They had stopped the bus service to the nearest town and they had cut off the water supply. But the villagers were a determined group of people. They were not allowing themselves to be intimidated easily. They had tried negotiating with the government department responsible. I had attended one of these meetings where we were trying to urge the government to abandon its racist ideological obsession because they were going to be inflicting untold suffering on God's children simply because they were black. All to no avail. The villagers had brought their plight to the Supreme Court. Their legal action failed. And so this was a last shot.

We held a moving service through the night. A soft rain was falling and it was chilly. In the middle of the night one of the villagers got up to pray. Now remember that this man would have his home demolished on the following day and he with his family and their household effects would be bundled into a government truck and they would be conveyed to somewhere else where they did not want to go. Well, he got up and prayed a prayer I will never forget for he said, 'God, thank you for loving us so much!' Incredible. But then so is this beautiful but oh so sad land, our motherland, South Africa.

Another story. It was the mass funeral of 17 victims of the massacre at Uitenhage when about 21 people were shot and killed on the 21 March – the anniversary of Sharpeville when some 69 people, protesting peacefully against the Pass Laws, were killed again by the police, and most of them were shot in the back running away. At the funeral in Uitenhage there were over 100 000 mourners. It was a volatile and tense situation. The police kept a very low profile which helped to keep things reasonably calm. I was sitting on the dais with church and community leaders and Dr Alan Boesak was next to me. In front of us behind the row of coffins were two young women sitting on the grass. They had their arms clasped round each other's waist. Now that is not particularly noteworthy, two women side by side hugging each other, except this, that one was black and the other white. They were out of earshot from us. I whispered to Dr Boesak referring to this interesting duo, 'That is the kind of South Africa we are all striving for' and as if they could hear the two women seemed to tighten their hold on each other. Incredible – but so is this beautiful but oh so sad land, our motherland, South Africa.

At that same funeral in Uitenhage I saw yet another extraordinary thing. There was a young white couple. You would have thought most white people would have been scared to come to such an event. But not so this young couple. Not only had they come, which would be a courageous thing in itself, but they had brought their two young children, the older of whom could not have been more than five years old. In that heaving, emotional and volatile mass of humanity came this couple. They wanted to move to another part of the arena and wonderfully the crowd standing shoulder to shoulder managed to open a path for them to pass through and as they did so people broke into warm smiles whilst they patted the children as they passed with their parents, unscathed, unmolested on such a day when a whole community was mourning some of their number so brutally mown down. Incredible – but so is this beautiful but oh so sad land, our motherland, South Africa.

ALIENATION AND POLARISATION

In the Old Testament, the story of Genesis describes the horrendous aftermath after the sin of Adam and Eve. There is alienation, division, separation, animosity and disharmony. Adam and Eve hide themselves from God, they quarrel, there is enmity between them and the rest of creation. The snake will bruise their heel and they will crush its head. The land now brings forth thistles and weeds and cultivating it is a drudgery, not a pleasant and fulfilling occupation. John Hick in his *Evil and the God of Love* says of this whole scene that it was crying out for atonement (at-one-ment, that is, reconciliation).

Almost always the consequence of sin is to divide, to break up, to cause to disintegrate, to separate, to alienate, to split apart. And apartheid partakes of this centrifugal nature of sin for it is in fact the essence of sin to separate. That is why we have said that apartheid is fundamentally, in its very nature evil, immoral, and unChristian. It is utterly sinful without remainder. It claims that what invests any person with value is a biological attribute, a total irrelevance, the colour of a person's skin. As if this were able to tell us anything worthwhile about that person. The colour of my skin can no more indicate that I am intelligent, compassionate or good humoured than another equally arbitrary attribute such as the size of my nose. This is quite contrary to what the bible says, which is that what invests each one of us with infinite worth is the fact that we are each created in the image of God.

Apartheid asserts that we are fundamentally irreconcilable, that we are made for separation, alienation and indeed enmity, when the bible declares unequivocally that we are created for fellowship, for to-getherness, for community, for interdependence. It is not good for man to be alone. In our African languages we say a person is a person through other persons; that we do not come into the world fully formed human persons, but have to learn how to walk, to think, to eat as human persons. We have to learn how to be human through association with other human beings. The most fundamental law of our being is interdependence; we are made for a delicate network of relationships and all kinds of things go horribly, badly wrong when this fundamental law of our being is broken. Apartheid denies a central tenet of the Christian faith – 'God was in Christ reconciling the world to Himself . . .' (2 Cor.5: 19). 'Christ has broken down the middle wall of partition . . . ' (Eph.2: 14) – that Christ has effected reconciliation between God and us and amongst ourselves, for 'He is our peace' (Eph.2: 14). Apartheid has brought untold and unnecessary suffering on millions of God's children, treating them as if they were less than human simply because they were black. Just think of all the anguish that has come as a result of the Race Classification Act, or of the Group Areas Act. Sophiatown is no more, a vibrant black township just outside Johannesburg which was demolished in the first flush of the Nationalist election victory of 1948. It has been replaced by a white township sensitively called Triomf, which, as if to rub salt into the wound in the black soul, retains the street names of the old Sophiatown.

District Six in Cape Town is now rubble. So-called coloured people will not easily forget the trauma they underwent with the destruction of this noteworthy part of Cape Town. Can we imagine the pain suffered by those who were caught in the snares of contravening the Immorality Act or the Prohibition of Mixed Marriages Act when something beautiful such as the love that subsisted between two persons could be made to seem sordid because it had to be furtive.

Think of all that our country has suffered as a result of Bantu Education and other instances of the deliberate policy of providing those who are not white with an inferior education. The Soweto uprising of 16 June 1976 had as its immediate cause all the problems relating to a gutter education, most immediately being an attempt to force Afrikaans as a medium of instruction. Our country has not yet recovered, for we are still in the throes of unrest fuelled by a perception that blacks are destined to be objects and not subjects in the land of their birth, talked *about*, legislated *for,* organised, and so on, having things done *for* and *to* them but never *with* them, the culmination of the politics of exclusion where blacks have been turned into aliens in the land of their birth, having to make do with only 13 per cent of the land with the whites always having the lion's share. Although only some 20 per cent of the population, whites luxuriate in 87 per cent of the land. A white child has eight times more per annum spent on its education than one black child over the same period. Black political organisations which had striven peacefully and non-violently to bring the plight of blacks to the notice of the authorities have been banned so that out of sheer desperation and as a last resort they are being compelled to opt for the armed struggle.

We are experiencing a civil war of low intensity in South Africa. The government is trying to maintain control through states of emergency that sanction an abrogation of what minimal human rights can be said to exist in our land. There is a plethora of draconian laws that allow for detention without trial even of children as young as 11 years of age because the present socio-political dispensation is based on injustice and inequality which can be defended only by equally unjust and evil methods. The base is fundamentally unstable and volatile. We must spend unconscionable amounts on defence and exporting instability and destruction to our neighbouring countries to destabilise them.

We are a deeply divided people. You can declare without fear of contradiction that usually what pleases most whites is almost certainly guaranteed to displease most blacks. If a Thatcher election victory in Britain makes whites ecstatic, then one can be sure that the same event rendered most blacks gloomy. And yet . . . what a wonderful country we have with a tremendous potential to become one of the greatest countries in the world, if only we could get rid of apartheid.

A POST-APARTHEID SOUTH AFRICA

This land has truly magnificent people. There are several young whites such as those who are members of the End Conscription Campaign who at great cost to themselves, are refusing to serve in the SADF because they believe that this Defence Force serves to defend something intrinsically indefensible – apartheid.

I never cease to be amazed that there are so many white people who genuinely want fundamental change in South Africa, that is, political powersharing in a non-racial, democratic and just South Africa. I am amazed that they should want this to happen when the present dispensation ensures that they enjoy quite substantial privileges simply because they are white. I would I am sure have needed an extra-ordinary access of grace to want to overturn a system that provided me with such privilege and power.

What a marvellous country we would be if apartheid were ended. Just think of all the resources that are wasted in opposing or defending apartheid which would be released to be used for the good of all South Africans, black and white. Just think of all the savings we could make by not duplicating services as we are doing at present. We have no less than 15 education departments serving a population of some 30 million inhabitants. Because of inferior discriminatory education we actually have a shortage of skilled man and woman power, the result of short-sighted political decisions to satisfy racist obsessions. Many of God's children have not been able to develop their full potential. Many schools in the white areas are standing half empty whilst schools in black areas are overpopulated and poorly equipped.

What a marvellous launching pad a liberated South Africa would be to help the sub-continent, indeed the whole of Africa into the twenty-first century with all the natural resources, the technological expertise that God has endowed us with so richly. The world is waiting for the day when we will resolve our man-made crisis to welcome us back into full membership of the family of nations. We would have no academic, cultural and sporting boycotts, or political and economic sanctions. We would be welcomed back warmly instead of being the pariah of the world. We would provide the world with a paradigm to solve its own problems because in South Africa we have nearly all the problems of the world in miniature – the tension between the developed affluent Western world and the developing indigent Third World, the problem between people of different races, and so on.

The Church has a golden opportunity to become what Harvey Cox has called a 'verbum visible' to demonstrate what human community is intended to be, what it can be. What we would be describing is a reversal of virtually everything that has obtained under apartheid in much the same way as the story of the first Christian Pentecost in Acts 2 has been seen as a reversal of all that happened in the story of the Tower of Babel, Gen. 11. The Church community would show forth that we have nothing to fear from our differences, our uniqueness as people of different backgrounds, cultural, ethnic, political, religious and social; that far from these making for separation, they would contribute to a real and deep unity, for it is precisely that which makes interdependence essential. Nobody can ever properly be completely self-sufficient, for to be self-sufficient in an absolute sense is to cease to be truly human. That is the point of Paul's imagery of the Church as the body of Christ (1 Cor.12–14; Romans 12 *et al.*). It is the rich diversity that makes for unity. It is precisely because the different organs *are* different that they can constitute a body at all. One huge nose could never be an organism, could never be a body.

Race is not the most distinctive attribute of a human being. Our distinction stems from the fact that we are created in the divine image and are therefore of infinite worth. We are intended to be decision-making animals, sharing in God's creativity, animals who must be involved in all decisions that are important for our lives.

The Church can show forth that we are in the business of forgiveness for those especially among whites who fear that blacks will do to them what they have done to blacks if the situation is reversed. Many whites fear being caught in a vicious spiral of revenge. All I can say is that this does not appear to be the African way of doing things. One would have expected that Kenya after the Mau Mau uprisings would be the white man's graveyard come *uhuru*; but it did not prove so. The man who had at one time been depicted as the devil incarnate, Jomo Kenyatta, came to be seen as one of the most responsible and stable of African leaders. One should have expected that things would have gone horribly badly for white people in Zimbabwe after one of the most bruising bush wars of liberation. But it has not been so. Mr Ian Smith managed to remain in Parliament in a post-independence Zimbabwe until he recently resigned voluntarily.

One of my former colleagues in the SACC, Thom Manthata, after a lengthy spell in detention without trial, said at a party to celebrate his release 'Thank you for your prayers whilst we were inside, they helped us. Please let us not be consumed with bitterness'. This, coming from a young man who had every right to be embittered, represents one of the miracles of our wonderful country. Africans believe in something which is difficult to render in English. We call it *ubuntu, botho*. It means the essence of being human. You know when it is there, and you know when it is absent. It speaks about humaneness, gentleness, hospitality, putting yourself out on behalf of others, being vulnerable, it embraces compassion and toughness. It recognises that my humanity is bound up in yours, for we can be human only together. It means not nursing grudges, but willing to accept others as they are and being thankful for them. It excludes grasping competitiveness, harsh agressiveness, being concerned for oneself, abrasiveness – all these are excluded. In a fun 'election' carried out in the Johannesburg black newspaper, the *Sowetan*, blacks were asked to choose the ten people they would want to lead them. Predictably Nelson Mandela was head and shoulders above everyone else. But remarkably in that list Dr van Zyl Slabbert features and President P. W. Botha appeared in the first 20.

I see a South Africa where a P. W. Botha would work in a government with a Nelson Mandela, a South Africa totally non-racial, democratic and just; where people counted because they were human beings created in the image of God; where black and white would walk tall because all, black and white, knew they belonged in one family, the human family, God's family.

There is an old film called 'The Defiant Ones'. In one scene two convicts manacled together escape. They fall into a ditch with slippery sides. One of them claws his way to near the top and just about makes it. But he cannot. His mate to whom he is manacled is still at the bottom and drags him down. The only way they can escape to freedom is together. The one convict was black and the other white. A dramatic parable of our situation in South Africa. The only way we can survive is together, black and white; the only way we can be truly human is together, black and white.

I pray for the fulfilment of that tremendous vision in the Revelation of St John the Divine, chapter 7: 9–12:

> After this I looked, and there was an enormous crowd – no one could count all the people! They were from every race, tribe, nation, and language, and they stood in front of the throne and of the Lamb, dressed in white robes and holding palm branches in their hands. They called out in a loud voice: 'Salvation comes from our God, who sits on the throne, and from the Lamb!' All the angels stood round the throne, the elders, and the four living creatures. Then they threw themselves face downwards in front of the throne and worshipped God, saying, 'Amen! Praise, glory, wisdom, thanksgiving, honour, power, and might belong to our God for ever and ever! Amen!'

Index